The
Real
Poverty Report

The

Real

Poverty Report

IAN ADAMS
WILLIAM CAMERON
BRIAN HILL
PETER PENZ

M. G. Hurtig Limited
EDMONTON

M. G. HURTIG LIMITED, PUBLISHERS
10411 Jasper Avenue
Edmonton
Alberta

Printed and bound in Canada

Preface

The title of this book requires an explanation.

Until April 1971, we were staff members of the Special Senate Committee on Poverty, a committee composed of members of the Canadian Senate who had been given a million dollars and a mandate to inquire into the causes of poverty in this country, and to make recommendations for its elimination.

The committee was chaired by Senator David Croll. Senator Croll was, furthermore, almost the only committee member to deal with the research staff in any way. The other senators contented themselves with journeys from city to city in search of deprivation; Senator Croll was in charge of the committee report — or, rather, the staff who were producing it.

By April, it had become quite apparent to the four of us that the Senate committee was not going to live up to its mandate. Any attempt to discuss the actual production of poverty in Canada — the roles played by the tax system, corporate autonomy, collective bargaining and the rest — was systematically eliminated from the drafts of the report. After one especially harrowing session of unilateral (and, we felt, essentially political) editing, we decided that we would no longer contribute to the production of a document that was obviously intended to be useful more to politicians than to the poor. We submitted our resignations.

We subsequently produced an article in the *Last Post* that was, in effect, a preliminary report to the taxpayers. This book is our final report; it contains detailed criticisms of the institutions and policies that were described briefly in the article, and it contains solutions and a detailed course of action for the elimination of inequality in Canada.

The Senate report on poverty, which we have not yet seen, will be the kind of investigation the government considers appropriate to the issue. That is, it will be useful, not as a plan for real action against inequality, but as a rough guide to the kind of thinking that created inequality in this country in the first place. The government, of course, is perfectly entitled to produce any report it likes, or finds palatable — but in our view and, we think, in the opinion of most Canadians, this book will be the real report on poverty in Canada.

This book is an analysis of the economic system that keeps people **poor**.

Acknowledgements

The writers would like to thank Gilles Pacquet, Wallis Smith and Alan Moscovitch for help with library and office space; Heather Hill for specialized research; Susan Kent for editorial work; Morden Lazarus for much-needed financial assistance; and Christine Bowen for typing under the gun.

Contents

Introduction

To be poor in our society is to suffer the most outrageous kinds of violence perpetrated by human beings on other human beings.

From the very beginning, when you are still a child, you must learn to undervalue yourself. You are told that you are poor because your father is too stupid or too shiftless to find a decent job; or that he is a good-for-nothing who has abandoned you to a mother who cannot cope. And as you grow up on the streets, you are told that your mother is dirty and lazy and that is why she has to take money from the welfare department. Because you are poor, the lady from the welfare office is always coming around asking questions. She wants to know if your mother is living with a man, and why she is pregnant again.

If as a child you are going to survive, you must close these violences out of your mind and retreat into a smaller world that you can handle. And if throughout most of your childhood you are sick and rarely have enough to eat, your sickness and hunger will only make the larger world more alien to you and force you deeper into your own personal apathy. If your parents are Indian, black or Eskimo, then all these strikes against you are multiplied.

By the time you are a teenager you accept without question your teacher's advice that you are not really good enough to go any further with your education. You know that it would be a waste of time even to think about it because your parents couldn't afford to send you anyway.

From then on, as you go from one menial job to another, you

come to know that machines are more important than you are. In the newspapers you read that the government is spending millions of dollars on people like you but it is apparently all money down the drain.

During hard times when jobs are scarce, employers tell you that it is your fault that you don't have enough education, enough skills. Men and women with anonymous faces behind anonymous counters spend a lot of time telling you that it is your fault that you have never taken advantage of the opportunities that came your way. So you spend a lot of time hassling with the unemployment insurance people, the welfare department, and sometimes with the law. And nothing is going to save you from these bureaucracies, because you will never have enough money to get them, and the loan sharks and the bill collectors, off your back.

As you move through a succession of crummy apartments, where the rents are always just too high, your kids start growing up the same way you did — on the street. And you suddenly realize there is no way out, that there never was a way out, and that the years ahead will be nothing but another long piece of time, spent with an army of other sick, lonely and desperate old people.

For unless you are blessed with an exceptional stroke of good fortune or a driving natural talent that will get you out into the larger world of affluence and opportunity, then you will, like the majority of the poor, live on the street and die on the street — and very few will ever give a damn about you.

I

Poverty and Its Symptoms

I.1 POVERTY AND POWER

What are the consequences for a society that claims to have a democratic system, enjoys trappings of wealth and economic power spectacularly beyond the reach of most nations in the world, but allows one-fifth of its population to live and die in a cycle of unrelieved misery?

Any attempt to come to grips with these consequences must deal with one question first: Why is the general population so apathetic about the fact that great numbers of our citizens — by the most reasonable count, four and a half million — are left to endure a life of poverty, exploited by an economic structure that continually reinforces their position of inequality?

Inevitably this question leads to an examination of the apparatus that, in theory, serves as a mirror of the public consciousness: the mass media. For the media, and the politicians supported and protected by the media, daily determine the shape and limits of public acceptability.[1]

1. It remains an ironic tribute to the advertising industry's effectiveness that few people realize the existence and extent of the inequalities between the poor and the affluent.

Ten years ago, John Porter, the Carleton University sociologist and author of *The Vertical Mosaic,* judged that in 1955 the middle-class life style didn't really begin for the individual until he received $8,000 per year. From income data, he calculated that at that time only four per cent of all Canadians received that amount in annual income.

In 1970, Porter's middle-class-income line would amount to almost $18,000 per year. Because there has been almost no change in income distribution since 1955, it would be safe to assume that the mass media are still, for the most part, creating an image of an affluent society that is real only for that four per cent at the top.

The media, of course, do not operate as an independent institution. There is overpowering evidence that they are an extension and overlapping of the élite groups of business, bureaucracy and politics.[2] In public, the media pose as freewheeling investigative institutions, continually digging out ugly social truths about our society. But the media are hopelessly compromised. A recent insight into the extent of this compromise was revealed during the hearings of the Senate committee on mass media.

One of the most often-repeated criticisms during these hearings was that the corporations, which control the media through advertising agencies, create and sustain an image of a mythical middle-class Canada in which there is widespread affluence and equality of opportunity; and the all-pervasive implication is that all Canadians live and work in that world.

Jerry Goodis, president of a prominent and successful Canadian advertising agency, testified before the committee:

> The measure of editorial acceptability becomes "How does it fit?" or "Will it interest the affluent?" As a consequence, the mass media increasingly reflect the attitudes and deal with the concerns of the affluent. We don't have mass media, we have class media — media for the upper and middle classes.
>
> The poor, the young, the old, the Indian, the Eskimo, the blacks, are virtually ignored. It is as if they don't exist. More important, these minority groups are denied expression in the mass media because they cannot command attention as the affluent can.[3]

Ironically, Goodis's statement was fully supported by a brief from the most commercially successful radio station in Canada, Toronto's CFRB.

It is in the power of advertising agencies to exert a profound influence on the life style of the Canadian people. The adver-

2. John Porter, *The Vertical Mosaic* (Toronto: University of Toronto Press, 1965), part two, "The Structure of Power."
3. Evidence of Jerry Goodis before the Special Senate Committee on the Mass Media, Proceedings 21:10.

tising they create to a considerable extent sets the standards of taste and the levels of consumer demand for a nation.[4]

Other briefs still claimed that the media and the advertisers they represent only play simple and decent handmaiden to the demands of public taste ("We're only giving the public what they want"). But the extent to which the advertisers have vast financial control of the media was revealed in the committee's research:

> What is not only fair but vital to realize . . . is that advertising is the overwhelming, the first, the chief source of revenue for the media; our research indicates that 65 per cent of the gross incomes of newspapers (70 per cent of the gross incomes of magazines) and 93 per cent of the gross income of the private broadcasting industry comes from that source.[5]

More to the point, this advertising revenue does not flow from widely based sources in the society, but instead comes from a narrow corporate élite. The committee discovered that the mass media derive seventy per cent of their advertising revenue from one hundred major Canadian companies (more than half of which are controlled by US interests), and that almost forty per cent of advertising agencies are now controlled by US interests.[6]

It is fairly easy, then, to understand why the media avoid critical investigation of the implications of concentrated corporate power. It is also easy to understand their refusal to spend much time talking about the inequality of income distribution; after all, they feed off the first and reinforce the second.

If the media were indeed called upon to examine in any detail how corporate power is wielded in its own narrow interests, as opposed to the collective social advantage, they would soon have to confront their own hypocritical position. For from any such investigation would come an uncomfortable conclusion: the forces in our society that sustain and enrich the media must be broken down and their powers distributed more equally throughout society. But the press

4. Special Senate Committee on the Mass Media, *Report* I (Ottawa, 1970): 245.
5. Ibid, 1:243; see also 2:120.
6. Ibid. 1:246.

ignore the core problem of inequality and the radical solutions that will have to be applied to make the structure of society more equal. Instead, the press behave like the proverbial barber's cat, full of piss and wind. They go on endlessly to document the brutalities of poverty and the inadequacies of existing social programs, and then hail each new band-aid adjustment to these programs as much-needed reform in the right direction.

To the accusation that these reforms are too little too late, and do nothing to break down the barriers that prevent the poor from taking power from the élite group, the media and the politicians reply that the slowness of change is the price to be paid for maintaining a democracy; and that this penalty must be paid in order to protect the democratic system's broader values of political equality.

This manoeuvre simply uses the idea of democracy as a mask for plutocrats and plutocracy in an undemocratic system. It is allied with Jean Paul Sartre's description of the affluent,

> who have it in their power to produce alterations for the better but instead work assiduously to perpetuate ancient swindles while professing humane goals.[7]

The real role of the press is to disguise the basic inequalities in the system. If the media did a proper job of exploring the basic inequalities in our society, they would open the door to the inevitable confrontation that precedes radical political changes. But the media are too much a part of the power structure even to attempt to bring this about. It is also impossible to escape the recognition that the shallow liberalism espoused by the two major parties, the bureaucracies and business, will never provide the energy to eradicate poverty in our country. At best it will continue only to fight a desperate holding action against equality in order to maintain the status quo, and to keep the urgently needed social services for the poor to a bare minimum.

The political and business élites, then, have effective control over the media in Canada; and that control intensifies the dan-

7. Quoted by F. Lundberg, *The Rich and the Super Rich* (New York: Bantam Books, 1968), p. 793.

gerous consequences of inequality, extending to minority control of the Canadian parliamentary system.

The media are so effective in obscuring social realities that most Canadians still have no political comprehension of their objective best interest. We apparently have the lowest state of political awareness in the English-speaking world.[8] The majority of voters, especially the low-income working class, continue to elect their oppressors by voting for the political fantasies projected by the media — as in slogans for a Just Society.

And this is done despite the fact that since 1867, legislation passed by Parliament has continually been in the main interest of the business élite. By comparison, social legislation and expenditures have been strikingly low. Canada has over the years allocated more for military expenditure than it has in the area of social welfare — despite the fact that we have never made any pretensions to be a military power; evidently this is the one type of government expense favoured by businessmen.[9]

In a recent study done by two political scientists, it was pointed out that the legislative demands

> . . . to which Parliament is attentive come disproportionately, in fact, almost exclusively from a very small and narrow segment of society. Second, the policy decisions that successive cabinets have made disproportionately reflect the interests of this narrow élite. Third, the proponents of policies from outside of Parliament [the corporate and bureaucratic élites] and those who ratify and legitimate these proposals within Parliament [MPS and cabinet ministers] frequently are *de facto* the same people, even though their formal roles may be analytically different.[10]

8. Robert R. Alford, *Party and Society: The Anglo-American Democracies* (Chicago: Rand McNalley, 1963), p. 284. See also Howard A. Scarrow, "Distinguishing between Political Parties: The Case of Canada," *Midwest Journal of Political Science* 10, no. 1 (Feb. 1965): 61-67.
9. A. Kornberg and D. J. Falcone, "Societal Change, Legislative Composition, and Political System Outputs in Canada," in *Political Elites and Social Structures in Parliamentary Democracies*, Louis Edinger et al (Boston: MIT Press, 1972), p. 65.
10. Ibid.

This is not difficult to understand — a study for the 1966 Committee on Election Expenses indicates that

> . . . something in the order of 90 per cent of the Liberal Party's income is derived from industrial and commercial firms and from businessmen clearly associated with particular companies.[11]

Ironically, the official report of the committee showed no interest in this aspect of democratic inequality, which shows quite clearly that the poor — without access to such funds — are barred from the parliamentary process. Instead the committee report went on to recommend "legislation that will suppress any parasitic element that might weaken the democratic mechanisms . . . and prevent parties and legislators from adopting legislation that is in the public interest."[12] The committee, it seems, were worried about the underworld gaining control of elected members. The affluent, interestingly enough, never seem to consider themselves a "parasitic element."

Obviously, then, the whole structure of élitist control in our country undercuts the basic premise of democracy. All energies are directed towards the maintenance of a political power structure that closes its eyes to the brutalities and irrationalities of an economic system in which the increasingly powerful tools of science and technology are utilized chiefly for private interest.

The result is that the needs of society as a whole are ignored. And the needs and demands of the poor are treated with contempt. (When we attempted to incorporate the views of Toronto aldermen John Sewell and Karl Jaffary — two politicians actually trying to do something for the poor who elected them — into the official report for the Special Senate Committee on Poverty, Chairman David Croll demanded that their names and the views they presented before the committee in public hearings be struck from the report. "They don't represent anyone," said Senator Croll — who holds not an elected position, but an appointed one.)

The British social scientist R. H. Tawney has written that democ-

11. Quoted by H. S. Crowe, "Liberals, New Democrats and Labour," in *Essays on the Left,* Laurier Lapierre et al eds. (Toronto: McClelland & Stewart, 1971), p. 210.
12. Committee on Election Expenses, *Report* (Ottawa, 1966).

racy is unstable as a political system as long as it remains a political system and nothing more. Conflict between the working-class majority and the privileged few is inevitable,

> . . . a struggle which while it lasts produces paralysis and which can be ended only by the overthrow of the economic and social privilege or the loss of political equality.[13]

For a timely illustration of how much we live with Tawney's perceptions one only has to recall the statement made by Prime Minister Pierre Elliott Trudeau after the implementation of the War Measures Act in October of 1970; needed, so he said, to protect us against the terrorists who were attacking ". . . our democratic system, from which all benefits so generously flow."

But the police caught no terrorists because of the special powers granted them under the act. For that they fell back on standard police procedures.[14] What the police did — with the sanction of federal cabinet ministers, provincial premiers and city mayors — was suddenly to equate socialists and separatists with terrorists. To this end they arrested hundreds of Québécois who wanted to do what the liberals of our time cannot bring themselves even to consider — to bring about, through the democratic process, a change in the economic power structure.

An affluent society that continues to tolerate widespread poverty and inequality of opportunity is in very real danger of losing its democratic ideals. It was not intended that the arguments and proposals in this book should find their place in the timid attempts at structural reform that are the hallmark of our liberal brokerage politics.[15] We hope instead that they will help to create the will for social and political revolution.

---

13. R. H. Tawney, *Equality* (London: George Allen and Unwin, 1931), p. 197.
14. R. Haggart and Aubrey Golden, *Rumours of War* (Toronto: New Press, 1971).
15. For a discussion of liberal brokerage politics, see A. C. Cairns, "The Electoral System and the Party System," *Canadian Journal of Political Science* 1 (Mar. 1968): 55.

I.2 MEASURING POVERTY

Although it may astound many members of the affluent class, the simple truth is that people are poor because they don't have enough money. There may be other reasons for poverty — lack of education, opportunity and so on — but these are all consequences of not having enough money to maintain an adequate standard of living. And by "adequate," we do not mean enough for bare survival.

An adequate income is one high enough to purchase the goods and services that will allow an individual or a family to participate fully and equally in society. If they cannot, then those individuals and families with inadequate incomes — the poor — are being materially deprived of goods and services the mainstream of society considers necessary for a stable and productive life.

In other words, poverty is relative to the living standard the rest of society enjoys. Where the practical difficulty lies, however, is in the attempt to measure the gap between those who enjoy an acceptable standard of living and those who cannot attain it.

In attempting to define poverty the American social critic Ferdinand Lundberg has written:

> Anyone who does not own a fairly substantial amount of income-producing property or does not receive an earned income sufficiently large to make substantial regular savings, or does not hold a well-paid, securely tenured job is poor. He may be healthy, handsome, and a delight to his friends — but he is poor.[1]

As Lundberg points out, the most solid foundations of a satisfactory standard of living are assets and accumulated wealth. That kind of economic power can assure freedom and security far beyond the resources of a simple weekly wage.

There are other forms of income in kind: ownership of a house, certain employee fringe benefits, and farm produce for the farm family. All of these guarantee a material standard of living that is beyond that of a straight income measurement. Other components of society's living standard are the free and subsidized public serv-

1. Lundberg, *The Rich and the Super Rich*, p. 23.

ices which, for the most part, seem to be exploited more by the afflu-ent than by the poor. To arrive at a true measurement of the average standard of living, then, a detailed and comprehensive accounting has to be made of the total amount of wealth, money income, and also income in kind, that is available in society. And only when this is done can one draw a poverty line that is relative to the general standard of living. Such a poverty line looks not just at the poor but at the whole of society, and brings out the true proportions of inequality.

So far poverty lines have made a passing bow to the idea of rela-tivity, but then they have gone on to leave out all the financial cushions that are available to the affluent class, and to bastardize the concept further by leaving out an escalator that would keep the poverty line in step with society. The result is that poverty is always defined in terms of essentials alone.

This is exactly what happened to the poverty line produced by the Economic Council of Canada — the calculation everyone now seems to use when they are attempting to get a handle on poverty in this country. Even though the ECC acknowledged that poverty was relative to society's general standard of living,[2] it still went ahead to produce a poverty line based on a notion of subsistence.

The council said that a family that had to pay seventy per cent or more of its income for the basic necessities of life — food, cloth-ing and shelter — was living at or below the poverty line. A decade ago, this came to $1500 for a single person, $2500 for a two-person family, $3000 for three persons, $3500 for four persons and $4000 for a family of five or more.[3]

However, no agency in Canada maintains a regular survey of spending patterns that would enable the ECC to keep the poverty line abreast of the average standard of living. So the council and the Dominion Bureau of Statistics were forced to fall back on the Consumer Price Index.[4]

This means that the living standard that the 1961 poverty line represents is kept frozen, and only adjusted for increases in the *cost* of living. (The cost-of-living index merely tells you what the same

2. ECC, *Fifth Annual Review* (Ottawa, 1968), p. 104.
3. Ibid, pp. 108-109.
4. Ibid, p. 109.

basket of goods costs over a period of time. It gives no indication of the real growth in the *standard* of living after rising prices have been accounted for in the growth of incomes.) As a result, the ECC poverty line does not rise with the general standard of living and so violates its original concept, that of poverty as relative to the standard of living enjoyed by society as a whole. In other words, the ECC poverty line has automatic obsolescence built into it, and denies the relevance of the concept of inequality that is fundamental to a relative poverty line.

Once this interior contradiction is understood, it is exasperating to watch the enthusiasm of the press in its use of the ECC poverty line to show how many people moved out of poverty during the year. This, of course, is one extremely dangerous consequence of the semi-official acceptance of this particular poverty line. Because it is static it creates the illusion that, as incomes alone rise, poverty is disappearing on its own. This sort of reasoning led the Dominion Bureau of Statistics to say:

> In the years from 1961 to 1967 there has been a gradual decrease in the incidence of low income for non-farm families, and for unattached individuals between 1963 and 1965.[5]

And more recently to add:

> The preliminary estimates for 1969 incomes indicate that the incidence of low income among families decreased from 18.6 in 1967 to 17.13 per cent in 1969. Although the number of total families increased by 7.6 per cent (an addition of almost 344,000 families) over the 2 years, the number of low-income families increased hardly at all (842,000 in 1969 compared to 840,000 in 1967.[6])

This, interestingly enough, happened during a period when, first, there was no talk and no action about anti-poverty programs and,

5. DBS, *Statistics on Low Income in Canada, 1697,* cat. no. 13-536 (Dec. 1970): 16.
6. DBS, *Income Distributions by Size in Canada, 1969 (Preliminary Estimates),* cat. no. 13-542 (Mar. 1971): 7.

subsequently, a lot of talk but still no action. Of course the suggestion that poverty, according to the illusory ECC line, is going away all by itself is ludicrous. The same proportion of the population is remaining in the same state of relative deprivation as long as the distribution of money does not change. And as the population as a whole grows, so does the number of the poor.

There are two other objections to the ECC poverty line: The first is that it does not make any allowance for living costs of the sixth and subsequent members of large families. No explanation has been given. Presumably the decision to go no further is a matter of statistical convenience, or perhaps it is even the manifestation of a middle-class prejudice against large families.

The second is the deceptive air of technical objectivity about the ECC poverty line, designed, it seems, to hoodwink the uninformed. The council has buried at a deep technical level what is really nothing more than an arbitrary decision on the part of some researcher to say that if a family were spending seventy per cent of its income on basic essentials, it would be living in poverty. There is simply no logical or statistical evidence to support such a conclusion.

I.3 THE RELATIVE POVERTY LINE

Instead of the misleading measurements just described, we propose a poverty line drawn at one-half of the average living standard of Canadians. This has several sensible arguments going for it. The reasoning behind the first is right out front for everybody to understand easily: people are living in poverty if their income gives them a standard of living that is fifty per cent lower than the average standard of living of society as a whole. This clearly ties the poverty line to the standards enjoyed by the rest of society; the whole concept of inequality is emphasized in a Relative Poverty Line.[1]

1. This is not an original proposal. It has been suggested in both the United States and Europe. In Britain, Peter Townsend has suggested the use of one-half or two-thirds of the median income as the poverty lines. And in the US, Victor Fuchs suggested using fifty per cent of the median income. The only difference is their suggestion to use the *median* rather than the mean we use to arrive at an average living standard. To use the mean gives one the added advantage of being able to project what kind of equality would be possible if

Average income, however, does not take into account family size. In 1969 the average income for all families was $8900; a couple living on that income is obviously a lot better off than a family of seven. What is needed, then, to answer the needs of family size, is a "living-standard equivalence scale."

While we have already said that we reject the ECC's concept of an arbitrary percentage — seventy per cent — as the basis for a poverty line, we feel that it does provide some indication of what income levels are required for families of different sizes to enjoy the same standard of living. The ECC considered that $1500 provided the same standard of living for a single person as did $2500 for a couple, or $3500 for a four-member family.

From this set of figures we have set up a scale on which a single person has three "living-standard equivalence points," a couple has five points, and every additional family member one additional point.[2]

A family of four, then, needs twice as much income as a single person to maintain a similar living standard, and a family of seven three times as much.[3]

How this works for three different "family" units is shown in table I.3.i. The first unit consists of a single person with $6000; the second of four persons with $10,000; and the third, of seven persons with only $4000. The total income is $20,000. The total number of living-standard equivalence points is twenty, and average income per living-standard equivalence point is $1000.

all national personal income were redistributed. See Peter Townsend, "The Meaning of Poverty," *British Journal of Sociology* 14 (1963); and Victor R. Fuchs, "Toward a Theory of Poverty," *The Concept of Poverty* (Washington, 1965), pp. 69-91.

2. It will be apparent that we rejected the ceiling that the ECC and DBS have placed on the poverty-income line at the family size of five. Instead, we attributed the same additional living costs that apply to the third, fourth and fifth family members to additional family members.

3. This procedure may somewhat overestimate the needs of large families, but probably not by much. The *Guides for Family Budgeting* of the Social Planning Council of Metropolitan Toronto (1967-68, pp. 58-60) indicate that household costs per additional family member do not decline to any significant extent beyond a family size of three. However, they do not include housing costs and there may be some savings in costs per additional family member by larger families in this spending component. Nevertheless, the living-standard equivalence scale we are using is obviously not far out, particularly since landlords discriminate against large families.

TABLE I.3.i
Illustrative calculation of the average living standard for a hypothetical population of three families

Family size	Actual income $	Liv std equiv pts	Average liv std	Actual as % of average
1	6000	3	3000	2000
4	10,000	7	7000	157
7	4000	10	10,000	40
Total	20,000	20		

For all three units to be at the same average living standard, the single person needs $3000; the four-member family, $7000; and the large family, with seven persons, needs $10,000.

This may appear complicated, but compared to other methods in existence it is decidedly simple.

On this scale, we have calculated the average income per living-standard equivalence point for Canada, shown in table I.3.ii. The poverty line per living-standard equivalence point is half of that average. If you multiply the appropriate number of living-standard equivalence points for each family size, the results are 1971 poverty-income lines of $2170 for the first family member, $1450 for the second member and $720 for every additional member. This estimation was made on the basis of the 1961 income-distribution data and the (partly projected) growth in personal income per capita since then. This growth rate can be used in the future as a temporary escalator to update the poverty line.

Obviously, this is not an extravagant poverty-income line. $5100 for a family of four in 1971 is only slightly higher than the ECC one. So it is worthwhile, at this point, to make a few comparisons. In table I.3.iii we have ranked three poverty lines: the one we are proposing, which we call the Relative Poverty Line, the ECC/DBS line, and a line arrived at from the results of a public-opinion poll commissioned by the Senate committee on poverty.

The public-opinion poll shows that most people in Canada apparently thought a family of four in 1970 required a minimum income of $6500, which represents two-thirds of the average living standard.

TABLE I.3.ii

The poverty-income line (one-half the average income) adjusted for family size [a]

		1961 [b] $	1965 [c] $	1967 [d] $	1969 [e] $	1971 [f] $
		AVERAGE INCOME				
1 liv std equiv pt		734	931	1008	1289	1448
Family of 4 (7 liv std equiv pts)		5100	6500	7600	9000	10,100
		POVERTY-LINE INCOME				
1 liv std equiv pt		367	465	544	644	723
Family size	Liv std equiv scale					
1	3	1100	1400	1600	1900	2200
2	5	1800	2300	2700	3200	3600
3	6	2200	2800	3300	3900	4300
4	**7**	**2600**	**3300**	**3800**	**4500**	**5100**
5	8	2900	3700	4400	5200	5800
6	9	3300	4200	4900	5800	6500
⋮	⋮	⋮	⋮	⋮	⋮	⋮
10	13	4800	6000	7100	8400	9400

a. To adjust the average income for family size, the living-standard equivalence scale shown in the second column under "poverty-income line" was used. The necessary data on economic family units were obtained from DBS, "Population Sample: Economic Families," *1961 Census of Canada*, bulletin SX-10, cat no 98-524 (Feb 1967), and a special tabulation from 1966 census data with extrapolations to later years based on changes in the size structure of census families, published in DBS, *Estimates of Families in Canada*, cat no 91-204.

b. Data for average income obtained from DBS, *Incomes of Non-Farm Families and Individuals in Canada, Selected Years 1951-1965*, cat no 13-529 (June 1969), table 4, but modified to apply to the total population on the basis of the difference between the data for the non-farm population and the data for the total population in 1965 (DBS, *Income Distributions by Size in Canada, 1965*, cat no 13-528, tables 13, All).

c. For source, see previous reference.

d. Source: DBS, *Income Distributions by Size in Canada, 1967*, cat no 13-524 (Dec 1970), table 1.

e. Source: DBS, *Income Distributions by Size in Canada, 1969 (Preliminary Estimates)*, cat no 13-542 (March 1971), table 2.

f. Projected by using a projection of the growth in personal income per capita.

TABLE I.3.iii

Comparison of the proposed Relative Poverty Line with the ECC — DBS poverty line and the results of a public opinion survey

Family size	1961		1970		
	Relative line	ECC-DBS line [a]	Relative line	ECC-DBS line [b]	opinion poll [c]
1	1100	1500	2100	1900	3200
2	1800	2500	3400	3200	4900
3	2200	3000	4100	3900	5700
4	2600	3500	4800	4500	6500
5	2900	4000	5500	5200	7400
6	3300	4000	6200	5200	8200
⋮	⋮	⋮	⋮	⋮	⋮
10	4800	4000	8900	5200	11,500

a. ECC, *Fifth Annual Review* (Ottawa: Queen's Printer, 1968), pp 108-109; and Jenny R. Podoluk, *Incomes of Canadians* (Ottawa: DBS, 1968), p 185.

b. Updated by the Consumer Price Index. This is the method used in the *Fifth Annual Review* (p 109) and DBS (i) *Income Distributions and Poverty in Canada, 1967 (Preliminary Estimates)* and (ii) *Income Distributions by Size in Canada, 1969 (Preliminary Estimates)*, cat no 13-542 (March 1971), pp 6-7.

c. Public opinion survey conducted by the Canadian Institute of Public Opinion for the Special Senate Committee on Poverty. The respondent was asked whether a certain income level (the ECC poverty-income line for 1961 updated by the personal expenditure per capita and with the ceiling at the family size of five removed) was adequate, too high or too low for his own size of family unit. The result presented is the poverty-income line presented to the survey respondents plus the median disagreement with this line, which turned out to be "$650 too low." This means that the results have the living-standard equivalence scale, which is implicit in the ECC poverty-income line, built into them. If this were removed and only the respondents for a particular family size were counted, the line would be $3000 (1), $5200 (2), $6200 (3), $7200 (4), $7800 (5), and the remainder identical with the results in the table. These figures were not used because of a bias due to the fact that larger families tend to have lower living standards and poorer respondents specified lower poverty-income lines.

The Relative Poverty Line shows $4800 for a family of four, which is fifty per cent of the average living standard.

The built-in obsolescence of the ECC/DBS poverty line becomes readily apparent. In 1961 the ECC/DBS line was actually higher than the Relative Poverty Line. But because it does not have the standard--of-living comparisons built into it, the ECC line quickly falls behind, so that by 1970 it has been passed by the Relative Line, which contains the standard-of-living escalator.

The Relative Poverty Line, at fifty per cent of the average standard of living, classifies four and a half million Canadians as living in poverty — twenty-one per cent of the population.

Any poverty line drawn across society must always be recognized as arbitrary. There will always be families living just above the poverty line. And for them the realities of poverty are obviously just as desperate as they are for those at the poverty line. For this reason we have calculated a Near-Poverty Line at two-thirds of the average living standard. This puts it on a par with the public-opinion poll.

The Near-Poverty Line puts another fourteen per cent of the population in poverty, for a total of thirty-five per cent — seven and a half million Canadians.

We do not by any means think that the Relative Poverty Line is perfect. It can be improved upon in many ways.

First, work needs to be done on a more accurate determination of the living-standard equivalence scale. Family size, obviously, is not the only variable in living costs. Variables such as age and type of work must all enter the picture.

Secondly, the average income per living-standard equivalence point was derived from the Survey of Consumer Finances, in which incomes, in particular investment incomes, are under-reported. This means that the figures in the table are an underestimation of the average living standard, and consequently an underestimation of the poverty line.

Thirdly, the data on income distribution is given *before* taxes. If it were possible to get data on net income after taxes, a poverty line after taxes could be used to arrive at a more accurate figure for the number of poor.

Finally, the Relative Poverty Line we are proposing here is in fact a poverty-income line, and not what is finally required, a *poverty living-standard line*. But to arrive at that, more reliable statistics are needed on property and wealth. These must be included in the calculation of an average living standard. However, we see those points as future improvements that will not undermine the basic concept: a poverty line based on one-half of the nation's average standard of living.

I.4 THE VIEW FROM THE BOTTOM

Probably the best way to look at the enormous difference in life styles between the poor and the rich in this country is to look at it from the bottom — to compare what the poor receive with what the rich receive. To do this properly we should have detailed and comprehensive information about just who owns and controls wealth and assets. But in this country it seems that hardly anyone is interested in collecting detailed information on wealth, although welfare payments to the destitute are kept constantly and highly visible.

Consequently, the best proof we have of the estimate of the gap between the poor and the rich is based on an examination of the distribution of national personal income. To illustrate the point, we have prepared several charts and tables. Table I.4.i, for example, shows how the average national personal income — which would be the point of total equality — is used as a measurement to gauge who gets how much, in terms of the total income available in society.

TABLE I.4.i
Estimated income distribution of families in Canada, 1969 [a]

Income group	Income share as % of total income (less than)	Average income $	Group income average as % of average of total income
Poorest 5%	1	1000 - 1500	10-15
Poorest 10%	2	1500 - 2000	20
Poorest 20%	6	2500 - 3000	30
Second low 20%	13	6000	60
Middle 20%	18	8000	90
Second high 20%	23	10,000	120
Highest 20%	40	18,000	200
Highest 10%	25	22,000-23,000	250
Highest 5%	15	25,000-30,000	300+

a. These estimates are based primarily on the assumption that the families reported (as a proportion) for each income class in DBS, *Income Distributions by Size in Canada, 1969 (Preliminary Estimates)*, cat no 13-542 (March 1971), were evenly distributed within the classes. For the open-ended income classes at the top and the bottom, the 1967 averages for these classes (minus $150 for "under $1000" and $37,000 for "$25,000 and over") were used. Because of these assumptions the estimates are too rough to warrant decimal points in the income shares.

The table shows, for example, that the average family in the poorest fifth receives only thirty per cent of the average income. If this is broken down a little more, by taking the poorest of the poor, we find the poorest one-tenth receive only twenty per cent of the average income. At the same time, the most affluent fifth of families in our country receive twice the average income; and the top five per cent receive an incredible three hundred per cent of the national average income.

This gives an immediate image of how fantastically lopsided our society is when viewed through the single dimension of the distribution of national personal income. The figures reveal an enormous gap between the poor and the rich just in terms of income received — a gap that could only become much greater if the missing data on wealth were included. To give some indication of this we will in a moment turn to some international comparisons.

This is only the first glance at the income-class structure. Refinement of the analysis to take family size into account in no way reduces the inequalities. This refinement is done with the same system of living-standard equivalence points that was described earlier in the description of the Relative Poverty Line. (See table I.4.ii.)

Even in terms of income distribution alone, there is evidence to show that the gap of inequality is probably even greater than it appears, simply because the affluent have better ways of hiding their income. The disparity shows up this way: the Dominion Bureau of Statistics has cross-checked the data received from the Consumer Finance Survey with those of the National Accounts; and DBS has come to the conclusion — after making allowances for a few conceptual differences in both surveys — that certain sources of income are seriously under-reported.

Wages and salaries tend to be almost one hundred per cent truthfully reported; eighty-six per cent of government transfer payments are reported; but investment income, which is concentrated among the rich, is another story. DBS reports that the wealthy "under-report" their investment income by as much as fifty per cent. Obviously, the wealthy do not care to reveal their wealth.[1]

1. DBS, *Income Distributions by Size in Canada, 1967,* cat. no. 13-534 (Dec. 1970): 71.

TABLE I.4.ii
The estimated distribution of income for families and unattached individuals, standardized for and weighted by family-unit size[a]1967

Income group	Income share as % of total income	Group income average as % of average of total income
Poorest 20%	5.9	30
Second-low 20%	11.9 - 12.0	60
Middle 20%	16.6 - 16.7	83 - 84
Second-high 20%	23.0 - 23.2	115 - 116
Highest 20%	42.2 - 42.6	211 - 213
Total	100.0	100

a. The family units were ranked by their income per living-standard equivalence point (for explanation see I.3). Each *person* in the family unit was then counted in making up the five quintiles.
b. The procedure by which these estimates were obtained was to use the total-dollar figure for a particular income group of a particular family-unit size together with the figure for the number of families to estimate any skew in the distribution of families within the income class. This is an improvement over the procedure used in table I.2.i, which refers to 1969 and for which no total-dollar figures were readily available. The ranges in the estimates come from alternative assumptions about the incomes per living-standard equivalence point of family units in the $25,000-plus category.
Source: Special DBS tabulation based on data from the 1967 income-distribution survey.

It is of value here, we think, to make some international comparisons. This isn't easy; different concepts and methods are used in the countries of Western Europe and the US. It is safe to say that the economic and social structure of the US is more closely related to ours than that of any other country in the world. Inequality in the United States closely resembles our own. This cannot be fully substantiated because, as we have mentioned before, there is little attempt in this country to obtain information about the ownership of wealth; but we are probably not very far behind the US, where "the top one per cent owned a third of all wealth in 1962."[2]

There is evidence that the inequality of national personal income

2. Edward C. Budd, *Inequality and Poverty* (New York: Norton, 1967), p. xxi.

distribution is not as bad in the industrialized countries of Western Europe as it is in Canada.[3] Even so:

> Today, less than 2 per cent of adult persons in Britain own 50 per cent of total personal capital; 10 per cent own nearly 80 per cent; while 75 per cent own less than 9 per cent.[4]

Another hard fact emerges from the data: this wide difference in income distribution has remained almost constant for more than twenty years.

This backs up an earlier argument that the population of the poor, in proportion to the whole of Canada, remains constant. Table I.4.iii shows that the poorest fifth of Canadian families (non-farm) have been consistently restricted to a share of the national income that ranged between six and seven per cent. The top fifth of Canadian families have maintained, since 1954, an income share of thirty-eight to thirty-nine per cent.

Some people have apparently come to think that these inequalities of income distribution are rigid and follow their own immutable laws. But there is evidence to suggest that during the depression of the thirties and World War II, income distribution did narrow somewhat; income distribution for the poor and the rich may not yet be in divine hands.

To find out how many single persons, family heads and children are living in poverty, we have prepared Table I.4.iv, which gives a composite picture of these families and individuals. The figures illustrate some of the starkest aspects — children, for example, outnumber any other group; some 1,750,000 under the age of sixteen are living in poverty.

Two myths about the poor are due for demolition. First, that the poor do not want to work because they are lazy; and second, that the poor are mostly on welfare.

3. Whatever attempts have been made suggest that Canada and the United States have more unequal distributions of income than the industrialized countries of Europe. John H. Chandler used as the measure of inequality the lower limit of the most affluent fifth. (For non-farm families in Canada in 1969, the corresponding figures would be $4600 and $12,110. See table I.4.iii. The resulting ratio of .38, however, is not comparable to the figures presented by Chandler because of conceptual differences.) He estimated that Canada's income distribution is roughly the same as that of the US.
4. Giles Radice, *Democratic Socialism* (New York: Praeger, 1966), p. 65.

TABLE I.4.iii

Shares of total non-farm-family income received by non-farm families ranked by income, 1951 – 1969

YEAR	Lowest fifth	Second fifth	Middle fifth	Fourth fifth	Highest fifth	Total
	% SHARES OF TOTAL INCOME					
1951	6.1	12.9	17.4	22.4	41.1	100.0
1954	6.5	13.5	18.1	24.4	37.5	100.0
1957	6.3	13.1	18.1	23.4	39.1	100.0
1959	6.8	13.4	17.8	23.0	39.0	100.0
1961	6.6	13.5	18.3	23.4	38.4	100.0
1965	6.6	13.3	18.0	23.5	38.6	100.0
1967[a]	6.9	13.3	17.9	23.5	38.4	100.0
1969[a]	6.9	13.0	18.0	23.4	38.7	100.0

	UPPER LIMITS ($)				Average $
1951	1,820	2,700	3,480	4,640	3,535
1954	2,220	3,240	4,150	5,680	4,143
1957	2,380	3,600	4,680	6,350	4,644
1959	2,650	3,920	5,000	6,690	4,968
1961	2,800	4,270	5,460	7,180	5,317
1965	3,500	5,250	6,810	9,030	6,669
1967[a]	4,090	6,060	7,930	10,650	7,756
1969[a]	4,600	7,050	9,280	12,110	9,056

a. Estimated on the assumptions that families are evenly distributed within the published income classes and that the proportionate relationships between non-farm and total-relative income shares and non-farm and total-upper limits and averages that prevailed in 1965 also applied in 1967 and 1969.
Sources: DBS (i) *Incomes of Non-Farm Families in Canada, Selected Years, 1951 — 1965*, cat no 13-529 (June 1969), table 12; (ii) *Income Distributions by Size in Canada, 1965*, cat no 13-528 (Oct 1968), tables 13, All; *1967*, cat no 13-534 (Dec 1970), table 3; *1969 (Preliminary Estimates)*, cat no 13-542 (March 1971), table 2.

The truth is that the poor work hard; many of them are moonlighters holding down two jobs in an attempt to make ends meet. In doing so they are caught in a vicious circle. For they never have enough time and money, or energy, to take advantage of education programs that would enable them to improve their skills and their wages.

Almost two-thirds of poor persons in 1967 were in family units whose major source of income was either wages and salaries or

TABLE I.4.iv
Estimates of poor persons by family status, 1971[a]

FAMILY STATUS	Poor persons as % of total pop by sex of head [b]			000 of persons in poor family units by sex of head [c]		
	MEN	WOMEN	TOTAL	MEN	WOMEN	TOTAL
Single	1.1	1.8	2.9	250	400	600
Family heads	3.8	0.7	4.5	850	150	1000
Children[d]	7.1	0.9	8.0	1550	200	1750
Other dependents	4.9	0.7	5.6	1050	150	1200
Total	16.9	4.1	21.0	3650[e]	900	4550

a. Based on the poverty-income line shown in table I.1.ii. It consists of one-half of the average living standard.
b. Derived from 1969 income-distribution data supplemented with more detailed data from the 1961 census and demographic data from the 1966 census.
c. Rounded to the closest fifty thousand. The population projector for 1971 is 21,689 thousand.
d. Under sixteen years of age.
e. The components do not exactly add up to the totals because of rounding.

Sources: DBS (i) *Income Distributions by Size in Canada, 1969 (Preliminary Estimates)*. cat no 13-542 (March 1971), table 2; (ii) *Estimated Population of Canada by Province*. cat no 91-201; (iii) *1961 Census of Canada*. bulletin SX-10, "Population Sample: Economic Families," cat no 98-524 (Feb 1967), statements 2, 4; (iv) *1966 Census of Canada*. bulletin 2-14, "Households and Families: Household and Family Status of Individuals," cat no 93-614 (Apr 1970), table 1; and
    J. R. Podoluk, *Incomes of Canadians* (Ottawa: Queen's Printer, 1968), appendix to chapter 8.

income from self-employment. These are the *working poor*. They are *not* on welfare.[5]

In two-thirds of all poor families the head of the family was working.[6]

Out of all the family heads who are working full time year-round during the year, one in ten were in poverty.[7] This also applies to single persons.

As we can see, the poor are condemned to a life of running extremely hard on the same spot.

Finally, Canadians should once and for all get it into their heads

5. DBS, *Low Income 1967*, tables 1, 12, 13.
6. Ibid.
7. Ibid.

that welfare recipients are not people who do not want to work. The majority of those who receive welfare are by the strictest criteria outside the work force. They are the aged, the physically handicapped, widows and mothers who are single heads of families.

These people normally form the great bulk of those on welfare. They do not work simply because they are not able to do so. Their position should not be confused with that of the marginal few who do not want to work, or that of those who cannot find work because of a general recession in the economy. And even then welfare is very hard to get. In Halifax during the winter of 1970-71, when Atlantic-region unemployment had risen to 11.0 per cent, a single able-bodied person had to establish his right to obtain welfare by producing a document with the signatures of ten employers, each certifying that there was no work available to the applicant.

II

The Production of Poverty

II.1 THE MYTH OF COMPETITION

To be born in Canada is not necessarily to be born equal to all other Canadians. And to be born in the wrong place in Canada, to the wrong parents, into the wrong race, is almost certainly to be introduced into a life of endless humiliation and mindless drudgery.

Most Canadians would agree that the children of the rich have an easier time of it, perhaps, in terms of schooling and security. But, at the same time, most Canadians would agree that to be the son of a poor man is not necessarily, or even probably, to be locked into poverty; that nobody, after all, has to be poor if he is willing to work; that in the end, affluence is a matter of effort and character. One recent survey discovered that about half of all Canadians think that poverty is self-imposed.[1] In other words, poverty is not something that happens to the poor; the poor, in their perversity, *choose* to lead lives of desperation and sorrow.

The poor know that they have very little choice in any part of their lives, and none at all in the determination of their standard of living. But the affluent retain their faith in the fairness of the Canadian economy, which has, after all, been more than fair to them.

The conviction that the economy is competitive, that it rewards equally for equal amounts of talent and drive, grew out of a strong faith in the individual, which reached its flowering in the last century. Individualism, in the main, was a reaction to feudalism, and maintained that economic freedom — which feudalism did not provide

---

1. See "The Real Poor in Canada — And Why We Don't Know Who They Are," fifth Maclean's-Goldfarb report, *Maclean's* (Jan. 1971).

— was an absolute prerequisite to personal freedom and national prosperity. In North America, the frontier provided an opportunity to exercise that freedom; and so faith in individualism, and the freedom of the market, was ingrained in the American and Canadian characters.

This view of life has persisted, almost in the form of a mass religion, well into the twentieth century. It has needed only minor adjustments. As the frontiers disappeared, the race evolved from a race for land into a race for skills; and the government evolved into a kind of umpire, providing skills and knowledge to the best of each generation, according to their ability and initiative.

This faith in competition between individuals shaped the whole of economic theory of the nineteenth and early twentieth centuries. Traditional economists assumed that men pursued material wealth as hard as they could, and that the best thing a government could do was to stay out of their way — in other words, that a market that allowed as much competition as possible was the best kind of market for everyone. Supply and demand would be regulated by changes in prices; and everyone would be reasonably happy.

The Great Depression of the 1930s indicated that a lot of this was wishful thinking. The untrammelled free-enterprise economy obviously had *not* kept supply and demand in balance, but instead had produced a lot of unemployment. Prodded by the disciples of British economist John Maynard Keynes, governments were forced to stop running their budgets like small-town druggists and to start taking a hand in the regulation of the economy.

But only to a point. After Keynes, a "neo-classical synthesis" took hold. This theory accommodated itself to the need for government to balance the economy — essentially, to act as a benign overseer to make sure that prices and employment levels stayed reasonably stable — but advised that government leave the rest of the economy to look after itself. Government was not encouraged to do anything to maintain a balance between various markets within the economy; that is, government was to stay strictly away from any attempt to balance demand for various goods, services, raw materials, machines or types of workers (except, lately, for supplementary efforts in the areas of manpower and regional development).

The policy of letting the economy look after itself (except in times of inflation or unemployment) was assumed to be best for everybody, including the workers. For competition was supposed to act as an equalizer, as far as wages were concerned.

Workers, ran the theory, will constantly pursue better jobs with higher wages; the employers with the better jobs, reacting to the rush of applications, will tend to push their wages down, and therefore will have no particular inclination to install machinery when low-wage workers can do the same job more cheaply.

The employers with the low-wage jobs, on the other hand, will find that nobody really wants to work for them, and will have to raise their wages in order to compete for workers (and perhaps, install machinery to economize on the high-priced help).

At the same time, employers will tend to move their plants (or whatever) to areas where low wage rates are usual; and they will design their plants to make the most use of low-wage workers, and economize on high-wage workers. That process boosts the demand for people to fill low-wage jobs, and so will tend to raise the wages for those jobs; people who specialize in high-wage jobs will find that a lot of their jobs have been mechanized away from them, and will cut their demands for high wages in order to get employment at all. So the market, left to itself, will tend to narrow the gap between high-wage and low-wage jobs, until some day the gap has disappeared, and all is well.

A similar mechanism in the competitive model acts to equalize and hold down profits; for high-profit industries attract new investment, which expands production, and so brings down prices and profits along with them.

The theory of equalization through competition was — and is — ingenious. But things do not seem to be working out that way.

In I.4, we cited figures to indicate that income is distributed very inequitably in Canada. But that inequality of income was measured after transfer payments — in other words, after the government had done its (indifferent) best to narrow the gap between incomes generated by the labour market.

A picture of the inequality in that market *before* government transfer payments (welfare cheques, pensions and so on) is given in table II.1.i. The figures are worse — not much worse, because government transfer payments are skimpy at best — but noticeably worse than the figures given in chapter I. The lowest fifth of Canadian family units (including unattached individuals), before transfer payments, took in only *one-tenth* ($700) of the overall *average* income in Canada; the second lowest fifth only half the overall average income.

TABLE II.1.i

The distribution of income before transfers through taxes and income-security payments among families and unattached individuals, 1967

INCOME GROUP a	Income share as % of total income	AVERAGE INCOME	
		$ b	% of average of total income
Poorest fifth	2.4	700	12
Second fifth	10.3	3,150	52
Middle fifth	18.0	5,500	90
Fourth fifth	25.4	7,700	127
Highest fifth	43.9	13,350	220
Total	100.0	6,087	100
Top 5%	16.5	20,050	330

a. The family units are ranked by gross income, ie, by income after social-security payments, rather than by income before transfer payments. This means that the figures understate the degree of inequality.
b. Rounded to the closest multiple of $50, excepting the average of total income.
Source: DBS, *Income Distributions by Size in Canada, 1967*, cat no 13-534 (Dec 1970), tables 31-33.

Some people argue that these inequalities in the labour market are not serious because the people in the bottom fifth of the economy aren't *in* the labour market — that is, they don't work, and get by on transfer payments. But table II.1.ii, which shows the distribution of income for those Canadian *individuals* — not families — who receive most of their income in wages, salaries or from self-employment, indicates that there is just as much inequality within the labour market itself. The range of Canadian incomes is substantial, then, between high-wage workers and low-wage workers, as well as between high-wage workers and people who get by on transfer payments. The more valuable fringe benefits are given to high-wage workers; if these were calculated, and, of course, if investment income (for which satisfactory data are not available) were included, the gap would become even wider.

TABLE II.1.ii
Estimated income distribution of individuals whose major source of income was either wages and salaries or income from self-employment in 1967 [a]

| INCOME GROUP | Income share as % of total income | AVERAGE INCOME | |
		$ [b]	% of average of total income
Lowest fifth	2	500	10
Second fifth	11	2,500	53
Middle fifth	18	4,200	90
Fourth fifth	25	5,900	126
Highest fifth	44	10,400	221
Total	100	4,700	100
Top 10%	28	13,000	277
Top 5%	17	16,300	346

a. These estimates are based on the assumption that the individuals reported for each income class in DBS, *Income Distributions by Size in Canada, 1967*, cat no 13-534 (Dec 1970), table 49, were evenly distributed within the classes. For the open-ended income classes estimated averages based on 1967 family data were used. Thus for the bottom class ("under $500") minus $250 was used as average. For the top class ("10,000 and over") the following percentage distribution was assumed:

$10,000 — 14,999	74.1%
$15,000 — 24,999	22.2%
$25,000 and over	3.7%
$10,000 and over	100.0%

For the class "25,000 and over" an average of $37,000 was assumed.

b. Rounded to the closest multiple of $100.

In 1969, almost one in ten Canadian workers made no more than $1.50 per hour (when the federal minimum wage was $1.65), and many of the workers in that bottom tenth made a lot less. The figures are given in table II.1.iii.

And the figures in that table underestimate the seriousness of the problem; for the data used by the Department of Labour excluded all businesses with fewer than eight employees, and, in fact, most businesses with fewer than twenty. Businesses with a relatively small

TABLE II.1.iii

The distribution of wage rates in jobs covered by the federal Department of Labour's survey, 1969

HOURLY EARNINGS [a]	Distribution of wage-and-salary earners	Wage rates as % of average of total income [b]	Distribution of wage-and-salary earners
up to $1.00	0.6%	0 - 50	4.6%
$1.01 - 1.50	8.5%	50 - 70	16.7%
$1.51 - 2.00	18.4%		
$2.01 - 2.50	20.5%	70 - 90	22.0%
$2.51 - 3.00	20.2%	90 - 110	21.2%
		110 - 130	19.0%
$3.01 - 3.50	16.9%	130 - 150	10.1%
$3.51 - 4.00	8.7%		
$4.01 - 4.50	3.5%	150 - 200	5.6%
$4.51 - 5.00	1.3%	200+	1.0%
$5.01 - 6.00	0.8%		
$6.01+	0.5%		
Total	100.0%	Total	100.0%

a. Wages and salaries paid on a basis other than hourly were converted to their equivalent.
b. $2.65/hr.

number of employees account for a great number of the lowest-paying jobs in Canada, especially in low-income regions. The data also excluded occupations that were uncommon in the industries surveyed; and executives, professionals and managers were left out entirely.[2] In other words, the survey knocked off both the lowest and the highest ranges of Canadian wages, and arrived at a nice, rounded average — with most of the real inequality left out.

But one thing is clear even from these figures — that the competitive economy, which is supposed to be narrowing wage inequalities, is really doing nothing of the kind; for there are very sharp differences in earnings in Canada.

The following sections of chapter II describe the competitive model in more detail, in specific and successive areas. In each of these areas — wages, job security and training, capital, profits and

2. Canada Department of Labour, *Wage Rates, Salaries and Hours of Labour, 1969* (Ottawa, 1970), p. 5. Incidentally, DBS does *not* publish any analysis of the distribution of wage rates within industries — just a list of average wages for those industries. And so overall wage inequality is ignored.

so on — the competitive model does not fit the realities of the Canadian economy. It has been useful, not as a description of reality, but as a convenient blind for monopoly power.

II.2 PERMANENT UNEMPLOYMENT

Some jobs in Canada pay much less than others; and, by the same token, some jobs are a lot less secure than others. An annual unemployment rate of six per cent does not mean that everyone in the work force is unemployed for six per cent of the year. It means that a minority of the work force is unemployed for a great deal longer than that.

A special labour-force survey for the Dominion Bureau of Statistics in 1964, when the unemployment rate was 4.7 per cent, revealed that the burden was borne by only fifteen per cent of the work force. And that, in turn, meant that a worker unlucky enough to lose his job faced, on the average, about seventeen weeks, or one-third of a year, without employment.[1]

So the loss of a job is likely to lead to a long stretch of time without much money coming in. High-wage workers who become unemployed have had a chance to store up money against the event; low-wage workers have not, and it is the low-wage workers, as table II.2.i indicates, who are most likely to lose their jobs.[2]

As unemployment figures rose past the six per cent mark in the winter of 1970-71, the government started to run into heavy political flak. The critics, however, usually did not realize that the six per cent figure hid a picture of unemployment that was a lot more dismal than they realized. For government statisticians, in measuring unemployment, pre-cook the results by excluding people who are actually unemployed but do not fit the government's narrow definition of unemployment.

1. Sylvia Ostry, *Unemployment in Canada, 1961* (Ottawa: DBS, 1968), p. 23.
2. The argument applies to low-wage jobs, and not generally to low-wage industries, although some correlation is obvious. Generally, the industries most vulnerable to economic recessions are the machine-producing, construction and consumer-durable industries, all of which tend to have rather high wages. Those who earn low wages in a high-wage industry, of course, catch hell in a recession — or so the figures argue.

TABLE II.2.i
Average unemployment rates, by occupation, Canada 1961-66

OCCUPATION	Unemployment rate %
White-collar occupations	1.8
Service and recreation	4.3
Primary occupations	5.2
Craftsmen and productions process workers	6.2
Transportation	6.9
Labourers	16.4
All occupations	5.1

Source: Sylvia Ostry, *Unemployment in Canada* (Ottawa: DBS, 1968), table 9A, p 17.

Government statisticians count as "unemployed" only those who, first, have had no work of any kind during the week before they are questioned and, second, are actively looking for work.

Those who have become depressed by long-term unemployment, and have dropped out of the labour market, are not counted as unemployed, even though their situation is at least as hopeless as those still in the labour market.

Those who picked up a little work during the week, even an hour's worth, are considered to have been employed for that week, and the part of the week they did not work is not counted in the statistics.

Those who have taken part-time jobs because they couldn't find full-time work are counted as employed.

And those who have had to take jobs in which they can't use their training — the Toronto PhDs who spend the winter driving cabs, for example, because jobs they are qualified for aren't available — are counted as fully employed, although they are *not* employed to their potential.

The longer a worker is unemployed, furthermore, the more likely he is to stay that way. Skills, in the end, after a long stretch without a job, become rusty; his drive to look for work declines; and finally he slides into the category of "hard-core unemployed."[3]

Workers who are kept out of the labour force for any length of time may not only lose the knack of doing their jobs, but may also

3. See Adrian Sinfield, *The Long-Term Unemployed* (Paris: OECD, 1968), pp. 51-58.

lose touch with improvements in the methods used to do those jobs; if they ever do become employed in their trade again, they will likely have to begin at the bottom and work their way up. Other workers may lose their jobs simply because technology has complicated the jobs so much that workers can't cope with the new demands. Workers who are knocked out of their jobs through technological change of this kind — not just automation, but complication — lose not only one specific job but their entire trade, and may drop out of the work force entirely, completely demoralized and robbed of their crafts by the advance of technology.

The present unemployment rate, then, is creating an army of hard-core unemployed workers, who will find it difficult to nail down a job even when the economy picks up again. Many of them will never work again; yet they are unemployed through no fault of their own.

In an economy that did not deliberately or inadvertently generate unemployment, industry would be forced to dip down into the ranks of the hard-core unemployed to find workers to train for jobs.

When, on the other hand, there is generally inadequate demand in the economy, as there is now, the number of jobs vacant will fall short of the number of workers available to fill them. And if there is a mismatch of jobs and workers — that is, if the jobs available are not suitable for the kinds of workers available to do them, for reasons of location or skills — the unemployment rate will show it. In Canada, we are faced with both kinds of unemployment; both can be traced directly to the federal government, which has failed to overcome the lack of demand in the economy through misuse of stabilization policy, and has failed to impose any kind of economic co-ordination to make sure that jobs and workers are fitted to each other.

None of this, of course, is new; structural unemployment rates — that is, unemployment caused by defects in the economy — rose steadily between the early 1950s and mid-1960s. The total rise may amount to as much as one per cent of the total labour force.[4] And the federal government is doing next to nothing systematic about it.

4. See Peter Penz, *Structural Unemployment: Theory and Measurement* (Ottawa: Canada Department of Manpower and Immigration, Program Development Service, 1969), p. 87.

II.3 WAGE INEQUALITY

The more secure jobs in the Canadian economy are the more highly paid ones; and the range of wages is wide. Table II.3.i demonstrates that employed managers earn twice as much as the average worker, and professional and technical workers one and two-thirds as much; service and recreation workers earn one-quarter *less* than the average, and farm workers and loggers one-third less than only about a half of the average wage.

TABLE II.3.i
Average income and earnings of major occupation groups, 1967

OCCUPATIONS	AVERAGE INCOME		AVERAGE EARNINGS OF FULL-YEAR WORKERS	
	$	% of average of total income	$	% of average of total income
Managerial	8,653	205	8,267	179
Professional and technical	7,158	170	7,673	166
Miners, craftsmen, etc.	5,334	126	5,617	121
Transportation and communication	5,169	122	5,404	117
Sales	4,392	104	5,071	110
Labourers	3,617	86	4,410	95
Clerical	3,895	90	4,314	93
Services and recreation	2,994	71	3,488	75
Farmers, loggers, fishermen	3,311	78	3,020	65
Total	$4,222	100%	$4,631	100%

Source: DBS. *Income Distributions by Size in Canada. 1967.* cat no 13-534 (Dec 1970). tables 41, 42, 49.

When the categories are broken down a little further, the figures turn up wide disparities in income for various groups. For 1961, the average income for fish canners, curers and packers was $1606; the average income of doctors and surgeons was a staggering $15,093. Farm labourers earned an average of $1695; owners and managers in machinery industries, $9564.[1]

1. Jenny Podoluk, *Incomes of Canadians* (Ottawa: DBS, 1968), table 4.12, pp. 74-78.

The average wage varies widely from industry to industry, even for those wage-earners working on an hourly rate. In 1968, the average wage in the petroleum and coal-products industry was $3.63 per hour; for hotel, restaurant and tavern workers it was $1.49 per hour. Construction workers earned, on the average, $3.42 per hour; workers in laundries and cleaning and pressing shops got $1.51.[2]

Part of this gap, of course, is due to training and skills; doctors have a lot more study and investment behind them than fish packers have. But that argument won't answer for the entire gap; even unskilled workers in high-wage industries do better than equally unskilled workers in low-wage industries. (Economist Sylvia Ostry analyzed the 1957 wage rates for labourers in Ontario and found that, within the general area of manufacturing, the highest-wage industries paid labourers about fifty per cent better than the lowest-paid industries did.[3]) Furthermore, fish packers logically should be paid a premium for sticking to their jobs, which are a lot less pleasant than doctoring.

And doctors are more likely to be the sons of doctors than to be the sons of fish packers; that, in part, explains why poverty tends to be handed on from generation to generation. The relationship between education and earnings is explored in VII.2; but there is an extra dimension to the relationship—that is relevant here, for in a society that reveres diplomas, credentials, degrees and certificates, many employers demand that their workers have high educational qualifications, even if those qualifications aren't required for the job at hand. In times of labour surplus, when employers are besieged with applications, some of them may use the high school or university graduation requirement simply as a screening device (one that may remain for a while even if demand for labour picks up again); other employers may simply feel that the best-educated applicant is the best person available, regardless of what that person will be required to do.

One particularly tough barrier between the poor and occupational training is the arrangement of responsibility for training in the labour

2. DBS, *Review of Man-hours and Hourly Earnings, 1966-68,* cat. no. 72-202 (1969), table 5.
3. Sylvia Ostry, "Labour Economics in Canada," in *Labour Policy and Labour Economics in Canada,* H. D. Woods and Sylvia Ostry (Toronto: Macmillan, 1962), table 58, p. 467.

market. When employers are responsible for training, they naturally choose those who are closest to the skill level required, and who will pay off best — the young and the already partly skilled. The older workers and the totally unskilled get left out, and they have no resources to finance independent training.

But education, training or experience is not the whole story; some people who have invested years mastering skills of complexity and precision suddenly find that those skills are no longer in demand. Nobody would argue that industrial fishing from small boats is a simple or undemanding way to make a living. The trade takes brains, experience and courage. But the fact that fishermen have skills that are more advanced than other workers won't help if somebody figures out how to mechanize the whole fishing industry, and/or if the market suddenly becomes saturated with fish. In other words, education and the acquisition of skills are all very well, but they pay off only if the market considers them valuable.

The institutions that have beaten, or at least can cope best with the laws of supply and demand, are in a position to affect the relationship between education, skills and wages. Industries that are cashing in on a monopoly, for example, and that employ a majority of workers with a specialized skill, will drive up the price for workers with that skill in other industries. In other words, whole categories of workers can benefit from corporate concentration of economic power — in the same way that other categories of workers suffer from it.

At times, in certain industries, this becomes all encompassing. The medical profession, for example, has a complete and perfect monopoly over the medical market, and exploits it as much as is compatible with the profession's dignity; there is considerable formal and informal price fixing in the medical world, and the results are reflected in medical incomes. A nice life, if you can get it.

II.4 ECONOMIC POWER: CORPORATIONS

If Canada's economy really worked on a competitive basis, and if free competition did tend to even out inequalities in wages, then wages would be a lot more even than they are now. But Canada's economy is doing a lousy job for low-wage workers. Either Canada does not have free competition, then, or free competition doesn't do what it's supposed to, or both. In any case, the competitive model doesn't fit the facts.

But the competitive model still swings a lot of weight with many government policy makers; and these policy makers, furthermore, act as if the model represented reality. The model itself, then, plays a role in the Canadian economy, by influencing government decision. It's worth a closer look.

According to the free-market theory, if for any reason there is a real difference in wages within the economy, three things will happen: capital will shift around, workers will change their jobs, and there will be adjustments in the techniques of production.

The workers, in theory, will jettison their low-paying jobs and go after the high-paying ones, perhaps after a bit of training or some other form of occupational upgrading; so employers in industries that pay low wages will find themselves without workers. In order to get workers, those employers raise their wages (likely passing the costs along to the consumer by jacking up prices), or they automate part or all of their production lines in order to get more productivity out of fewer employees. Employers in industries that pay high wages, on the other hand, discover that workers are jamming their personnel offices, and they can afford to bring their wages down — or at least to hold the line on increases. So wages in the long run will tend to even out.

The movement of capital in the competitive model is roughly the same. Physical capital, like plants and equipment, is more or less fixed in one spot. But financial capital is not. Savings — that is, money for investment — will tend to go to industries that look as though they are going to pay off; and industries that pay low wages tend to look that much better in terms of potential profit. So the capital is pulled into low-wage industries, which use the money to expand their production. That expansion means that more workers are needed, and some of them will have to be attracted from other industries; so wages have to be raised. But high-wage industries, where wages are squeezing profits, look less attractive to the money men. Eventually they will not be able to expand further, will not require many more workers than they already have, and will grant smaller raises in pay. The movement of capital, then, like the movement of labour, should tend to even out differences in wages.

Profits, in the competitive model, are treated in the same way; in theory, the movement of capital should also work to equalize profits, the earnings of capital. Industries with high profits attract the capital, expand production, and therefore make more of whatever it is they are making. The new abundance of their products drives the price of those products down, and the profits in the industry along with it. Competition, then, is supposed to keep the profiteers in line.

Technology can be fitted into the competitive model as well. For employers will tend to avoid using high-priced skilled workers if they can get the same result more cheaply with unskilled workers and a little machinery. So demand for highly skilled labour will slacken off, and demand for unskilled or semi-skilled labour will pick up; wages for the highly skilled worker will decline, and wages for the un- or semi-skilled worker will rise.

There are a few adjustments to be made within the broad outlines of the competitive model to account for the fact that not all economic decisions are made exclusively on the basis of the dollar.

Working conditions, for example, are important; some workers will accept significantly lower wages if their places of work are pleasant; if they find their work satisfying; if it is secure, or prestigious, or offers a chance of promotion. And, similarly, jobs that are dangerous, unpleasant, monotonous, insecure or offer no chance of promotion may have to pay more. (Capital, of course, will tend to avoid risky investments in the same way that workers avoid risky jobs; so the promise of a premium on profits from risky ventures is necessary to finance those ventures in the first place.)

At the same time, since not all workers are interchangeable, employers will prefer some workers to others, and pay more money for their services. Trained workers can ask more in wages than workers who have to be trained. Workers with innate abilities applicable to certain jobs are more likely to get those jobs. (A man applying for a job as a football tackle, for example, who has both played football before and stands six-foot-four, will be preferred to a man who has not, and does not.) If everybody has roughly the same access to training, the wage differentials between trained and untrained workers will about equal the amount it costs a worker to get his training, which is generally not steep if averaged over a worker's lifetime. This should work itself out so that premiums for training, which opens up fairly pleasant jobs, are offset by premiums that must be paid to workers for sticking at crummy jobs in crummy conditions.

And finally, in the theoretical free-competition economy, profits are held down to the general level of wages. If they are not, workers will either go into business for themselves, or at least save enough to invest in high-profit enterprises. Capital will become more plentiful, and profits will decline in relation to wages.

The competitive model is a theory of immense elegance: it is internally consistent; it leaves no economic factor unconsidered; and it is easy to understand. There is only one thing wrong with it, and that is that it does not work.

For if the competitive model — in the stripped-down version presented here, or in the one with all the options provided by its adherents — did bear any relation to reality, the structure of wages and profits in Canada would be a lot more equitable than it is; and, furthermore, it would be heading visibly towards complete equality for all. In fact, the wages paid in the Canadian economy are quite unequal, and there is no evidence to show that this inequality is decreasing. None of the mechanisms that are described in the competitive model seem to operate as they are supposed to; for example, the crummiest jobs in the Canadian economy, which should be paying high wages in order to attract workers at all, are in fact offering the crummiest wages.

Some of the reasons for these inequalities are to be found in the "skill mix" in various industries — that is, the number of highly skilled workers in relation to unskilled workers in any one line of work. High-wage industries usually have higher concentrations of highly skilled workers than low-wage ones. But differences in skill mix do not tell the whole story; for workers with equivalent skills are still paid worse in generally low-wage industries than in high-wage ones. In other words, if you're in the wrong industry, it doesn't much matter how many skills you have — your wages will be lower than if you switched to doing the same sort of thing in the right kind of industry.

If the competitive model held water, the Canadian economy would generally not be able to tolerate major differentials in wages nor the simultaneous existence of a high rate of unemployment and a lot of vacancies in the job market.

Canada's economy has been able to do precisely those things. The economists with faith in the competitive model explain this quite simply: workers, they contend, do not like to move from place to place, or from job to job. Workers are not well enough informed about better jobs in other locations; and even those who do find out about better work elsewhere are generally not willing to uproot their families and move on to another location.

This argument may solve the problem as far as the competitive model goes, but it doesn't jibe with the facts. Canadian workers are quite mobile; during the period 1952-56, for example, more than half of all workers covered by unemployment insurance changed their jobs (on the average) at least once a year. This was higher than the rate for American workers; and Americans, in relation to workers in other countries, are fairly mobile themselves.[1] Low-wage workers, certainly, are willing to move around.[2] So, when Prime Minister Trudeau (who evidently retains an orthodox faith in the competitive model) told an unemployed worker in the winter of 1970-71 that he would find a job for him in northern Ontario, he was not proposing a serious solution to the problem of unemployment, but merely ducking the issue by attacking an individual.

Moving to northern Ontario, in fact, is unlikely to help. The competitive model assumes that unemployment is aggravated by the unwillingness of workers to pull up stakes and move to outlying regions. But Canadian workers move around a lot during good times, when unemployment is low, from one job to another. Labour mobility drops during bad times, even though more workers are unemployed. If workers are willing to move when they have jobs already, then they should be even more willing to move when they do not have jobs; and so the fact that mobility drops in bad times means that jobs in outlying regions dry up at the same time as other work does. (In 1951, a relatively good year, the worker turnover rate was about ninety-two per cent of the total number of jobs in the country; in 1954, during a slump, the rate had declined to seventy-

1. Ostry, "Labour Economics," pp. 344-345.
2. DBS, *Hiring and Separation Rates in Certain Industries*, cat. no. 72-006.

eight per cent. It rose again to eighty-six per cent in 1956, a good
year, and fell again to seventy-three per cent in 1958, a bad one.[3])

But even high mobility rates do not mean that workers are moving
from low-wage to high-wage jobs, as the competitive model would
assume. A lot of the moving around is from one low-paying job to
another. Access to high-paying jobs is limited, and not merely by
lack of training; for if high-wage industries really needed workers,
they would be doing a lot of training of workers themselves. The
problem is not that workers don't want to move around within the
economy; the trouble is in the economy itself.

If the problems of wage differentials were caused by the unwillingness of workers to move or change jobs, then the highest wages
would be paid in those industries that are expanding and need to
coax more people into working for them. Sylvia Ostry thinks that
this is in fact happening, at least some of the time.[4] Barry Bluestone,
on the other hand, analyzed US data for the period 1947-66, and
couldn't make any relationship between demand for labour and high
wages stick; he found several low-wage industries that had expanded
production at an above-average clip, but raised wages *less* than the
average.[5] So employers do not depend on the payment of high wages
to attract new workers; at least, not all the time.

There is another hitch. When the productivity of an industry rises,
wages can be raised, profits increased, prices lowered, or all three at
once. So, according to the competitive model, when firms become
more productive, they will cut their prices and force their competitors
to follow suit. This does, in fact, seem to happen in low-wage, competitive industries, inasmuch as productivity gains are not reflected
in the growth of wages.[6] Bluestone found that

> . . . the productivity gains in the low-wage industry are not
> reflected in relative wage-rate changes in low-wage industry.
> Rather than contributing to higher wages, productivity increases
> are either being absorbed into broader profit margins or other-
> wise into lower prices due to raging competition.[7]

3. Ostry, "Labour Economics," p. 342.
4. Ibid, pp. 455-457.
5. Barry Bluestone, "Lower-Income Workers and Marginal Industries," in
Poverty in America, Louis A. Ferman, Joyce L. Kornbluth and Alan Haber
eds., rev. ed. (Ann Arbor: University of Michigan Press, 1968), pp. 291-292.
6. Ostry, "Labour Economics," pp. 457-458.
7. Bluestone, "Lower-Income Workers," p. 293.

The ploughing of productivity into price cutting happens, of course, only when there is competition between firms. In industries where there is no competition worth speaking of — in monopolistic or oligopolistic industries, controlled either by one firm or by a small group of firms — increases in productivity get skimmed off as profits. This, ironically, does pay off for the worker; owners of companies in a monopoly or oligopoly situation generally do pay decent wages.[8] (Companies may be reacting to union pressure, or ensuring that their work forces remain good ones, or simply being careful about public relations.)

The real connection, then, is not between labour demand and high wages, but between industrial concentration and high wages.[9] Companies that can do just about as they please in the market can also afford to pay, and generally do pay, relatively high wages. Furthermore, companies that have a great deal of this kind of control over their markets are generally large, and use a relatively small amount of labour to turn out their products — that is, they are "capital intensive," and use a lot of hardware, or anything else that requires money as opposed to labour, to make their cars, or boats, or whatever. Small companies, on the other hand, generally use a lot of labour and relatively little capital to turn out their products or provide their services. They are labour intensive, usually highly competitive and, as a rule, don't pay their workers much.

The small, labour-intensive businesses are the ones that behave most like businesses in the competitive model; and they are also the ones that pay low wages. The large, capital-intensive businesses don't have to worry much about competition, so they can pay high wages to their workers and pass the costs of the high wages along in the price of the products. (It won't raise the price much, because there's not a lot of labour involved in the final products anyway.) If these large businesses *were* truly competitive in the way that the competition model assumes they are, they would be forced to pass the benefits of increased productivity along to the consumers, rather than keep it in profits or pay it out to the high-wage workers. Those consumers, of course, include the low-paid employees of the small, competitive firms — so, those low-wage workers are not only being

8. See Ostry, "Labour Economics," p. 459; Bluestone, "Lower-Income Workers," p. 297.
9. Detailed information on this relationship is given in appendix I.

paid badly, but they're actually subsidizing the wages of people who are being paid a lot better. Poverty, then, at least in this sense, is the result of an imbalance of economic power between businesses and, by extension, the people who work for those businesses.

The number of workers who get a crack at high-paying jobs is severely restricted. Monopolies and oligopolies tend to keep a strict watch on the number of products they are turning out, in order to make sure that they are receiving maximum prices for each of those products. If the monopolies or oligopolies were made competitive, more products would be turned out as a result of the competition and extra high-wage jobs would be created. So the competitive-model ideal of worker movement from low-paying to high-paying jobs doesn't work out in reality; for where there is not much industrial competition, there just aren't enough high-paying jobs to go around.

The competitive model premise that capital moves into high-profit industries and so makes them competitive sounds as though it ought to be right, but it runs into trouble in the real world. For when those high-profit industries are monopolistic and capital intensive, it may take a tremendous amount of money to set up in competition with them; and they may cut prices, temporarily, in order to force any new competition out of business. The established companies, more-over, have likely used advertising to create loyalty to brand names, which may be too solid or expensive to weaken, and so form another barrier to competition. Governments help out with restrictive patent laws which are discussed in III.5. So no new competition can get off the ground; the profits stay where they are; the number of jobs remains restricted.

High-wage industries, then, tend to be capital intensive, profitable and not very tolerant of competition. Low-wage industries are very competitive, use a lot of labour and aren't very profitable. So much for that aspect of the free-competition model.

The American economist Robert T. Averitt has identified two economies within the United States that split along roughly the same lines as those described above: the *periphery economy,* which tends to be labour intensive, competitive and low paying; and the *centre economy,* which tends to be capital intensive, non-competitive, and high paying.[10] The two economies are, of course, not entirely

10. See Robert T. Averitt, "The Dual Economy," in *The Dynamics of American Industry Structure* (New York: Norton, 1968), pp. 6-7.

separate; in fact, many large corporations, charter members of the centre economy, own or control businesses in the periphery economy in order to safeguard their supply lines. Automobile manufacturers, for example, may own or control auto-parts manufacturers and act as their sole customers—but wages in the auto-parts companies will remain a lot lower than wages in the auto manufacturers' main plants.

The corporations that control the market tend to avoid any flat-out expansion of their production ("capital widening") in order to prevent the market from being swamped; they can therefore keep the prices of their products as high as possible. But the market control exerted by the high-wage industries also puts limits on capital deepening, or mechanization, in the low-wage industries — the mechanization that was supposed to act as an equalizing device in the competitive model. For low-wage industries, which are competitive, are forced by their competition to pass along any benefits from increased productivity to the consumers, instead of keeping it in profit; the high-wage industries of the centre economy are not forced by competition to do anything at all, so profits from increased productivity — including the benefits of technology — can be kept in the family.

Sooner or later, a lot of money winds up inside the corporate structures; and Canada's tax laws, which tend to be quite gentlemanly towards corporations (see V.2), have encouraged the concentration. For income from dividends — that is, profits that are distributed every so often to the shareholders — have been taxed in Canada at a stiffer rate than capital gains, which are realized when shareholders finally sell their stocks.

The shareholders, understandably, have encouraged corporations to hold on to their earnings, rather than pass them out in highly taxed (well, *relatively* highly taxed) dividends; the earnings get poured back into the corporations and the corporations themselves become more valuable, which drives up the value of their stock; and when the shareholders sell the stocks, they get their share of the boodle at a lower tax rate.

If the money were passed out in dividends on a regular basis, smaller businesses, which need credit, could have a crack at it; instead, the money is kept inside the corporate walls and the capital and credit market is reduced in effectiveness. (And, of course, as long as a certain level of profitability is assured, the members of the "technostructure," as John Kenneth Galbraith has called it — that is, the top brass of the corporations — can do what they please. They are, in effect, laws unto themselves; and the smaller businesses can go whistle for capital.)

The retained earnings of the corporations tend to be spent on technological improvements. These improvements not only do not open up more jobs to be filled by workers graduating from low-wage industries, but they cut down on the relatively highly paid jobs available within the high-wage industries. Galbraith points out that the technostructure

> . . . seeks technical progressiveness for its own sake when this is not in conflict with other goals. More important, it seeks certainty in the supply and price of all the prime requisites of production. Labour is a prime requisite. And a large blue-collar labour force, especially if subject to the external authority of a union, introduces a major element of uncertainty and danger. Who can tell what wages will have to be paid to get the men? Who can assess the likelihood, the costs and consequences of a strike?
>
> In contrast mechanization adds to certainty. Machines do not go on strike. Their prices are subject to the stability which, we have seen, is inherent in the contractual relationships between large firms. The capital by which the machinery is provided comes from the internal savings of the firm. Both its supply and cost are thus fully under the control of the firm.
>
> . . . Thus the technostructure has strong incentives, going far beyond considerations of cost (which may themselves be important) to replace blue-collar workers.[11]

Of course, all technological development is accorded a certain degree of class by the corporate psyche, and, in the world of corporations and large industry, technological skill has come to be an objective in its own right, not entirely subject to considerations of profit. This is not completely based on considerations of prestige, for basic research is essentially a gamble, and a difficult one to hedge even

11. John Kenneth Galbraith, *The New Industrial State* (New York: New American Library, 1967), pp. 245-246.

with long-term planning. And to the extent that inventions are made by small businesses or individuals, they are generally bought up by large corporations. In any case, technology, at the corporate level, picks up a momentum of its own.

The result, of course, is that technology, and the investment that applies technology to improve production, has become almost exclusively the stamping-ground of the corporations. The effects of that are twofold: first, credit and financing are denied to industries in the periphery economy; second, high-wage jobs in the centre economy become less accessible to low-wage workers. So workers are stuck in the periphery economy, and the resulting oversupply of labour holds down wages that are low enough already.

This pattern holds true both in Canada and in the United States; but in Canada the problem is compounded because the national economy is largely run from abroad. In 1965, according to the Dominion Bureau of Statistics, American investment in Canada amounted to almost fourteen billion dollars; and, as Charles Taylor has pointed out, that figure is almost certainly an underestimate.[12]

This is distasteful to the nationalists. It is also directly harmful to the Canadian economy, for it aggravates the shrinking of high-wage jobs in at least three ways.

First, resources tend to be shipped from Canada to the United States *before* they are processed; the high-wage jobs, in the secondary refining and manufacturing industries which depend on those resources, are kept for American workers.

Second, the presence of American subsidiary manufacturers in Canada has created a kind of "miniature replica" effect, which is directly harmful to the Canadian market. Charles Taylor outlines the problem this way:

> A small country like Canada can only hope to be competitive internationally in manufacturing by specializing in certain product lines into which it can afford to put the research and development resources needed to stay a world leader. But the joint effect of the tariff and the American corporation has been to lead us away from this pattern. The result has been the

12. Charles Taylor, *The Pattern of Politics* (Toronto: McClelland & Stewart, 1970), p. 71.

creation in Canada of a kind of replica in miniature of the American manufacturing company, or certain parts of it, notably consumer-durables manufacture. This cannot but be inefficient. The *locus classicus* is the refrigerator industry. The 400,000 units sold each year in Canada could probably be most efficiently produced by two plants. Instead there are nine, seven of them American-controlled subsidiaries. This number of productive units makes sense on the American market but is madness here. In addition, the branch plants often try to duplicate the full range of models produced in the United States which further increases costs. And in this respect too our reliance on foreign investment has been feckless.[13]

And third, a corporation that is fully controlled by a parent corporation in the United States is vulnerable to its parent's control over pricing policies, which can be used to draw money out of the Canadian economy and pump it into the American one. This is done quite neatly by overpricing the services sold to the Canadian junior plants by the American senior ones, and underpricing the products going from the Canadian plants to the American ones. So whenever the American corporations want a bit of working capital, the Canadian subsidiaries can be counted on to provide it.

(Heavy American investment has, of course, produced economic distortion in other ways; the fact that Canadian industry is disproportionately located in southern Ontario, according to economist Michael Ray, can be largely traced to the influence of American senior plants, which want their Canadian junior plants where they can get at them.[14])

In the end, then, the only sensible attitude consumers can have towards corporations is one of intense hostility; for corporations that are able to control their markets are stealing the consumers blind. Consumers are in effect taxed without representation through rising prices, so that corporations can finance research and development and underwrite the expansion of their empires. In a competitive situation, prices would be lower. But the people who run corpora-

13. Ibid, p. 82.
14. Cited in T. N. Brewis, *Canadian Economic Policy,* rev. ed. (Toronto: Macmillan, 1965), p. 41.

tions look upon competition in the same way Australian ranchers look at rabbits — cute, but too expensive.

The control of markets by corporations pays off for the workers who are lucky enough to work for those corporations; industries in the centre economy have no real reason to fight to hold the line on wages, if the price of increasing them can be passed along to the consumer. (The work force, in return, is expected to be reliable and co-operative; long-term planning must be made secure.) Of course, what the workers in the centre economy gain as workers, they lose to some extent as consumers, for they pay the same rising prices as everyone else.

The principle of competition is almost sacred in our society. But as far as the working poor are concerned, competition, as it is practised in Canada, is death. For the economy discriminates against workers in competitive industries in favour of the workers and owners of powerful, non-competitive corporations.

The competitive model, in short, does not represent reality; and government policy makers should stop pretending that it does.

II.5 ECONOMIC POWER: UNIONS

Canadian unions certainly talk a good game. At the 1970 convention of the Canadian Labour Congress, for example, it was declared that poverty was a bad thing, that equality was a good thing, and that unions should probably be doing something about both:

> The Canadian Labour Congress in convention declares that the elimination of poverty must be a major goal for Canada. The continued development of natural resources, the growth of industry and the increase in productivity must be directed not only at providing greater corporate wealth or improving the incomes of those who are already well off, but must contribute effectively to raising the living standards of those who are segregated, by their lack of means, from the mainstream of Canadian life. A major redistribution of the national income is essential with a larger proportion going to those who are classified as being poor.

> . . . Organized labour cannot . . . disclaim any responsibility of its own in the war against poverty. The trade unions have a role to play. They can and must bring the advantages of trade union organizations and collective bargaining to the large mass of wage and salary earners who are the victims of low wages and inferior conditions of employment.[1]

This, of course, was what trade unions were all about in the first place. For unions grew out of the discovery by workers that concentrated ownership gave industrial bosses great power, and that the only way to match that power was to organize. As John Eleen, the research director of the Ontario Federation of Labour, has pointed out,

> . . . trade unions were the first armies in the war against poverty. They came into being fighting economic and social injustices.[2]

And if anyone suggests that, somewhere along the way, the army fighting the war against poverty eased up a little, the trade union movement is reproachful:

> . . . it is difficult for trade unionists to understand the often-levelled accusation that organized labour is concerned only with the welfare of union members. For from its very beginnings, the trade union movement has been a consistent and articulate spokesman for the weak, the exploited and the helpless — for the unorganized as well as organized workers.[3]

The declarations of the trade union movement are certainly honourable; but, in the long run, the unions may not have done very much for the poor, or to narrow the gap between the poor and the affluent.

Most people assume that unions are involved in a fight to get more of every industry dollar for the workers, and therefore are

1. See *Canadian Labour* 16 (July-Aug. 1970): 29-34.
2. *Canadian Labour* 14 (Aug. 1969): 17.
3. Editorial, *Canadian Labour* 14 (Sept. 1969): 3.

cutting down on that share of the national product that goes to profit. In fact, nobody has really proved that unions do anything of the kind. Sylvia Ostry, for example, points out that the data necessary to make a historical analysis of the question are not available in Canada, and then notes that

> . . . a large body of American research supports the view that unions have had a negligible influence in this area although this opinion is certainly not unanimous.[4]

The relationship between the share of the national product allotted to labour, and the share allotted to profit, may be determined by many things: technological change, for example, or changes in the supply of or demand for labour, or capital, or both. Stephen Peitchinis, a University of Calgary economist, notes that American and British researchers do not agree on the effectiveness of unions in this area, but adds that he can find no proof that unions have any consistent influence at all:

> . . . trade unions may have influenced labour's share of the national income from *time to time;* but there is no evidence that their political activity [that is, their organizing and bargaining activity] has had any influence on the share in the long run. Whatever gains unions may have made "from time to time" at the expense of other factors of production, by taking advantage of the periodic emergences of hard-market environments, were wiped out when periods of soft-market environment returned. It would appear, therefore, that *as long as management has control over factor combinations and product mixes used in processes of production, and so long as, from time to time, the product market permits them to increase prices, occasional income redistributions caused by both economic and non-economic forces will be corrected at the first opportune moment. What we get in the long run, in effect, is a photographic enlargement of the income pie rather than its redistribution.* The significant change in the industrial and occupational distribution of the labour force, and the rapid increase in the

4. Ostry, "Labour Economics," p. 416, n. 43.

proportion of the labour force in paid employment, largely account for the upward trend in labour's share since 1946.[5]

In fact, trade unions may have contributed greatly to inequality in the overall wage structure in Canada, by gaining more for union members than the unorganized workers could manage to wring from their employers.[6]

Only one-third of Canada's paid workers (outside agriculture) are union members.[7] Some of the other two-thirds are professionals and other well-paid workers, but certainly, most of Canada's low-wage workers are unorganized.

And their unorganized status keeps their wages down; for being a union member certainly does not hurt wages, and is likely to improve them.[8] Moreover, in an industry that is extensively organized, when unions manage to negotiate higher wages, the wages in the unorganized part of the industry may rise as well. So unions can affect the whole pattern of wages inside an industry, whether all the workers in that industry are unionized or not.

There are a number of reasons for the low level of unionization in most Canadian industries. For one thing, Canadian unions have to operate under a number of odd legal restrictions, which are discussed in III.3. And North American management generally is more hostile to union activity than European management; there are still scraps, in both Canada and the United States, over workers' rights to collective bargaining.

Furthermore, there are a number of specific factors that make the organization of low-wage workers, in the eyes of most unions, only more trouble than it is worth. For one thing, many of them are scattered around in small businesses, and are difficult to get at. For another thing, low-wage workers move around a lot, which means that union officials must constantly check back to see that unionized

5. S. G. Peitchinis, *Canadian Labour Economics* (Toronto: McGraw-Hill, 1970), p. 437. See also the (Woods) Task Force on Labour Relations *Report* (Ottawa: 1970).
6. Ostry, "Labour Economics," pp. 463-466.
7. Canada Department of Labour, *Labour Organizations in Canada* (Ottawa, 1969). If teachers, civil servants and police are added, the figure reaches about forty per cent.
8. Ostry, "Labour Economics," p. 467. The differences in the averages between specific industries varied from negligible to thirty per cent.

members and shops stay that way. And the very fact that low-wage workers are paid low wages makes it difficult to finance any kind of organizing drive without help from outside; there is very little money to be made in unionizing the poor.

So unions in Canada have not directed much activity in the direction of the low-wage worker; instead, at the moment, they are concentrating on organizing white-collar workers who may need collective bargaining less, but are easier to handle and are worth a lot more in union dues. Organization of white-collar workers, in fact, may be vital to the continued existence of unions; for the relative overall economic importance of blue-collar workers, low-paid ones in particular, is declining as corporations replace undependable workers with dependable machines and loyal junior-executive types to run them.

Furthermore, Canadian unions are not paying off as well as might be expected even for many of those workers who are organized. Wages paid for various jobs differ considerably from one industry to another. Certainly workers in the automotive and construction industries get paid a lot more than workers in the textile and clothing industries, even though both industries are unionized; and the differences cannot be explained away by variations in the skill mix.[9]

All collective bargaining, of course, is affected by the particular economic environment the bargaining takes place in; so the power of a union depends a great deal on the state of the industry it is involved with. Canadian unions, in particular, have allowed differences in economic environment to determine what happens to individual contracts, for contracts are not negotiated across industries or for the same occupation in all industries, but between unions and specific businesses.

About three-fifths of all bargaining contracts cover one plant only.[10] This is characteristic of North American unions; contracts are hammered out for each individual employer, which results in a tremendous variety of wages between one plant and another, and between one industry and another, even for jobs that demand

9. There is very little Canadian data in this area; the conclusion here is lifted from American data, and certainly there is no Canadian evidence to indicate that it is out of line with the facts.
10. Alton Craig and Harry Waisglass, "Collective Bargaining Perspectives," *Rélations Industriels* (Oct. 1968), p. 582.

roughly the same level of skill and effort. Two American economists, Arthur Ross and Paul Hartman, have concluded:

> Although collective bargaining is now fairly firmly established in the United States, the structure of bargaining is perhaps the most decentralized in the world.
>
> Canada's bargaining system is almost a carbon copy of that in the United States. There is some multi-employer bargaining, almost no industry-wide bargaining, except where one firm constitutes the industry; and the great majority of contracts cover the employees of single firms.[11]

In Western Europe, bodies similar to the Canadian Labour Congress have tremendous power, because they act as co-ordinators for industry-wide collective bargaining and can get the same deal for workers across industries, even across national economies. The Canadian Labour Congress, however, trains union officials, does research, advises government, but provides no guidelines for collective bargaining at all. As Stuart Jamieson points out, workers in competitive industries in Western Europe are a lot better off:

> In Britain, West Germany and the Scandinavian countries, by contrast, the vast majority of organized workers are covered by master agreements negotiated on a nation-wide scale between industrial unions and employer associations or industry federations.[12]

In some industries, there is an informal connection between the settlement negotiated in one plant and the settlement in another; if automobile workers in Oshawa manage to nail down a settlement for six dollars an hour, auto workers in Hamilton are unlikely to settle for five. But this pattern holds true only in the centre economy. In the periphery economy, every union must scramble for itself.

Centralization of collective bargaining, and of unionization in

11. A. M. Ross and Paul T. Hartman, *Changing Patterns of Industrial Conflict* (New York: Wiley, 1960), p. 166.
12. Stuart Jamieson, "Labour Unionism and Collective Bargaining," in *A Social Purpose for Canada*, Michael Oliver ed. (Toronto: University of Toronto Press, 1961), pp. 362-363.

general, leads to increased equality of wages. In other words, Canadian low-wage workers are paying a price for the fragmentation of Canadian unions.[13] Table II.5.i gives an indication of the connection between centralized bargaining and equality in wages.

TABLE II.5.i

Comparison of the wage-bargaining systems and wage structures of six countries in the 1950s

COUNTRY	Centralization of wage bargaining	Wage-rate disparities
Denmark	high	low
France	high	low
Italy	high	low
Australia	high	moderate
Britain	low	moderate
United States	low	high

Source: John T. Dunlop and Melvin Rothbaum, "International Comparisons of Wage Structures," *International Labour Review* 70 (Apr. 1955): table 3, p. 355.

Unions exist, more than anything else, to get money for their members, so unions tend to set up shop where they have a reasonable chance of being successful. In capital-intensive, non-competitive industries, as noted in the previous section, wage increases are easier to come by; for industries with a high degree of control over their markets and no particular reason to hold down prices will tend to grant wage increases and then pass the tab along to the consumer in higher prices.[14] Some corporate managers, in fact, grant wage increases and then blandly jack up the prices of their products more than the wage increases warrant. Unions can be helpful.

These hefty wage settlements may persuade the managers involved that more machinery is required to reduce the relatively minor share of labour costs involved in their products even further, and so put a lid on the number of jobs in their plants. At the same time, the constant price increases will force some consumers to look around for

13. Centralization, of course, does not necessarily have to come from the unions; it may come from direct government determination of wages; or through a labour court; or see John T. Dunlop and Melvin Rothbaum, "International Comparison of Wage Structures," *International Labour Review* 70 (Apr. 1955): 351.
14. See II.4.

partial substitutes for the high-priced monopoly products, or to go without them entirely. And high-wage jobs available to workers moving from low-wage industry vanish.

The rising prices, furthermore, often bring the government into the act. In times of inflation, federal planners put the screws on the economy, and produce a lot of unemployment. The workers who become unemployed are generally not the same workers who negotiated the wage increases, and indirectly caused the price increases; the inflation fighters, as we have pointed out, are generally low-wage workers who are paying the price for the rising wages of unionized workers who have high wages already.

The low-wage workers are generally not unionized because in the periphery economy, wage increases are hard to make stick, and unions are largely beside the point. The only successful unions in highly competitive industries are those that have managed to tie up an entire industry. (If every business in a competitive industry is unionized, and all can be made to pay higher wages, the competition remains at the same level, and nobody gets priced out of business.)

All other things being equal, corporate managers would probably prefer that unions had never been invented; there is still a kind of hostile hangover from the old days, when the interests of corporations and unions were obviously opposed. Still, it is possible for corporations to accommodate themselves to the existence of unions without too much pain, for unions provide valuable services. They act as safety valves for the work force and, through grievance procedures, head off trouble before it becomes serious. And they tend to minimize any possibility that government will intervene unless there is a disaster. As Robert Averitt points out, in connection with American unions:

> The combined political power of center labor and center business makes it difficult for government to assume more than voluntary last-minute arbitration. . . . The appeal of the present system of resolving central labor disputes over any other system involving government led *Fortune* magazine to proclaim that "Labor Unions Are Worth the Price."[15]

15. Averitt, "The Dual Economy," p. 146.

Of course, when corporations come up with a new wrinkle that seems to reduce their need for unions or gives them increased power over them, the mutual understanding falls apart. As Ed Finn, a Canadian labour specialist, points out, the evolution of conglomerates has given corporations even more power than before in relation to their workers, and less reason to fear strikes:

> . . . The Proctor-Silex Co., at Picton, Ont., was able to sustain a 10-month strike by the International Union of Electrical, Radio and Machine Workers because it is part of a conglomerate that includes Smith-Corona, Singer, and the Friden Corp. . . . production stoppage at any one plant hardly disturbs the overall corporate structure, especially when business can easily be transferred elsewhere.[16]

American ownership complicates the Canadian economy and reduces job possibilities for Canadian workers. So does continental unionism. Most large Canadian unions are, in fact, subsidiaries of American unions, and are patterned after their senior partners; a kind of "miniature replica" effect, similar to the one in the corporate field, hampers any attempt to bring unions in Canada together. Similarly, when high-wage workers in Canadian industry push for the same wages as American workers in the same union, they aggravate the inequality of incomes in Canada. And Canadian unions tend to act in the same way as the American unions, to operate their unions as businesses concerned with securing high wages and fringe benefits for union members, and *not* with organizing low-wage workers, or pushing for more equal wages.

A number of professional associations have managed to get by very nicely without centralized collective bargaining or, indeed, bargaining of any other kind; various groups that control the professions are legally entitled to fix fees and control accreditation without being subject to anti-combines controls or any kind of public regulation.

The members of such associations are in the particularly fortunate position of being both employer and employee; a doctor, when he

16. Ed Finn, "Unions and Conglomerates," *Canadian Dimension* 6, no. 5 (Oct.-Nov. 1969): 13.

sets his bill, is determining both a price and a wage, and a medical association that puts a floor on his charges is price fixing in a splendidly efficient way.

These professional associations put a limit on who may join, and impose rigid standards for membership. The Ontario Royal Commission Inquiry into Civil Rights observed that

> Those professions or occupations which have been granted self-governing status are charged with a responsibility not only to see that persons licensed are qualified, but that all qualified applicants are licensed . . . it must be recognized that each of the self-governing bodies have been given a statutory monopoly through its licensing powers. What has to be guarded against is the use of the power to license for purposes other than establishing and preserving standards of character, competence and skill.[17]

Trade unions occasionally act in the same manner, using their powers in this area to require extremely long periods of apprenticeship and training, and keeping out all but the most determined — and the most able to survive for a while on low wages. Many unions charge exorbitant rates for admission, which hit low-wage workers hardest. Furthermore, the use of seniority in a fragmented system of bargaining means that an older worker who is laid off will have to start again at the bottom level in any new job; and the fact that most pensions cannot be transferred from job to job gives older workers real reason to stay in low-paying jobs, simply because their security in retirement will be endangered if they go after a job with higher wages.

Workers with any seniority, then, tend to be tied to their jobs, unable to move on to better ones, despite the high worker mobility between one low-wage job and another; high-wage unions and professional associations intensify the problem by insisting that any newcomer put in a good deal of time at the bottom of the ladder. (These barriers are actually becoming stiffer in some areas. The Association of Professional Engineers of Ontario, for example, has

17. Cited in ECC, *Interim Report on Competition Policy* (Ottawa, 1969), p. 152.

announced that it will phase out its program of independent study, which could be entered into by high school students, and demand that any aspiring engineer, from now on, graduate from university.[18])

As Galbraith has noted, high-wage industries have every reason to eliminate blue-collar workers, and substitute for them white-collar workers who are inclined to be a little more respectful towards the corporations because they conceive of themselves as administrators and not workers at all. Technology, then, as used by the corporations, poses a direct threat to the unions. Another threat is the growing public impatience with inflation, which becomes sharper with every high wage settlement, consequent price hikes and profit expansion; that impatience has prepared the way for tough anti-union intervention by the government.

So the unions are in trouble. Although they seem to be committed to the ideals of equality and democracy, they have accepted direction from senior unions in the United States; they have abandoned the low-wage worker; they have refused to push for centralization of the fragmented union pattern in Canada; and they have left themselves open to repressive action from government.

II.6 REGIONAL AND RURAL POVERTY

If the free-competition view of the world is unrelated to reality, and if Canada's economy is organized into two distinct areas — the centre economy and the periphery economy — then, logically, some areas of Canada should be economically worse off than others. In fact, regional disparities in Canada are critical.

For certain regions of Canada produce poverty, and other regions of Canada produce affluence. The division is not absolute; in Ontario, which enjoys the highest standard of living in Canada, a million people are living below the poverty line. But, all things being equal, you are more likely to be poor in Newfoundland than in Ontario; and, since all things are *not* equal — since the government of Canada has done very little that is sensible about regional dis-

18. See "Professional Engineers Will Require Degrees," Toronto *Globe and Mail* (8 July 1971), p. B2.

parities — poverty has become accepted as a natural and inevitable way of life in many areas of the nation.

The gap between the rich and the poor provinces is a wide one and can be shown numerically. Table II.6.i gives a schedule of average personal income for each province — income that includes all welfare payments, unemployment-insurance benefits, old-age pensions and other transfer payments:

TABLE II.6.i

Personal income as a per cent of the average of total Canadian income

PROVINCE	1961	1963	1965	1969	1970
Newfoundland	57.8	55.4	55.9	56.8	55.4
Nova Scotia	77.9	76.0	75.6	77.4	79.4
New Brunswick	68.1	67.5	68.5	70.7	71.5
PEI	58.5	58.6	60.4	61.5	62.4
Quebec	90.2	88.1	89.9	91.0	90.4
Ontario	118.3	117.1	116.6	115.5	115.7
Manitoba	95.8	95.8	95.3	97.8	97.7
Saskatchewan	71.0	99.2	90.9	84.9	86.4
Alberta	99.6	98.1	96.4	98.3	100.1
BC	114.3	112.2	113.0	109.4	107.1

Sources: DREE, *Major Economic Indicators, Provinces and Regions* (Ottawa, 1971), table 4:2.

These raw figures can be made a little more meaningful; table II.6.ii breaks down both personal income and earned income (that is, income without transfer payments, dividends, interest and so on) in each province, and expresses them as percentages of the highest average provincial income in Ontario.

The average earned income — the money earned by the average worker — in Prince Edward Island and Newfoundland was *less than half* that of the average worker in Ontario, on a per capita basis.

Things have been this way for approximately fifty years;[1] and, as economist Marvin McInnis has pointed out, the situation is not getting much better:

1. Marvin McInnis, "The Trend of Regional Income Differentials in Canada," *Canadian Journal of Economics* 1 (1968): 446.

TABLE II.6.ii
Personal and earned income per capita, as a per cent of the Ontario figures, 1969

PROVINCE	Personal	Earned
Newfoundland	47.9	45.1
PEI	54.0	48.9
Nova Scotia	68.5	66.5
New Brunswick	61.8	59.5
Quebec	78.0	77.5
Ontario	100.0	100.0
Manitoba	84.4	83.0
Saskatchewan	74.7	72.3
Alberta	86.5	86.5
BC	92.6	90.6

Calculated from DREE, *Major Economic Indicators, Provinces and Regions* (Ottawa, 1971), table 2.4.
Note: "Earned income" is personal income less government transfer payments less interest, dividends and miscellaneous investment income of persons.

> On the basis of the evidence the trend of regional income differentials in Canada appears to have been roughly a constant; there has been neither convergence or divergence.[2]

Jobs pay less in depressed regions; and the chances of getting one of those low-paying jobs are relatively thin. Unemployment rates in the Atlantic regions and in the province of Quebec, as shown in table II.6.iii, consistently run a lot higher than the ones in Ontario and the Prairies. In other words, when the crusaders in Ottawa deliberately jack up the unemployment rate in order to fight inflation, the poorer areas of Canada pay for it.

And the bill is higher in those regions than is indicated by simple unemployment statistics; for in depressed regions, a lot of people have simply given up the struggle and dropped out of the labour market. This factor shows up in measures of the "labour-force participation rate." T. N. Brewis has noted:

2. Ibid.

TABLE II.6.iii

Unemployment rates, %

YEAR		Atlantic	Quebec	Ontario	Prairies	BC	Canada
1961		11.3	9.3	5.5	4.6	8.5	7.2
1962		10.8	7.5	4.3	3.9	6.6	5.9
1963		9.6	7.4	3.8	3.7	6.4	5.5
1964		8.2	6.3	3.3	3.1	5.3	4.7
1965		7.4	5.4	2.5	2.6	4.2	3.9
1966		6.4	4.7	2.5	2.1	4.6	3.6
1967		6.6	5.3	3.1	2.3	5.2	4.1
1968		7.3	6.5	3.6	2.9	6.0	4.8
1969		7.5	6.9	3.1	2.9	5.0	4.7
1970		7.6	6.9	4.3	4.4	7.7	5.9

Source: DREE, *Major Economic Indicators, Provinces and Regions* (Ottawa, 1971), table 2.4.

As might be expected, high unemployment rates tend to be associated with low labour force participation rates.[3]

Table II.6.iv confirms the point. One person in ten who could at least look for work in Ontario is out of luck in the Maritimes — so far out of luck that he doesn't even show up on the unemployment charts. If the unemployment statistics were balanced out — that is, if enough people in the Atlantic region had gone looking for work to bring the labour-participation rate up to the Canadian average — the unemployment statistics for 1970 for the Maritimes would have been almost 16 per cent, instead of 7.6.

The jobs, many of them, aren't where the people are. Thirty-seven per cent of all Canadians live in the Atlantic, Prairie, or British Columbia regions, and only twelve per cent of non-local or non-primary manufacturing jobs (that is, skilled jobs in large industries that can afford to pay decent wages) are found in those regions.[4]

A lot of workers in depressed regions don't try to buck the odds; instead, they move on to the affluent areas. And a number of policy makers have decided that the fast way to narrow regional disparities is to encourage — even, one way or another, to force — this kind of

3. T. N. Brewis, *Regional Economic Policies in Canada* (Toronto: Macmillan, 1969), p. 18.
4. Ibid, table 1:4, p. 16.

TABLE II.6.iv.

Participation rate

YEAR		Atlantic	Quebec	Ontario	Prairies	BC	Canada
1965		48.2	53.2	56.7	55.5	53.9	54.4
1966		48.6	54.3	57.2	55.8	54.9	55.1
1967		48.5	54.9	57.6	55.8	55.8	55.5
1968		48.2	54.3	57.8	56.8	56.1	65.5
1969		48.0	54.5	58.0	56.9	56.7	55.8
1970		47.6	54.3	58.0	57.1	57.3	55.8

Source: DREE, *Major Economic Indicators, Provinces and Regions* (Ottawa, 1971), table 2.1.

migration. But these interprovincial flows are not adequate for purposes of regional economic adjustment.[5]

In fact, the shuffling around necessary to even up the average earned income for each province would almost certainly destroy most of the provincial economies. Table II.6.v gives an idea of the size of the problem.

TABLE II.6.v

Population of provinces equalized by migration

PROVINCE	Equalized	Actual
Newfoundland	273,000	(518,000)
PEI	63,000	(110,000)
Nova Scotia	595,000	(766,000)
New Brunswick	415,000	(624,000)
Quebec	5,430,000	(6,013,000)
Ontario	8,905,000	(7,637,000)
Manitoba	949,000	(981,000)
Saskatchewan	749,000	(942,000)
Alberta	1,613,000	(1,600,000)
BC	2,259,000	(2,137,000)

Source: Calculated from DREE, *Major Economic Indicators, Provinces and Regions* (Ottawa, 1971); figures in brackets are population in 1969 (est); hypothetical population is based on "earned income" in 1969.

5. T. J. Courchene, "Interprovincial Migration and Economic Adjustment," *Canadian Journal of Economics* 3 (Nov. 1970): 573.

The Department of Regional Economic Expansion has decided that migration is not the answer. Instead, it proposes to concentrate on boosting wages and jobs within each region

> . . . so that economic growth takes place mostly by movement and change within each region, rather than by massive attrition of whole regions.[6]

There will have to be a lot of movement of industry before equality is achieved. High-paying industry — manufacturing, in particular — is concentrated in the central provinces, and the manufacturing that is located in depressed regions pays low wages. Table II.6.vi outlines the gap between the rich regions and the poor ones and indicates a further concentration in Ontario between 1961 and 1969.

TABLE II.6.vi

Percentage of employment in manufacturing, by region, 1961 and 1969, and average wage in manufacturing, 1969

REGION	Employment 000	1961 share %	1969 share %	Average wage $
Atlantic	76.8	4.6	4.5	4995
Quebec	527.0	33.6	31.2	5542
Ontario	836.9	47.8	49.5	6228
Prairies	119.8	6.9	7.1	5888
BC	130.7	7.7	7.7	6591

Source: DREE, *Major Economic Indicators, Provinces and Regions* (Ottawa, 1971), tables 3.3, 3.1.

T. N. Brewis has calculated that eighty-eight per cent of manufacturing (aside from primary and local manufacturing, which don't pay as well) is located in Ontario and Quebec;[7] and only about sixty-four per cent of all Canadians live within reach of those manufacturing jobs.

The public services to citizens of depressed regions are consequently starved for money. As table II.6.vii demonstrates, regions with no jobs and no industry have very little to tax.

6. Canada Department of Regional Economic Expansion, *Salient Features of Federal Regional Development Policy in Canada* (Ottawa, 1969), p. B7.
7. Brewis, *Regional Economic Policies,* table 1:4, p. 16.

TABLE II.6.vii

Per capita dollar yield of one percentage point of income tax

PROVINCE	Personal	Corporate
Ontario	$3.14	$3.40
BC	2.98	3.29
Quebec	2.21	2.39
Saskatchewan	1.89	1.82
New Brunswick	1.27	1.38
PEI	.91	1.00

Source: Taken from "Federal-Provincial Grants and the Spending Power of Parliament," Government of Canada working paper on the constitution (Ottawa, 1969), p 30.

These factors — low wages, high unemployment, low labour-force participation, small tax base — all interlock, so the incidence of poverty, set out in table II.6.viii, is a lot higher in some provinces than in others.

TABLE II.6.viii

The incidence and distribution of poverty by region, 1967 [a]

REGION	Poor persons as % of total population	% distribution of all poor persons
Atlantic	38.0	18.1
Quebec	22.9	33.9
Ontario	12.8	22.2
Prairies	22.6	18.6
BC	15.2	7.2
Canada	20.0%	100.0%

a. Based on the Relative Poverty Line presented in table 1.3.ii. Source: Raw data from the 1967 DBS survey of consumer finances. These figures were presented in *Income Distributions by Size in Canada, 1967*, but using the ECC/DBS poverty line.

While the tax base — which is the main factor in financing public services — is a lot smaller in the Prairies and in Atlantic regions than it is in Ontario and Quebec, yet there is a greater need for public services in a region where jobs don't pay much and don't last long; the poverty in depressed areas, therefore, is intensified.

Education and training are crucial in the avoidance of poverty;

but because the tax base in poor areas is small, there is less money available for education and training, and so the problem grows.

But why do these disparities exist? How did they come about? Are there genuine deficiencies in the ways people work or in the ways industries work in the depressed regions that would explain the starvation of these areas?

A study for the Economic Council of Canada turned up none of the obvious ones. The regional differences in industrial or occupational distribution, in the age of the labour force, in the hours people worked, in the amount of schooling they got, and in the numbers of people who lived in the city as opposed to the country, were substantial, but not substantial enough entirely to explain away the disparities in earnings:

> . . . even at the level of mere statistical distribution, the factors examined do not account for much of the observable variation in earnings; something more basic must be sought.[8]

The answer that seems to hold up best is that small flaws were built into Canada's economy right at the beginning and, as the economy grew, these flaws magnified themselves into seriously imbalanced growth. One writer has found

> . . . a systematic relation between national development levels and regional inequality or geographic dispersion.[9]

In other words, when any country, Canada included, begins its economic growth, flaws in the distribution of the factors of production — that is, labour and capital —tend to exaggerate the differences between regions.

One of these unbalancing forces is migration. Generally, a region that is a little less prosperous than its next-door neighbour will lose the very best of its workers to that neighbouring region, where their talents can be rewarded more liberally. The people that move will be

8. Frank T. Denton, *An Analysis of Interregional Differences in Manpower Utilization and Earnings* (Ottawa: ECC, 1966), p. 13.
9. J. G. Williamson, "Regional Inequality and the Process of National Development: A Description of Patterns," in *Regional Analysis*, L. Needlerman ed. (Harmondsworth: Penguin, 1968), p. 155.

vigorous and entrepreneurial, the educated and skilled, and of productive age.[10]

These are exactly the same people who have been invested in most by the region that has trained them and is now losing them. The Maritimes, Newfoundland, Saskatchewan and Manitoba have all seen waves of emigration, in which these provinces lost their expensively educated young people to the central provinces or to British Columbia. This pattern has been quite consistent in the Atlantic provinces and in Saskatchewan.[11]

Those who move are young;[12] the depressed area has no chance to recoup even a little of its investment in them before they move on. Not only that, but the region has lost their potential contribution to its recovery as well. And the process is cumulative; for as the region falls further behind, more young people — who are more mobile than their elders — will be encouraged to leave.

The British economist J. G. Williamson has suggested that sooner or later, as economies mature into truly national ones, these differentials will tend to work themselves out;[13] more unskilled workers will begin to move into places like Toronto from the Maritimes (which does seem to be happening now), and the differences in wages themselves will begin to narrow.

But there is more to regional economics than labour alone, and, therefore, more to regional disparities; there is reason to suspect that Canada's financial institutions are not doing much to overcome regional disparities, and may, in fact, be reinforcing them.[14] It is difficult to tell with any precision; for the agencies responsible for keeping these institutions in line (the Bank of Canada and the Department of Insurance) are not doing anything in the way of collecting information about the behaviour of financial organizations on a regional basis — nor is the Dominion Bureau of Statistics. (Several provinces made earnest recommendations to the Royal Commission on Banking and Finance that information of that kind be gathered.[15]

10. Ibid, p. 102.
11. See Leroy O. Stone, *Migration in Canada* (Ottawa: DBS, 1969), pp. 89-100, 153-172.
12. Ibid, p. 74.
13. See Williamson, "Regional Inequality."
14. Submission of the Government of Manitoba to the Royal Commission on Banking and Finance (1963), p. 9.
15. Ibid, p. 14.

As far as can be discovered, no national organization has any intention of doing so.)

What these institutions are probably doing — and nobody has made a strong case to disprove it — is pulling savings out of low-income areas and investing them in the centre economy.

The Canadian Life Insurance Officers' Association provided a small insight into the problem in its submission to the Royal Commission on Banking and Finance. From information in that brief, it is possible to calculate the relationship between life insurance premiums and assets in each province, and so to figure out where money gets pumped into life insurance companies, and where it gets pumped out again. This information is set out in table II.6.ix, and it indicates that the companies are investing heavily in the more developed areas of the country. (It would not be necessary to do all this sleuthing, of course, if these companies were required to report their premium income and their new investment each year.)

TABLE II.6.ix

Estimated percentage distribution of life-insurance premiums and assets by province

PROVINCE	(1) Assets	(2) Premiums	(1) ÷ (2)
Nfld	0.8	0.9	89
PEI	0.2	0.3	67
NS	2.1	3.3	64
NB	1.5	2.2	68
Que	24.2	27.0	90
Ont	43.6	43.0	101
Man	4.6	4.2	109
Sask	3.0	3.0	100
Alta	8.5	6.3	135
BC	11.0	8.6	128

Source: Canadian Life Insurance Officers' Association, *Submission* to the Royal Commission on Banking and Finance (Ottawa, 1963), table 5a, p 69, for assets; figures are for 1960. For premiums, Superintendent of Life Insurance for Canada, *Report for the Year Ended December 31, 1961* 1 (Ottawa, 1962), table xxii, p 88a. The figures relate to 1961.

Trust companies would probably be involved in much the same kind of investment if they were not heavily regulated by the government for the protection of the people who have money in them. As it is, most trust companies invest their clients' assets in low-yield government bonds and mortgages wherever the trust companies happen to be, and so probably don't do much good or much harm in terms of regional disparities.

Almost no hard information is available about the investment behaviour of chartered banks in Canada, nearly all of which have their headquarters in Montreal and Toronto. But there is a lot of reason to think that they tend to invest in the same way as life insurance companies, putting money into affluent or expanding areas at the expense of weaker ones.[16] The government of Manitoba is fairly certain that the banking system is not meeting the needs of emerging areas:

> The chartered banking system's traditional outlook and centralized control, and its traditional policies and practices in general have not favoured balanced regional growth in Canada.
> . . . the application of "blanket" policies cannot have a uniform impact on each region. For the transitional economies with a high proportion of small business, and where few alternative sources of capital funds are available, the effects are most significant.[17]

Without data to prove the point either way, it is reasonable to go along both with theoretical suspicions and with the impressions of those people responsible for the economies of low-income regions, and say that Canada's banks are *probably* making regional disparities worse. In any case, it is up to them to prove that they are not; and if the information is not forthcoming, the federal government should force them to provide it.

As noted above, Williamson argues that the imbalances in the flow of productive factors will tend to reverse themselves over time.

16. See J. K. Galbraith, *The Economics of Banking Operations* (Montreal: McGill University Press, 1968), ch. 4. Given a constant reserve requirement, when lending increases in economically expanding areas, the banks will sell securities in other areas to keep their cash position in line with legal requirements. "In effect," as Galbraith points out, "the areas buying the securities are supplying funds to the expanding areas." (*Banking Operations*, p. 210.) It is precisely this area in which no data are available. We do know, however, which areas of Canada have been expanding.
17. Submission of the Government of Manitoba to the Royal Commission on Banking and Finance, p. 9.
18. Williamson, "Regional Inequality," p. 107.

Labour, apparently, is already doing this, and, theoretically, capital should follow along.[18]

One of the major obstructions in the way of this crucial reversal is, and has been, national economic policies that from the beginning have favoured the development of the centre economy over the development of the periphery. The concentration of economic power in the centre has led to a distortion of prices: goods manufactured in the centre economy and exports to the periphery have been overpriced, and goods travelling the other way underpriced.

Canada's economy, then, contains vast disparities between various regions, disparities that directly affect the livelihoods of the inhabitants of those regions, and that cause a high incidence of poverty. Canada's financial institutions are not helping, and are probably hindering any effort to lessen those disparities. In any case, there is no sign that the regional problems in this country are becoming any less severe.

II.7 DISCRIMINATION

Poverty in Canada is not spread smoothly throughout all groups. On the contrary. If you have the misfortune to be a woman, an Indian, an Eskimo or a French-Canadian, your chances of being poor are greater — much greater — than if you were young, white, male and English speaking.

The effects of discrimination vary according to the group that is being discriminated against. Women tend to live longer than men, and so presumably enjoy better health, but their incomes, in the kinds of work they can find, are much lower. The old obviously *have* lived longer than many, but their incomes are very small, and their living conditions generally miserable. And almost all Indians, Eskimos and Métis spend their lives in a world of complete degradation.

The statistics for Canada's native peoples indicate just what a century of systematic oppression can do. These are from a 1965 study:[1]

1. Jim Harding, "Canada's Indians: A Powerless Minority," in *Poverty in Canada,* John Harp and John R. Hofley eds. (Toronto: Prentice-Hall, 1971), p. 240.

Over forty per cent of Indian and Métis *families* earn $1000 or less — the level of absolute deprivation for an *individual*. Seventy-five per cent of Indian and Métis families live on $2000 or less, in conditions of absolute deprivation.

In northern Saskatchewan, the average income of all Indian and Métis families is about $500 per year.

In 1961, only 15.9 per cent of all employable Indians and Métis were in the work force, as opposed to 37.5 per cent for the rest of the population. The bulk of this employment was seasonal, low skilled and low paying.

More than sixteen per cent of Indian and Métis families live in one-room shacks. More than half of them live in three rooms or less.

Only thirteen per cent of Indian and Métis homes have running water.

Only twenty-five per cent of all Métis and Indians get to the grade six level in elementary school. Of the seven thousand Indian students in Canada in 1962-63, only six per cent were in grades nine to twelve; the vast majority were in grades one to four. In 1962-63, there were only seventy Indian students beyond high school in Canada: six at university, a few more in professional schools, and the rest, the majority, in trade schools.

The health and mortality rates for Indians, Eskimos and Métis are all abysmal.[2]

The specific reasons for this squalor are too complex to be summed up quickly. But the general principle underlying them is clear:

> A strong argument exists for viewing Canadian people of Indian ancestry as a colonial people, who have been treated and in effect controlled by outside authorities over which they had no direct control.[3]

And the colonial principle has permeated every government and public attitude towards the Indian, even to the way the department responsible for their supervision was organized until relatively recently:

2. See VII.4.
3. Harding, "Canada's Indians," p. 243.

It is tragic and ironic that Canada's native population should be under the control of a branch of government in the Department of Immigration. Many people of Indian ancestry point to this irony as evidence of their colonial status. Canadians would perhaps be outraged if any other ethnic group in Canada existed under special control of one government branch, instead of having relations with all government branches as do other citizens.[4]

This paternalism is distasteful. It is also unsuccessful, even in providing the basic tools to raise Indians, Eskimos and Métis out of poverty:

Indians do not have the money to develop their reserves. They cannot, like other people, get it from the province and Indian Affairs doesn't have it. Credit available to Indians is minimal, often in sums too small to be useful.[5]

The Trudeau government has reacted to the failures of Canadian Indian policy, not by changing the nature of its relationship with the Indians, but by attempting to deny it. Jean Chrétien has proclaimed his intention to abolish his department within five years. The recent white paper on *Indian Policy* referred to the "anomaly of treaties within groups in society," made a passing reference to the native peoples' "sense of grievance," and then declared the government's intention to liquidate its obligations according to the letter of the law:

The terms and effects of the treaties between the Indian people and the government are widely misunderstood. A plain reading of the words used in treaties reveals the limited and minimal promises which were included in them.[6]

In other words, the white man gave the Indian a raw deal in the first place, and now intends to honour it.

4. Ibid, pp. 244-245.
5. Heather Hildebrandt, "The People Factory," in *Poverty and Social Policy in Canada*, W. E. Mann ed. (Toronto: Copp Clark, 1970), p. 320.
6. Cited in James A. Duran, "The New Indian Policy: Lessons from the US," *Canadian Dimension* 6, no. 6 (Dec.-Jan. 1969-70): 22.

This proposal was widely and sensibly attacked by the Indians, as being wrong in law and useless in application.

First, the bit about the "anomaly of treaties within groups in society" is a red herring; the Indian treaties were in fact contracts, in which promises were made in return for the use and possession of Indian land. The contracts were presented as an alternative to annihilation, but are nonetheless binding.

Second, the written memoranda of these contracts were never considered complete by the Indians and certainly did not represent the range of the government's commitment:

> When one considers the unequal competence in law between the negotiators for the Crown and the Indians, this insistence on observing only the letter of the agreement neglects the spirit in which the negotiations were conducted. The Indians of North America relied primarily on an oral tradition, and village elders still refer, in the case of certain numbered treaties in Canada, to oral proclamations made by the agents of the Crown. Given their non-European cultural background, the Indians considered the oral commitments as binding, if not more so, as the brief written terms of the treaties.[7]

Third, the decision to eliminate the contract was made by the government on its own, and did not reflect any of the ideas and opinions expressed by those Indians who had been — briefly — consulted. Harold Cardinal, in *The Unjust Society,* points out:

> Despite the impression deliberately fostered by the government all during 1968 and early in 1969 that the meetings between Indians and the government were only of a preliminary nature, the government decided in June of 1969 to publish an Indian policy paper. Even to publish such a policy paper ran absolutely counter to everything the government had been telling the Indian people for a year and a half. The fact that the government stood ready to countenance such a hypocritical reversal of its word gives the lie to all the pious Ottawa utterances of the so-called consultation period. To make matters

7. Ibid, p. 22.

worse, however, it is quite obvious that during the exact period in which the government was theoretically pursuing consultation, federal officials, in isolation from the people they were supposed to be consulting, were plotting unilaterally a policy designed to alter the future of every Indian in Canada.[8]

Fourth, an attempt much like Mr. Chrétien's to jettison the responsibility of a government towards the Indian population was made in the United States during the 1950s, and finally had to be abandoned.

The federal government, in its anxiety to "get the United States out of the Indian business," tried to shift responsibility for Indians to the states. The states weren't having any; and neither, likely, will most Canadian provinces, which have a miserable record in dealing with Indians' property and other rights. In this connection, one critic of Indian affairs remarked:

> In view of the US experience, Mr. Chrétien's plan . . . seems to be an ill-founded dream which, if executed, will be done over the objections of the Indians themselves.[9]

The problems of the Canadian Indian will not be solved by a shuffling of jurisdictions. And increased social-welfare programs will not help much. What is required, evidently, is a resolve to raise the Indians' standard of living — and on the Indians' terms.

French Canadians have already been putting the heat on the federal government; for their place within Confederation has certainly not assured them of economic equality, or anything like it.

But the federal government has consistently implied that the national aspirations of Quebec are irrational, and that the economic grievances of the Québécois can be fixed up with a little good will and bilingualism. Table II.7.i indicates that bilingualism will not fix the whole thing up; for French Canadians, in Quebec, are as colonized as the Indians are.

The findings of the Royal Commission on Bilingualism and Bicul-

---

8. Harold Cardinal, *The Unjust Society: The Tragedy of Canada's Indians* (Edmonton: Hurtig, 1969), p. 128.
9. Duran, "New Indian Policy," p. 21.

turalism, as summarized by *Le Magazine Maclean,* indicate quite clearly that fluency in both national languages is less important than membership in the English-speaking dominant group in Quebec — and that bilingualism is largely irrelevant:

> Unilingual English Canadians earn as much as bilingual English Canadians while French Canadians who speak only English (the assimilated) earn considerably more than bilingual French Canadians. And bilingual French Canadians earn considerably less than unilingual English.
>
> In total . . . unilingual English Canadians earn $5,502 while bilingual persons earn $4,772. In short, it isn't the knowledge of two languages that is beneficial to the French Canadian in Quebec, but rather the knowledge of one language — English.
>
> "In Quebec," the authors add, "as in the rest of the country, it is better to be a unilingual English Canadian than a bilingual French Canadian."[10]

TABLE II.7.i
Average income of salaried males in 14 ethnic groups, Quebec, 1961

ETHNIC GROUP	In dollars	Index
General average	3469	100.0
British	4940	142.4
Scandinavians	4939	142.4
Dutch	4891	140.9
Jewish	4851	139.8
Russians	4828	139.1
Germans	4245	122.6
Poles	3984	114.8
Asians	3734	107.6
Ukrainians	3733	107.6
Other Europeans	3547	102.4
Hungarians	3537	101.9
French Canadians	3185	91.8
Italians	2938	84.6
Native Indians	2112	60.8

From *Canadian Dimension* 5, no 8 (Feb 1969): 17.

10. As cited in *Canadian Dimension* 5, no. 8 (Feb. 1969): 17.

Unemployment and education statistics show the same relationship. To be French Canadian in Canada's French Canadian province is to be at a distinct disadvantage. And to be French Canadian in any of Canada's English provinces is to find existence in one's own language and culture impossible.

The recent report of the Royal Commission on the Status of Women came up with figures that show that women are generally short-changed in the labour market. The average annual income of Canadian female heads of families in 1967 was $2536; over forty per cent of all women not in families earned less than $1500. Women in all types of work earned less than men, and educational qualifications were worth less to women than to men.[11]

Simple recitations of figures cannot include any discussion of the various social prejudices directed towards minorities, or the causes of those prejudices. And there can be little detailed criticism of government policy towards minorities for, with the doomed exception of Canada's Indian policy, there is no discernible government intervention in these areas.

But the numbers alone prove that there is systematic oppression and exploitation of minorities in this country; to be a member of a minority is to live badly, to be shackled to a low-paying job, and to know that you will never get any further.

II.8 CONSUMER EXPLOITATION

The poor live constantly on the edge of disaster. Any illness, injury, breakdown or lay-off, expected or unexpected, will shove a family in poverty over the edge; for part of being poor is to have no security, and no margin for error.

At the same time, the poor are subject to the constant thievery, major or minor, that is inevitable in a society controlled by corporations: misleading advertising, ravenous finance practices, exploitative prices, shoddy manufacture and so on. The affluent have the resources to protect themselves against this kind of swindling, and so tend to see the dark side of consumerism as a kind of game

11. Royal Commission on the Status of Women in Canada, *Report* (Ottawa, 1970).

between the customer and the producer. But for the poor, the sudden breakdown of a new major appliance, or the discovery that a used car will cost a fortune in repairs, may be a catastrophe.

And, in fact, the poor are more likely to buy a lousy used car or a shabby appliance than the rich. They cannot afford to invest in quality, and in the end, they pay even for that. For entire business enterprises are set up quite' specifically to exploit the difference in purchasing power between the poor and the affluent; countless techniques have been evolved to make the exploitation more efficient; and used-car dealers, pawnbrokers, and owners of encyclopedia and kitchenware chains retire rich.

The exploitation is not limited to areas in which a little counselling from a home economist could prevent it; the poor are badly oppressed, for example, in the housing market, an area in which smart shopping won't compensate for lack of money.

According to a survey of a number of families on welfare by the Canadian Welfare Council, the poor on public assistance spend an average of forty-seven per cent of their budgets on housing (almost twice the twenty-five per cent considered reasonable) — and the allowances given in welfare budgets for housing don't come close to covering the need.

Furthermore, families on welfare are larger than the Canadian average, but live in smaller accommodation; over thirty per cent of welfare households have more than 1.6 persons per room, as opposed to about four per cent in Canada as a whole. Families on welfare in Canada are more than twice as likely as non-welfare families to be obliged to share their accommodation with others, and the houses available to welfare recipients are substandard in terms of piped water, baths, flush toilets and other things most Canadians consider necessities.[1]

All this does not necessarily imply that there is a housing shortage generally in Canada, and that the poor are getting the short end of the stick of a general shortage; for, although the Hellyer and the Central Mortgage and Housing Corporation task forces both argued that Canada was in a housing crisis, a recent study by

1. Canadian Welfare Council (now the Canadian Council on Social Development), *Some Preliminary Findings: The Housing Conditions of Public-Assistance Recipients in Canada, 1968*. Report to the Canadian Conference on Housing, 1968.

N. H. Lithwick indicates that in terms of housing stock, overall, Canada is not doing so badly.[2]

For one thing, in 1966, there was relatively little doubling-up; only about four per cent of all families did not maintain their own households, as opposed to thirteen per cent in 1951. In general the quality of Canadian housing, measured in terms of toilets, baths, showers and general repair has been improving.[3] And housing has become less urgent for many people; in 1966, for the first time, Canadians spent a higher percentage of the gross national product on transportation than on housing.

So the problem is probably not that there are not enough decent houses to go around; the problem is that the poor do not have enough money either to rent or to buy them:

> For the period 1961-1965 some crude estimates can be derived. For the lowest third of the income distribution, family incomes rose by 25% over this period while the price of homes they typically purchased rose by 35%. The next 50% of the income distribution had an income increase of 25%, with the price of homes they tended to buy rising by only 18%. It would appear that in this period, the poor were indeed made worse off by the trend in housing prices.[4]

So the housing market for the poor is quite different from the Canadian housing market as a whole; and although there may or may not be a housing shortage for middle-class Canadians, there is certainly one for the poor. Lithwick has pointed out that the problem is especially severe in the cities, where the creation of slums has become almost a routine process. The poor cannot reach the suburbs, where property values are kept high through zoning and where cars are a necessity; and, as industry moves out into the suburban areas, the poor are increasingly closed into jobless slums.[5]

The poor, then, have less to spend for housing, and so are forced into bad and crowded accommodation. But the economies involved in living in a slum may be illusory because, dollar for dollar, they

2. N. H. Lithwick, *Urban Canada: Prospects and Problems* (Ottawa, 1970), ch. 1.
3. L. B. Smith, *Housing in Canada* (Ottawa, 1971), pp. 9-10.
4. Lithwick, *Urban Canada*, pp. 27-29.
5. Ibid, pp. 34-35.

may be getting a worse deal than the affluent. Canadian data are not available on this subject, but American data are; and R. F. Muth has concluded, after a study of housing expenditures, that the poor, in relative dollar terms, are being taken for a ride.[6]

Corporations, as has been suggested in previous sections of this chapter, are essentially free to charge the prices they care to in the market. Since the poor pay at least as much as everyone else for products, they are victimized by corporations in the same way everyone else is.

There has been some expert suggestion, furthermore, that the poor pay more than the affluent for a lot of things. Canadian data on this question are, once again, not available. But an American study by David Caplovitz suggests that when the poor do not actually pay more than the affluent for products themselves, they do pay much more stiffly for the credit they need to buy them.

In fact, Averitt's distinction between the centre economy and the periphery economy might be translated into the centre market and the periphery market; for the retail services available to the poor do not really resemble those available to the affluent. Consumption is considered an index of respectability and personal worth in North America, and, for the poor, the only route to consumption is through credit. The affluent, when they use credit at all, have enough collateral to shop around for the best terms. The poor, who find credit a necessity but have few assets, are exploited by finance companies and revolving retail loan plans, and the prices they finally pay for goods, credit included, are astronomical.

The effect of advertising in all of this is difficult to calculate. Certainly, advertising creates false needs and then demands that they be met but, more important, the prevalence of advertising persuades the poor and the affluent alike that the way to be wealthy — and to appear to be wealthy — is to consume. Anything. Preferably something expensive; but, in the end, it is the process of consumption that counts. Caplovitz:

Americans in all walks of life are trained to consume *in order*

6. R. F. Muth, *Cities and Housing* (Chicago: University of Chicago Press, 1969). Muth concluded that the major part of the housing problems of the poor were due to a lack of effective demand (money); see pp. 307-335. He found some evidence that the poor pay more.

to win the respect of others and to maintain their self-respect.
. . . Compounding the force of a rising standard of living is the fact that most low-income families . . . have little opportunity to base their self-respect and the respect granted them by others on occupational, educational, or other accomplishments. And this poverty of opportunity may only reinforce the significance of consumption in that pattern which we have called "compensatory consumption."[7]

The poor pay ferociously for credit. And they are routinely swindled, stolen from, lied to, and oppressed by the consumer society. But the core of their problem, and the core of the problem for the nation as a whole, is that the foundation of the exploitation visited on poor and affluent alike is the illusion that consumption is a good in itself. Advertising, in its creation of spurious need, is the source of that illusion. And the power of advertising, in the final analysis, is the power of the corporation. "Consumer education," which seeks to help the poor shop wisely and stretch a dollar, is, then, largely irrelevant; the solution lies not in advising the robbed, but in catching the robbers.

II.9 THE INHERITANCE OF ECONOMIC POWER

If poverty is tied to a lack of money, then poverty implies a lack of savings. Saving is something you do with money you don't need at the moment, and the poor don't have all the money they need at any moment, much less money they can afford to sit on.

The poor either spend all their money on essentials or go into debt to buy things they might not need, but corporate advertising convinces them they need desperately — for spending, as noted in the preceding section, can actually be a compensation for poverty. In any case, the poor are not likely to have anything to save, or any real desire to save it.

In a society that does not provide for its old people, a man at

7. David Caplovitz, *The Poor Pay More* (New York: Macmillan, 1967), pp. 180-181.

the end of a career without savings is headed for a hard old age. And a young man with a wife and a family, who has not yet reached the years in which he is earning most and has not yet saved enough to buy a house or appliances, will scrape through hard years before he is comfortable.

The last factor, in particular, is important; for it leads to the deprivation of children. In chapter VII there is a description of the results of poverty for children — among them, inadequate education and poor health. And considerable sociological and psychological literature indicates that a childhood in poverty may produce a kind of "poverty syndrome," an acceptance of defeat and worthlessness that can lock a child, and eventually *his* children, into poverty forever.

If poverty is inherited, so is wealth; and the more wealth, the more rapid its growth.[1] Large savings grow at a faster rate, absolutely and relatively, than smaller savings, for among other things, the information necessary to make savings grow costs the same for the small investor and the large one, and therefore is relatively cheaper for the plutocrat. Furthermore, people with small nest-eggs will tend to watch them carefully, and pump them into safe but low-paying investments, rather than go for broke in high-risk, high-yield projects, as the multi-millionaire is able to do.

And, of course, the wealthy have an opportunity to save in the first place, which the poor do not. Once an affluent professional, say, reaches a certain level of savings, his bankroll becomes in effect another source of income — another job, one that will support him splendidly in his retirement, demands no effort, and will never vanish. It will remain, in fact, even after his death, especially if he has done very well; in 1966, more than sixty-five estates of over one million dollars were passed on, to the tune of $250 million.[2]

With wealth comes power. As James Meade points out:

A man with much property has great bargaining strength and a great sense of security, independence, and freedom; and he

1. See James Meade, *Efficiency, Equality and the Ownership of Property* (Cambridge, Mass.: Harvard University Press, 1965), pp. 44-45.
2. See Canada Department of National Revenue, *1968 Taxation Statistics* (Ottawa, 1968), table 2A, p. 162.

enjoys these things not only *vis-a-vis* his propertyless fellow citizens but also *vis-a-vis* the public authorities. He can snap his fingers at those on whom he must rely for an income; for he can always live for a time on his capital. The propertyless man must continuously and without interruption acquire his income by working for an employer or by qualifiying to receive it from a public authority. An unequal distribution of property means an unequal distribution of power and status even if it is prevented from causing too unequal a distribution of income.[3]

Analyses of the effect of wealth and economic power on actual political power are difficult to come by; there is no particular reason for the wealthy to describe the techniques of their influence for the benefit of the public. But certainly, a tiny Canadian élite does control a great deal of the Canadian economy, and that is, in fact, almost synonymous with the control of political power in Canada. John Porter discovered that

> . . . 907 individuals residing in Canada shared between them 1,304 (81 per cent) of the directorships in the dominant corporations as well as 118 (58 per cent) of the directorships in the nine chartered banks and 78 (58 per cent) of those in the life insurance companies.[4]

Porter argues, moreover, that in Canada (more than in the United States), shareholders exert real control over corporations;[5] and that holding companies can be linked together to allow élites to run businesses at a distance.[6]

In other words, the wealthy have a disproportionate voice — if, in fact, they do not have the *only* voice — in the operation of the Canadian economy and the Canadian nation. And to be wealthy, more than likely, is to be the son of a wealthy man; to be poor, to have been born in poverty, and to have been excluded from power and profit from the moment of birth.

3. Ibid, p. 39.
4. Porter, *Vertical Mosaic*, p. 234.
5. Ibid, pp. 244-245.
6. Ibid, pp. 255-263.

.10 SUMMARY

Equality of opportunity, then, is essentially non-existent in Canada. Poverty and inequality persist, and cannot be assumed away through any model of society that pretends that Canada is competitive.

Inequality of earnings, and even to a great extent inequality in education and skills, are the result of inequality of *power* — in industry, business, and the economy as a whole. Corporations are sovereign; unions are fragmented. Minorities are systematically excluded from the labour market, or kept at the bottom levels of the work ladder.

Unemployment both creates poverty and intensifies the poverty that already exists; and unemployment is itself created through government reaction to gains in income by the affluent.

Canada's society is a class society, organized around the division between the powerful and powerless — a division that perpetuates itself from generation to generation.

The myth of competition has served those who refuse to compete.

III

The Failure of Government

III.1 THE PHONY WAR

The most powerful illusion in this country is that Canadian governments are committed to democracy and to the value that is at the
heart of the democratic ethic: the principle of political equality.

According to this ideal the ultimate power rests, not with the few,
but with the whole of society.

> Control over government decisions is shared so that the prefer-
> ences of no citizen are weighed more heavily than the prefer-
> ences of any other citizen.[1]

The role of government, then, is to give equal consideration to all
and to be equally responsible to all citizens. From this ideal it follows
that democratic justice should most energetically be extended to the
poor; for the poor, more than any other group in society, need the
assistance of government.

In our country, nothing could be further from reality. The poor
have had to pay harshly for the way the economy is mismanaged.
They are the first to lose their jobs when unemployment is high, and
they suffer most from cutbacks in government spending. They are
also the ones to suffer most from the government's refusal to tackle
structural faults in the economy.

But the democratic illusion is so strong in this country that very
few speak out against these inequalities. And when they do, they are

1. Robert A. Dahl and Charles E. Lindblom, *Politics, Economics and Welfare*
(New York: Harper and Row, 1963), p. 41.

accused by the politicians of attacking democracy itself, even though the politicians are simply being called to account for their support of the privileged interests of the few who keep them in power. The most direct effect of government refusal to manage the economy has been to create a climate in which corporations have been given free rein to pursue their self-interests, without regard to society's interests; and most often the government itself has been left to pay the bills.

When we examine just what the federal government has ever done to adjust the inequalities in our society, we see that any official intentions have turned out, in the end, to be no more than the usual liberal rhetoric. There was, for example, a Declaration of War on Poverty in the throne speech of April 1965, and this led to the establishment of a Special Planning Secretariat to co-ordinate federal government efforts that related to poverty.

And eight months later, a national conference on poverty was held. But nothing came out of the conference — and that was the extent of the Pearson government's war. Two years later, when the federal government embarked on an austerity program and cut back government services, one of its first economies was to wipe out the Special Planning Secretariat.

This abandonment is typical of the government's irresponsibility towards the poor. The business of this chapter is to indicate just how little Canadian governments have done to fight poverty and the effect their economic policies have had in making life more difficult for the poor and easier for the affluent.

I.2 THE INFLATION-UNEMPLOYMENT TRADE-OFF

Full employment was promised in the Liberal government white paper on employment and income of 1946. But successive governments have never lived up to that promise, although politicians consistently talk about it before elections, and it once again became official policy in the 1965 legislation that created the Economic Council of Canada. Table III.2.i documents the failure of postwar government policies to provide jobs for every worker who wanted one.

TABLE III.2.i
Unemployment rate, Canada, 1946 — 1970

1946	3.8%	1954	4.6	1962	5.9
1947	2.6	1955	4.4	1963	5.5
1948	2.6	1956	3.4	1964	4.7
1949	3.3	1957	4.6	1965	3.9
1950	3.8	1958	7.0	1966	3.6
1951	2.6	1959	6.0	1967	4.1
1952	3.0	1960	7.0	1968	4.8
1953	3.0	1961	7.1	1969	4.7
				1970	5.9

Sources: Sylvia Ostry, *Unemployment in Canada* (Ottawa: DBS, 1968), table 1, p 1; and Canada Department of Finance, Budget Papers for 1971-72, in *Hansard* (18 June 1971): 189, for years 1967 — 70.

Some international comparisons — set out in table III.2.ii — make it even more obvious just how badly Canadian postwar governments have done in this area. In 1961, for example, when Canada was experiencing its highest unemployment rates since the depression of the thirties, other countries — France, West Germany, Great Britain, Japan and Sweden, for example — had unemployment rates substantially below two per cent. All of these nations, like Canada, are heavy trading nations; furthermore, in this country during the

TABLE III.2.ii
Unemployment rates for selected industrial countries, 1959—63

COUNTRY	1959	1960	1961	1962	1963
US	5.5%	5.6%	6.7%	5.6%	5.7%
Canada	6.0	7.0	7.2	5.9	5.5
France	1.4	1.3	1.1	1.2	1.5
West Germany	2.4	1.2	0.8	0.7	0.8
Great Britain	2.2	1.6	1.5	2.0	2.5
Italy	5.2	4.0	3.4	3.0	2.5
Japan	1.5	1.1	1.0	0.9	0.9
Sweden	2.0	1.4	1.2	1.3	1.4

Source: Arthur F. Neef, "International Unemployment Rates 1960—64." *Monthly Labour Review* 88 (Mar 1965): 258. These figures have been adjusted to US definition of unemployment.

years 1957 to 1968 the average rate of unemployment was 5.3 per cent.

These high rates of unemployment were not just the manifestations of unique phenomena, like the Canadian winter; they were the result of policies chosen by Canadian governments to fight inflation.[1] And inflation, we have seen from the decisions made during 1969 and 1970, has always been regarded as the greater evil. For government policy makers have in effect decided that the structure of the economy offers two black and white alternatives: a high rate of employment (inflation) and a relatively low rate of inflation (unemployment).[2]

Because government policy makers have not adopted substantial programs to deal with structural changes in the economy, and have not planned their policies except as reactions to events, they have been forced to approach the economy on the terms dictated by that trade-off: to fight inflation with unemployment. Given the very high rate of unemployment, they haven't even done much of a job controlling inflation, as is shown in table III.2.iii, which compares Canada's rates of inflation and unemployment with other countries. West Germany and the United States have lower inflation rates, while France, Great Britain and Austria have similar inflation rates combined with drastically lower unemployment rates over the period between 1959 and 1968. For 1969 the Canadian Consumer Price Index rate of increase was 4.5 per cent, and in 1970, 3.3 per cent.

This unhealthy preoccupation with inflation has not only created staggering unemployment but has also considerably weakened economic growth. A recent study of these three factors and their interrelationship suggests that the maintenance of a low inflation rate constricts growth, while the goals of full employment and of rapid

1. All levels of government must somehow be drawn into stabilization policy. For example, in 1969, when unemployment was 4.7 per cent and rising on the way to 5.9 per cent, the total government surplus was 2.2 billion. The federal government, which should know better, in fact ran a surplus of $776 million in that year. Even in 1970, with unemployment continuing to rise, the federal government could only manage a $12-million deficit. See Economic White Paper, *Hansard* (18 June 1971), tables 50, 52. Part of the problem is to be found in the distaste of provincial governments for deficit financing, which leads them to tie their expenditures to revenues, which makes them destabilizing. See R. T. Robinson and T. J. Courchene, "Fiscal Federalism and Economic Stability," *Canadian Journal of Economics* (May 1969).

2. This relationship is heightened as market structures become more oligopolistic. See Paolo Syles-Labini, *Oligopoly and Technical Progress* (Cambridge, Mass.: Harvard University Press, 1962); in particular, ch. 10.

TABLE III.2.iii
International comparison of inflation: unemployment performance

COUNTRY	Average unemployment rate 1969-68	Average rate of CPI increase 1959-68
US	4.9%	1.9%
Canada	5.3	2.1
France	1.3	2.8
West Germany	1.3	2.0
Great Britain	1.5	3.1
Italy	4.0	3.5
Japan	1.5	5.1
Austria	2.4	3.1

Sources: For unemployment rates, OECD, *Labour-Force Statistics, 1957-1968* (Paris, 1970), table II.
Consumer Price Index, *UN Statistical Yearbook* (New York, 1969), table 175.

economic growth are complementary.[3] This conclusion is supported by a recent American study carried out by the former chairman of the Council of Economic Advisers in a report for the Commission on Money and Credit.[4] The fight against inflation is, of course, complicated by our entanglement with the US economy, given our fixed exchange rate.[5]

The high levels of unemployment over the past five years can be seen as the direct result of the government's consistent choice of crude policy tools that fight inflation with unemployment, and sacrifice the

3. R. G. Bodkin, "An Analysis of the Trade-off between Full Employment, Price Stability and Other Economic Goals," *Canadian Economic Policy since the War* (Montreal: Private Planning Association of Canada, 1966).
4. Arthur Okun, *The Battle against Unemployment* (New York: Norton, 1965), pp. 47-52.
5. A brief account can be found in Derek A. White, *Business Cycles in Canada* (Ottawa: ECC, 1967), pp. 7-10. We do a lot of trading; the foreign-trade component of our GNP is 24%; while that of the UK is 20%; of Japan, 12%; and of the US 5%. Over 60% of all our exports go to the United States, and we get more than 70% of all our imports from the US. (L. Officer and L. B. Smith, "Stabilization Policy in the Postwar Period," in *Canadian Economic Problems and Policies* [Toronto: McGraw-Hill, 1970], p. 19.) There is a wealth of other connections that strengthen the relationship. (I. Brecher and S. S. Reisman, *Canada-United States Economic Relations* [Ottawa, 1957], pp. 63-64, lists some of them.)
    Although the dollar is actually floating right now, it has merely been freed to find a new level. Moreover, the government is using the foreign-exchange fund to stabilize it; and unless government intentions change, it will soon be repegged. It is against the rules of the International Monetary Fund to have a floating exchange rate.

overall economic growth rate by which the country prospers. Table III.2.iv shows the extent. The per capita GNE — which measures the growth in real income available to each of us — has been halved since the government went into the production of unemployment in a big way to fight inflation. The average growth in per capita GNE since 1967 has been 2.4%, while in the previous five years it averaged just about twice that.

TABLE III.2.iv
Changes in gross national expenditure, 1955-1970

YEAR	GNE 1961 dollars % change	Per capita GNE 1961 dollars % change
1970	3.3	1.7
1969	5.1	2.8
1968	4.9	3.7
1967	3.5	1.5
1966	7.0	4.7
1965	6.6	4.7
1964	6.9	4.7
1963	5.3	4.0
1962	6.9	4.7
1961	2.9	0.5
1960	2.9	0.0
1959	4.1	3.4
1958	2.2	-1.0
1957	2.8	-0.5
1956	8.7	7.1
1955	9.9	5.9

Source: Canada Department of Finance, Budget Papers for 1971—72, in *Hansard* (18 June 1971), tables 1,4.

This is because the government's overall economic policies have followed conventional liberal practice of non-intervention in the structure of the economy; the status quo has been maintained, and the social inequalities under which so many Canadians suffer have been reinforced. It follows, then, to ask why — and at what cost?

The unemployment rate for Canada in 1970 was 5.9 per cent. In February of 1971 there were 677,000 workers officially seeking jobs. Some 100,000 other workers were in manpower training courses and another 100,000 had dropped out of the official picture of "those seeking employment" simply because they realized that there were no jobs to be had.[6]

With almost a million workers unemployed, the earnings foregone on all goods and services in Canada amounted to a total of about $2 billion.[7] And, more important, this loss was concentrated in the low-income classes — the heaviest weight of the burden of recession is carried by the poor.

For unemployment is not evenly distributed through the labour force.

> . . . the group which is least able to bear the disaster of unem-
> ployment — the unskilled — carries the heaviest weight of the
> recession, while the burden of unemployment weighs least upon
> those for whom it is probably less of a financial hardship — the
> office and professional worker.[8]

And, within those low-income groups, unemployment weighs heavily on the young. If one were to look at workers as representing certain values of "human capital" — education, training, apprenticeship, experience, etc.—the young, who have the least capital invested in them, are the first to be shaken out of their jobs as unemployment rises. In February 1971, some 20.3 per cent of male members of the labour force aged fourteen to nineteen were unemployed. And, as everybody knows, unemployment is not distributed evenly across the country; if regional differences are taken into account, in February of 1971 one out of every four young men between fourteen and nineteen in the Atlantic provinces was unemployed.

There are many other costs of unemployment, some measurable, others not. For example, in 1970 the Unemployment Insurance Commission paid out more than $600,000,000 in benefits.[9] Obviously this money could have been used more productively — for job

6. Cy Gonick, "The Scourge of Unemployment," *Canadian Dimension* 7, (June 1971): 15.
7. We allow 1.5 per cent as the frictional level of unemployment, distribute the remaining 4.4 per cent regionally as they were in September 1970, and we average weekly wages and salaries for those regions. This overestimates this particular component of the cost of unemployment, but excludes many others.
8. Woods and Ostry, *Labour Policy*, p. 367.
9. "Activities of the Unemployment Insurance Commission," *DBS Statistical Review* (Nov. 1970), p. 43. Estimates were made of benefits paid for the last quarter.

development and worker training — than as a meagre subsistence benefit.

The costs of inflation are even more difficult to assess. First, it is important to point out that rising prices cannot be taken in isolation; incomes have risen faster than prices. Between 1949 and 1969, family incomes grew an average of 8.4 per cent per year. The Consumers' Price Index grew by only 2.8 per cent a year. Obviously, then, there has been a growth in real income, so inflation has not been that serious.

The consequences of inflation are alleged to be:
1. The impact on the poor and those with fixed incomes.
2. The negative effect on our international competitive position.
3. The weakening of overall efficiency in economic growth.[10]

A common fear related to the third point is that when runaway inflation takes place, then total economic collapse is around the corner. Aware that their money is losing value, people will hurry to spend it on goods and services, constantly pushing up the prices of those goods and services in demand.

But according to one of the world's leading authorities in the area, this cycle rarely becomes so serious that it leads to disaster.

> . . . the general flight from cash is hard to start; and there is evidence that it has never started until prices have doubled in six months or less.[11]

During the inflation battles of the past few years, politicians have constantly reminded us of the inflationary spirals of the type that led to the economic crashes in Germany in 1922-23, and in Hungary in May 1946. In both cases these were the result of blundering government policies, and the economic lessons learned there and in the depression of the thirties have produced techniques to stop inflationary spirals.[12] But more to the point:

10. J. C. Weldon, "Exercising Inflation and Unemployment," *Labour Gazette* 70 (Sept. 1970): 634.
11. H. J. Brown, *The Great Inflation* (New York: Oxford University Press, for the Royal Institute of International Affairs, 1955), p. 195. Cited in Tibor and Anne Scitovsky, "Inflation versus Unemployment," in *Inflation, Growth and Unemployment* (Englewood Cliffs, NJ: Prentice-Hall, 1964), p. 433.
12. See Earl Brunner and A. H. Heltzer, "What Did We Learn from the Monetary Experience of the United States in the Great Depression?" *Canadian Journal of Economics* 1 (1968): 334.

All the hyperinflation of history can be traced back to political upheavals rather than economic causes — war, revolution, or defeat.[13]

Who gains and loses from inflation? A recent Canadian analysis concludes that:

Recipients of wage and salary income or of self-employment income experience compensating changes in income . . . during all inflationary periods.[14]

A similar American study reinforces this conclusion.[15] It also shows that price increases since World War II of the goods normally consumed by the poor have risen less than those used by the middle class. In other words, inflation does not hit the poor as hard as unemployment, which is concentrated among them; but God help the poor if they try to dip into the middle-class basket of goods.

Inflation is thought to harm the national balance of payments by raising the cost of our export products until they can no longer compete with those of other countries. It is also supposed to make imports more competitive in the domestic market. This fear is valid only when there is a fixed exchange rate, which the government insisted on until 1970 when the rate was temporarily floated specifically to fight inflation.

The final chestnut about inflation is that it hurts those on fixed incomes. The Canadian evidence shows that:

While it was certainly true that the elderly, the poor and the recipients of transfer income and retirement pension all found their relative income positions deteriorating during periods of rising prices, it was also true that this occurred as well during the periods of price stability. The problem is clearly not that of

13. Scitovsky, "Inflation versus Unemployment," p. 450.
14. Rosalind Blauer, "Fixed Income and Asset Groups in Canada," mimeographed (Brock University, 1970), p. 16. The period in question is 1950-67; a general discussion can be found in G. L. Bach and A. Ando, "The Redistributional Effects of Inflation," *American Economic Review* 47 (Feb. 1957): 7.
15. Robin Hollister and John Palmer, "The Impact of Inflation on the Poor" (University of Wisconsin: Institute for Research on Poverty, 1969), discussion paper 4-69.

inflation but of society's grossly inadequate treatment of the elderly and the poor.[16]

Whatever harm inflation does to the poor on fixed incomes — pensioners, for example — is clearly the government's responsibility for not attaching sensible escalators to pensions. The government is fighting an evil of its own creation.

The alternative is to create a policy of full employment, then to tolerate a moderate level of inflation with adequate protection against its consequences. A full-employment market is of immense benefit to the poor.

> They gain relatively more than any other group, probably because of movements from part-time to full-time employment, and because of a narrowing of wage differentials between the employed poor and the non-poor.[17]

Our conclusion is that, contrary to federal government assumptions,[18] and the problem of pensioners aside, the evidence is overwhelming that the poor are not hurt as badly by inflation as they are by anti-inflation policies that create unemployment.[19] An American group working on the same problem concluded that

> . . . a drop of one per cent in the unemployment rate would remove a million to a million and a half people from poverty that would not have been removed otherwise.[20]

Obviously parallel results could be expected in Canada; for the relationship between poverty and unemployment is no different here than it is in the United States.

16. Blauer, "Fixed Income and Asset Groups," p. 20.
17. Hollister and Palmer, "Impact of Inflation on the Poor," p. 44.
18. An example of this assumption showed up in the recent white paper on income security for Canadians: "People in the weakest bargaining position suffer the most from price increases, since their incomes are relatively fixed." Canada Department of National Health and Welfare, *Income Security for Canadians* (Ottawa, 1970), p. 11.
19. Scitovsky, "Inflation versus Unemployment," p. 469; and Hollister and Palmer, "Impact of Inflation on the Poor," pp. 44-52.
20. Hollister and Palmer, "Impact of Inflation on the Poor," p. 44.

Despite all this evidence, successive Canadian governments have continually mismanaged the economy by using unemployment to fight inflation. In the past few years the Liberal government of Pierre Elliott Trudeau has been so successful that it has created an unemployment rate of over six per cent, and the real rate of GNP growth has been brought down to 3.3 per cent for 1970, as compared to 4.9 per cent for 1968 and 5.1 per cent for 1969. This, to hear the government, has been done in the interests of saving the economy and the poor. It is stupidity — or criminal hypocrisy — to club the national economy almost to death, putting hundreds of thousands of Canadians out of work, and then to claim the action was taken to save the aged poor on fixed incomes.

Finally, both inflation and unemployment can be seen as a form of taxation, because they reduce peoples' real income:

> It is very clear that the tax of unemployment is a very inequitable tax; it is not clear that the tax of inflation falls extraordinarily heavily on any population group; its impact may be spread rather broadly across the whole population.[21]

If this evidence is related to the international comparisons we have made, it does not seem extravagant to say that Canada has had rates of unemployment over the past twelve years that would have caused fallen governments, if not revolutions, in Western Europe.

There is no black and white choice between inflation and unemployment. For there are structural policies that can be used to fight inflation and unemployment at the same time. The government uses them. Two are manpower and regional development policies, but the government's particular use of stabilization policy seriously blocks their effectiveness, in ways that are more fully explained in III.3 and III.4.

The one structural attack the government does try to integrate with its stabilization policy is the incomes policy under the Prices and Incomes Commission.[22] Its purpose is to keep a rein on con-

21. Ibid, p. 48.
22. A recent evaluation of the effectiveness of the United Kingdom incomes policy suggests that better results are obtained without an incomes policy than with one when low levels of aggregate demand are employed. See R. G. Lipsey and Brian Parkin, "Incomes Policy: An Appraisal," *Economica* 37 (May 1970).

stantly increasing wages and prices by imposing voluntary guidelines. In doing so it is supposed to function as an important part of national stabilization policy.

But expecting voluntary guidelines to work in a free enterprise system — even a non-competitive free-enterprise system — is about as realistic as asking industry in that same system voluntarily to clean up the pollution it creates. The few anti-pollution programs that exist have not come into effect because of sudden social enlightenment on the part of corporations; they have come about as a consequence of threatened punitive legislation or actual lawsuits — the lawsuit the Ontario government has launched against Dow Chemical, for example.

The same applies to voluntary wage and price guidelines. They become, if anything, floors rather than ceilings. Wage and price guidelines simply do not work without coercion. It is true that the Prices and Incomes Commission can recommend that governments take coercive action. But the fragmentation of bargaining units and employers' associations make coercion impossible.

The government must certainly be aware of this, yet it has never proposed an agency that would enforce an incomes policy. But if ever such an agency were set up, the certification rulings of the labour boards would quickly neutralize its effectiveness, because their decisions make consolidation of the bargaining units within the economy impossible. This point is discussed in more detail in III.3.

An incomes policy, then, has all the impact of a puff of smoke on our present system. And the failure of voluntarism allows the government to proceed with the crude fiscal and monetary policies that create heavy unemployment.

> When co-operative saintliness is found not to exist, the government finds itself tempted to make good the moral defect by toughening its posture in the real (monetary and fiscal policy) sector.[23]

Finally, the attempt to impose a six per cent flat rate on the rises in wage incomes can only act to perpetuate or worsen the existing

23. Weldon, "Exorcising Inflation and Unemployment," p. 631.

inequalities of income distribution.[24] No attempt is made to consider wages and prices in terms of economic justice; and that, no doubt, scuttles the program in the eyes of the public. The only paltry concession the government made to equality was to allow relatively larger raises to wages below two dollars per hour.

III.3 LABOUR POLICIES

The government also intervenes in the economic structure with labour policies. These include manpower policies, industrial relations and minimum-wage legislation.

When Jean Marchand, then the minister of Manpower and Immigration, introduced the Occupational Training Act to the House of Commons (3 March 1967), he said:

> We want to provide a second chance to the people who need it most. These are the men and women who missed the chance to acquire a skill during their youth or whose skill has been made obsolete by technological change.[1]

During the 1969-70 fiscal year, some 300,000 adults received training in various programs that were supposed to up-grade their skills so they could seek better and higher-paying jobs. The total cost was about $250,000,000. Many of those who completed training did increase their income somewhat. But, as is the case with most programs, certainly very few of those who received Manpower training were among those who needed it most. There are just too many barriers; three are especially effective.

First, the Occupational Training Act and the order-in-council stating the regulations for that program both declare that no manpower course shall be longer than fifty-two weeks in duration. Manpower officials have gratuitously declared that this means that

24. One problem that an effective incomes policy of this type would cause is a distortion of resource allocation. Price changes are supposed to trigger off factor movement eventually, and a flat economy-wide ceiling of the six per cent type could actually lead to perverse factor flows. With the present incomes policy, we can breathe easy on this point.
1. *Hansard* (3 Mar. 1967).

no individual shall be permitted more than fifty-two weeks of basic academic upgrading.

Second, to be eligible for training, applicants must also have a specific occupational goal. This provision weeds out those who are demoralized and confused by the labour market. The lower the levels of education and skills, the more difficult it is to state a specific occupational goal. These people are unable to state their aims in a manner that would satisfy a Manpower counsellor holding the middle-class views of his bureaucratic institution. Moreover, the lack of detailed data on job vacancies prevents the counsellor from assigning any particular significance to an applicant's choice.

Finally, before a person can receive an allowance for manpower training, he must have been in the labour force at least three years prior to the application. This means working or actively seeking work for the past three years. This rule was explicitly designed to exclude the young from the program, even though they make up an enormous percentage of the total unemployed.

Through an arrangement with the provincial departments of education, Manpower buys seats in various educational institutions or private colleges. In many cases it also pays the person taking the retraining course an allowance ranging from $40 to $103 per week. These arrangements subtly erect another barrier to access by the poor. For there is no doubt that, in the eyes of Manpower counsellors, the poor are a "high-risk population." And because the competition for manpower retraining is high — only one in ten of all applicants is accepted — the inevitable "skimming" process takes place. Successful applicants are those with a level of skills and education high enough to guarantee success. The Frontier College brief to the Senate committee on poverty stated:

> No person requiring more than one year's academic upgrading (computational and written-language skills) is eligible for occupational training.[2]

Because almost all vocational-skills programs in Canada today require a grade ten prerequisite education (such as welding, car-

2. Frontier College brief to the Special Senate Committee on Poverty (16 Dec. 1969) 13:30.

pentry, electrical trades, plumbing), and because most academic-upgrading centres (known as Basic Training for Skills Development [BTSD] centres in Manpower terminology) can raise a student's functioning equivalent-grade level by about three grades in fifty-two weeks, very few persons with educational attainments below grade-seven level can gain entry into BTSD occupational training courses. Moreover, most adults who have received only seven or eight years' education as children function at a much lower level in their adult years. Such persons make up a very large element in our population. The vast majority of poor Canadians able to work would fall into this category. Some persons in this category do gain entrance to manpower programs, but usually this happens "in error" or because of a "sympathetic" Manpower counsellor.

Behind the obstacles that put manpower retraining programs beyond the reach of the poor is a larger problem. It is that a high unemployment rate, produced by the federal government's indiscriminate attack on inflation, makes manpower policies a largely futile effort. People are being trained for non-existent jobs; the best-skilled people are skimmed from among the unemployed to fill the relatively scarce vacancies, and the unskilled get left behind (with all the resultant bitterness expressed many times in the Senate committee proceedings).

The problems of manpower policies, however, cannot be attributed to the Finance Department. The Department of Manpower and Immigration is not able, either to produce information on current vacancies, or to predict the future trend of vacancies, let alone the wages that are likely to be paid in them. This means that they counsel people on career opportunities and buy training "seats" on the basis of little more than hunches.

More fundamentally, there is a distinct lack of concern for workers who are having a hard time in the labour market.

Again, from the brief by the United Community Services of the greater Vancouver area:

In the basic conflict within the Manpower Department between their two "clients," the employer and the employee, the BC Regional Office has opted to serve the employer. This philosophy was clearly expressed by a Manpower representative on an open-line show on December 2, 1969; he repeatedly told callers: "We have no responsibility to you; our responsibility is to the labour market." Asked by the interviewer if Manpower didn't sometimes assign a counsellor to help a person find a job, the response was "We'd love to, but we don't have enough staff."[3]

Of the male trainees in the retraining program in the fiscal year 1969, fifty-three per cent had grade eight or less (how much less has not been made clear by the department), though a staggering forty per cent of all male workers in Canada are in that category.[4] Obviously they should have much greater representation in the training programs, for these are the men who have the greatest difficulty adjusting to the labour market and finding decent jobs. They are also the people beating on the doors of the Manpower Department.

As Frontier College noted:

> We suggest that a large number of Canadians who "most need" the occupational training services of the Manpower Policy are denied access to occupational training by certain provisions in the present policy.... Of course, there are many "poor" Canadians whom the Manpower Policy cannot assist. But there are large numbers of "poor" Canadians who are able and anxious to work; those unemployed, under-employed, or seasonally employed, who lack the prerequisite education and job skills for secure employment. It is this group that the Manpower Policy fails in large measure to assist....[5]

The department's Manpower Mobility Program, for example, which pays people to move from areas of low labour demand into areas of higher demand, is an application of this same philosophy. The candidates for transfer are preselected on the same basis as the candidates for retraining. People retrained are the people most likely to succeed without retraining; the people selected to move are the

3. See United Community Services of the Greater Vancouver Area brief to the Special Senate Committee on Poverty, *Guaranteed Income or Guaranteed Employment? A Critical Examination of Income Maintenance and Manpower Policies* (April 1970) 33:7.
4. DBS, *Special Labour Force Study #1*, cat. no. 1500-503 (Oct. 1968), table 1.
5. Frontier College brief, 13:31.

people most likely to move in any case. The brief of the federal Department of Manpower and Immigration notes: "In general, the flow of assisted moves follows normal mobility patterns. The majority are under 35 years of age."[6]

The emphasis, as always, is on helping men with skills, not on helping men without them — swapping trained men around in response to labour demand, rather than creating new training programs for unskilled men before or after moving them.

The emphasis on supplying the needs of the employer rather than the employee has led to considerable suspicion and resentment among the unskilled and unemployed. A survey of the situation in Ottawa by researcher Michael Posluns of the Canadian Civil Liberties Association turned up reports of administrative truculence, arbitrariness and general lack of insight on the part of Manpower counsellors. A brief to the committee by United Community Services in Vancouver reported:

> During the past months, United Community Services has interviewed numbers of those receiving social assistance in regard to "hang-ups" in the welfare system; their comments about Manpower have been devastatingly critical. These criticisms are not without support; indeed, one social service administrator bitterly stated: "It is as though they had the brand of Cain on their forehead when Manpower finds out they are on welfare." The Director of the John Howard Society states: "Our referrals are quickly categorized by Manpower as 'untrainable' and therefore not adaptable to their procedures."[7]

Dr. Eric Robinson, principal of Frontier College, told the committee:

> In our experience in conducting adult basic education programs and community-education programs, we have on occasion been in confrontation, you might say, with the Department of Manpower and Immigration. Although we have discovered

6. Canada Department of Manpower and Immigration brief to the Special Senate Committee on Poverty (1969) 10: 377.
7. UCS brief, 13:7.

the splendid good-will that many manpower officers show, we have also encountered arbitrariness and rigid adherence to certain policies and practices which unarguably leave out large segments of the population of Canada who can benefit from basic training for skills development.[8]

Those "policies and practices," in themselves unreasonable, are rooted once again in the original premise of the Manpower Department — that the employer and the requirements of technology are to be served first.

Granted, it is difficult, frustrating and expensive to train the unskilled and illiterate up to market standards, particularly in a period of high unemployment. But it is not good enough merely to blame weakness of manpower policy on an obviously mistaken stabilization policy. Assisting and training only those whose skills are closest to the scarce job opportunities available is the easy way out, but it has serious long-term consequences. The unskilled become demoralized and lose those skills that they do have, but cannot apply.

An army of people without skills accumulates. When the economy returns to normal employment conditions, those people will not be well equipped to fill the new jobs. A long-sighted policy would try to make the unskilled competitive in the labour market, even during high unemployment conditions. It would serve not only equality, but also the economy's overall efficiency. But that policy is not generally adopted by the Manpower Department.

The types of training subsidies given to workers also reveal the government's subservience to corporate demands. Millions of public dollars are spent every year training workers in skills that are of use only to specific industries but that those industries have never troubled themselves to provide. Those dollars, in the absence of the Occupational Training program, would have been provided by those industries themselves.

There is evidence, too, that since the start of the training program, the little training industry once did has declined. Corporations are transferring even that small amount of their training costs over to public expense.

The department's refusal to seek out those in the labour market

8. Frontier College brief, 13:11.

who need special help is only further evidence of its unwillingness to do anything except find jobs for people on terms dictated by corporations.

Manpower centres are austere, bureaucratic institutions, usually located in areas far from concentrations of people with known employment problems. They keep regular nine-to-five hours, and execute decisions made at central head offices without any reference to the specific needs of the community.

There is almost no attempt to help workers move from one area and no attempt to train them for a job in another region where the employment prospects are good. The workers must either accept training where they live, or at the nearest place where the particular training course is offered. The only alternative for the worker is to move to an area where the job prospects are better, without acquiring any training or skills. He then becomes just another unskilled worker seeking a job in an industrial area that almost always demands specific skills.

The government has ignored the need to create training programs and to find jobs for the hard-core unemployed. There are only three exceptions to this general abdication of responsibility: the Vocational Rehabilitation Program, the various NewStart programs and the Gottingen Street Outreach Project in Halifax. All have low priority. The Vocational Rehabilitation Program suffers all the usual cost-sharing wrangles between governments. And in 1968-69 this program spent a parsimonious $8,000,000.

The Halifax Gottingen Street Outreach Project was a special Manpower office set up in a Halifax slum and staffed by specially trained residents. The project attempted to bring the usual Manpower services to the attention of the people in the area, and to provide them with any special help they might need to become employed. Despite the enthusiasm of the residents for the project, and its apparent success in finding work for them, the Manpower Department has not repeated the experiment elsewhere.

It is significant that the department has also refused to make public its own evaluation of the project.

The other exception is the NewStart Program, which began in 1967 when the federal Manpower Department set up a number of experiments in depressed regions. The aim was to try a developmental approach towards manpower retraining where the conditions were toughest.

The NewStart programs, however, were quickly starved of funds, and were caught in a bureaucratic squeeze between two government departments: the Department of Manpower and the Department of Regional Economic Expansion. Both departments were concerned with specific aspects of unemployment in depressed regional areas. NewStart finally came to rest under DREE, where, it seems, it was regarded rather uneasily by the department's administrators; and all NewStart programs are now in the process of being closed down.

NewStart was originally a bright and sensible idea. But it didn't fit in with that basic premise of the Manpower Department: that the requirements of employers are supreme and workers are just incidental to technological progress.

Until that premise is discarded, manpower programs will do little beyond training those who need it least, helping those who require it least, moving those who would have moved anyway, and tailoring the pay-offs for employers and not for the poor.

Some elements of the immigration program of the Department of Manpower and Immigration also tend to exacerbate income inequalities. While the department has tried to admit immigrants only in occupations that are in high demand (apart from sponsored immigrants), the method it has chosen reinforces income inequality. A job that is unpleasant and low paid will usually have a high turnover rate as people move out of it. This will register in the department's point-rating system as high demand for that job. Immigrants who want to come here can acquire as many as thirty of the fifty required points by having an occupation in one of these high-demand industries. The department does not look at wages, simply at vacancies.

The process of funnelling immigrants into such low-wage jobs has occurred on a large scale in the mining and fruit- and vegetable-processing industries. The Manpower Department has even assisted growers and packers by flying in temporary help from the West Indies. Without the explicit recruiting help of the Manpower Department both here and abroad, those industries would be forced to pay higher wages.

As any union man knows, organizing the unorganized in Canada has always been an exhausting battle. The problems of overcoming apathy and self-interest have always been compounded by the inhibiting laws that control certification of labour unions, as these laws are applied by the provincial labour-relations boards.

In a recent article, Ed Finn, editor of *Canadian Transport,* the publication of the Canadian Brotherhood of Railway, Transport and General Workers, described how industrial-relations laws stand in the way of any attempt by unions to do something about organizing low-income workers:

> As now worded, the nation's labour codes do not prevent unfair labour practices by anti-union companies. Despite clauses forbidding dismissal of workers for union activity, employers can intimidate and even fire employees almost with impunity. Even if a union wins a legal suit, the guilty firm is merely fined a token sum rarely exceeding a few hundred dollars.
>
> Other deterrents against organizing in our labour laws and procedures include long delays in processing certification bids, and the requirement that unions must sign up a large percentage of eligible workers before a representation vote can be obtained. In most provinces it is at least 51 per cent, which means in practice that a union must have 60 to 70 per cent to be on the safe side.[9]

There are other industrial-relations laws that work against the poor:

— Agricultural and domestic workers are excluded from the right to bargain collectively.

— Certification-voting procedures allow competing unions to split the vote, which may result in a disqualification of both unions even though a majority of workers have demonstrated that they want collective-bargaining rights.

— Under federal law a certified unit has no protection if the employer changes the name of his firm, merges or in other ways

9. Ed Finn, "Why Unions Can't Do More To Fight Poverty," *Toronto Daily Star* (16 Nov. 1970), p. 11.

transforms the structure of his business. Under such circumstances the collective agreement can be wiped out.[10]

Even more serious is the effective fragmentation of bargaining units that is maintained by the rulings of the federal and provincial labour-relations boards.

The boards will rarely certify bargaining units made up of blocs of unions and groups or associations of employers. And although some de facto agreements are being made in this way, especially in the construction industry, the legal position allows any employer to opt out of the agreement he has made with the unions. This leaves the union in the precarious position of having to accept agreements from employers' associations on little more than good faith:

> . . . there is a fair amount of multi-employer bargaining despite the existence of relatively few multi-employer certification orders. In Quebec and in Ontario, 81,000 employees are covered by agreements negotiated on a multi-employer basis although there have been no multi-employer certifications in these two provinces.[11]

The boards are even reluctant to certify bargaining units that would cover several plants owned by the same corporation.

> Most provincial boards, before approving certification applications for multi-plant bargaining units, insist that the plants covered by such units be located within close geographical proximity of not more than a few miles apart. The only provincial board that does not apply this criterion and is willing to certify multi-plant bargaining units covering plants in different cities, is the Saskatchewan board.[12]

The result of erecting all these barriers to effective union organization is that less than twenty per cent of all negotiating units

10. Task Force on Labour Relations, *Report* (Ottawa, 1970), pp. 86-88.
11. Edward E. Herman, *Determination of the Appropriate Bargaining Unit* (Ottawa, 1968), p. 132.
12. Herman, *Determination of Bargaining Unit,* p. 114.

involve several companies — only twelve per cent are with employer associations — and only slightly more than twenty per cent involve several plants of single owners. Almost sixty per cent of all bargaining units involve single plants.[13]

The most progressive development so far is the Quebec government's plan to develop "sectoral bargaining." Not only will this make it possible for unions to bargain with groups of employers, but the way is opened for central collective bargaining through a whole industry — it is in this direction that we propose the solutions discussed in chapter IV.

The purpose of minimum-wage legislation is to prevent the exploitation of labour and reduce poverty. And as such it could be a powerful tool in a government earnings policy to bring about a more equitable earnings distribution; but the government has never seen it in this light and there has never been any attempt to integrate minimum-wage legislation into a broader earnings policy.

In fact, minimum-wage legislation has been pursued with considerable timidity by governments that feared that if they pushed the minimum wage too high, they would incur the anger of business interests, or create unemployment by forcing employers to streamline their production processes through technological change, or go under completely. First of all, according to the professional literature on this subject, the danger of unemployment resulting from raising the minimum-wage level has been exaggerated. Secondly, even if younger and more vulnerable workers are laid off, a government committed to a dynamic and humane economy could help them move into new jobs. The older, less mobile workers would not be trapped at a poverty-wage level; for parallel government programs would provide increased capital for machinery, cut down on the work force and so encourage wages to rise.

But this kind of commitment is something Canadian governments normally shun. Instead they have kept minimum-wage legislation at a subsistence level. In 1970, the majority of provinces provided a minimum-wage level of less than forty-five per cent of the average wage. In the affluent provinces of Ontario and British Columbia, for example, the minimum wage was only $1.50, or about $3000 a

13. Craig and Waisglass, "Collective Bargaining Prospectives," p. 582.

year — below the Relative Poverty Line for a couple without children.

Even so, many groups have been excluded from the minimum-wage law: agricultural workers, domestic servants, apprentices, part-time workers and employees of nonprofit organizations.

The minimum wage has been further weakened by allowing different levels to be used for men and women, and between rural and urban areas. Saskatchewan and Nova Scotia have differentials between urban and rural areas. Quebec had such a differential until 1970. In Prince Edward Island, Newfoundland and Nova Scotia there is a differential in the wage floor for men and women. The latter, of course, is blatant sexual discrimination and the former only creates more problems by reinforcing regional wage disparities. Within the whole area of Canadian labour policy there is no application of a decent wage structure — income distribution is apparently irrelevant.

III.4 INVESTMENT AND REGIONAL DEVELOPMENT

Viewed from a national perspective, the whole structure of the Canadian economy is incredibly lopsided. The enormous gap that separates the rich, highly productive industries from the low-wage ones cries out for a vigorous government investment policy — a policy that would direct capital to the low-wage industries to improve both their productivity, and wages for workers.

But Canadian governments, for all the reasons touched upon in chapters I and II, maintain a hands-off policy towards corporate investment. Consequently, nothing has been accomplished in redressing the inequalities that exist between the have and the have-not industries and regions.

Major corporations, in devising what to produce and where, have no responsibility to ensure that different regions are equally benefitted. They do not set themselves the problem of what lines of production would be viable and profitable in the Maritimes, or eastern Quebec or northern Ontario. Nor can they be blamed for this; such decisions have no relation to the task they set themselves, which is to find profitable modes of expansion regardless of economic welfare.[1]

Corporations, even when heavily subsidized with public funds, demand and get almost as much freedom in planning as they want. This means little or no government planning. And so government subsidies given to industries to locate in depressed regions have not paid off very well for anyone except the companies. The government, apparently, has never seen the importance of moving investment into those areas on a scale that would really meet the needs of the region.

This involves a degree of government initiative in investment, including a large-scale use of instruments like a government investment fund, which once more over-steps the boundaries of corporate autonomy as now understood on this continent. The mobilization of capital for a public fund will require inter-ference with the normal channels of saving, such as insurance and trust companies and mutual funds, and the entrepreneurial role of the fund would seem to be an invasion by government of a function reserved for private business.[2]

The Industrial Development Bank is an institution that is sup-posed to make capital readily available to small businesses. But the interest charged, ten to eleven per cent, has discouraged customers. And the total loans outstanding in 1968 amounted to less than $400 million.[3] Compare this with the $7.6 billion made by chartered banks, and the $2.8 billion in deferred corporate income taxes — which amount to interest-free loans to big business. Obviously, the industrial bank is not going to save small business.

The federal government's system of investment incentives through tax concessions is a policy that is supposed to stimulate productivity and growth. Its impact on the economy has been examined by Eric Kierans, former minister in the federal and Quebec cabinets, and former president of the Montreal Stock Exchange — obviously

1. Taylor, *Pattern of Politics*, p. 42.
2. Ibid.
3. Bank of Canada Review, 1968 supplement to statistical summary (Ottawa, 1969), p. 117.

a man who has some experience of the inner workings of the machinery between corporations and government.

He points out that these tax concessions end up favouring powerful corporations, and are biased against small businesses in desperate need of capital:

> The small firm uses capital sparingly and economically and is less able to take advantage of the tax subsidies that go to larger competitors. The labour-capital output ratio is better balanced and the small firm does more, proportionately, to solve the priority Canadian problem, unemployment.[4]

In addition, tax concessions reinforce the grip large corporations have on the market:

> The system is an additional block to new entry into an industry since the tax advantages are valueless until a stream of profits is established which may take years. The existing firm benefits, not the new firm.[5]

All businesses, large and small, pay the corporation tax, but it is only the really powerful ones that make a large enough investment to be able to take advantage of the concessions. This, in the end, amounts to a transfer of capital from small business to large corporations. It all adds up to help for our friends at the top from the guys at the bottom.

And Kierans takes it one step further, saying that these tax concessions subsidize capital rather than jobs and thus contribute to Canada's unemployment problem.

The Canada Development Corporation

The Canada Development Corporation could have been a powerful tool for the government to use in the evening-out of industrial and regional inequalities. In its present form, and with its stated objectives, it amounts to a smoke screen to hide a headlong flight by the

4. Speech to the annual meeting of the Canadian Economics Association, Memorial University, St. John's, Nfld. (3 June 1971).
5. Ibid.

federal government from the responsibility for planning investment.

As a crown corporation, one of the main objectives of the CDC should be the expansion of employment in high-wage industries; it should pump life and technological change into the low-wage industries and thereby promote increased productivity and higher wages.

However, the whole idea of using the CDC as a force for greater government participation and responsibility in the Canadian economy has not been adopted. The objectives of the CDC are now to provide Canadian shareholders with a new vehicle to maximize private profits. It is going to do this with a project funded initially on public money — $250 million of it — but ultimately private partners will be allowed to control ninety per cent of the fund. In addition, $300 to $400 million worth of publicly owned assets in existing crown corporations will be transferred to private ownership.

Foreign capital has been welcomed to this country because governments have been afraid that Canada would never have enough capital for development of resources and industry. Enormous concessions have been made to keep US capital flowing into the country. And although there now appears to be a belated awareness of the need for economic independence within the Liberal party, Prime Minister Trudeau has publicly stated that we still do not have sufficient capital to do without large-scale US investment. There is evidence that Trudeau is wrong.

> Canada is not a capital-poor country at all. The extraordinary myth that the country lacks capital is based on a lack of another kind . . . managerial skills . . . Canada is one of the richest countries in the world with one of the highest rates of savings. Indeed, we export a lot of capital and at the present time a great deal of it is exported to the United States . . . it is calculated, for instance, that Canadian mutual funds are investing something like 45 per cent of their holdings in the American economy.[6]

It is also now evident that US corporations have been able to take control of the Canadian economy through the simple expedient of raising most of their money in Canada. When the United Church

6. Taylor, *Pattern of Politics,* p. 72.

sold Ryerson Press to McGraw-Hill, the US corporation got the money through loans from a Canadian bank. And this is not a recent development:

> . . . between 1957 and 1965, American-directed investment companies in Canada found seventy-three per cent of the funds they needed from retained earnings and depreciation; and a further 12 per cent from borrowing in Canada. Only 15 per cent of the funds came from the United States.[7]

Regional-Development Policies

One of the most bewildering inconsistencies about government regional-development policies is that they are formed in isolation of existing policies, and undermined by the prevailing monetary and fiscal policies.

For example, to 1 May 1971, the Department of Regional and Economic Expansion spent $140 million in industrial incentives grants. But this was at a time when the federal government was working hard and successfully to dampen the central economy. It is futile to attempt to get an industry going in the Maritimes when the markets for its products are depressed. This reality appears to have eluded the government policy makers. There are many similar contradictions in regional-development policy. Since Confederation there has been a consistent federal policy of trying to develop the central economy. The methods chosen have substantially worsened the terms of trade on which producers from these depressed areas have to deal with foreign and domestic markets. The products that come out of these regional areas are mainly primary. Their inability to find appropriate export markets is largely the fault of tariff agreements that favour the central economy with certain protections but discriminate against underdeveloped regions.

The 1969 federal task force on agriculture took up this point as central to agriculture's difficulties in finding export markets.

> International trade in agricultural products is of vital importance to the Canadian economy. Agriculture exports account for about 15 per cent of Canada's total exports. These represent

7. Kari Levitt, "Dependence and Disintegration in Canada," *New World Quarterly* 4, no. 2, p. 131. Quoted by Taylor, *Pattern of Politics*, p. 73.

an important contribution to sustaining our balance-of-payments position. More important, there are the opportunities to improve this position by enhancing the competitive position of Canadian agriculture and by the use of appropriate trade policy objectives and strategies.[8]

In its recommendations, the report said that the Canadian government must take further initiatives — "as opposed to merely reacting to others' proposals" — to get tariffs reduced on agricultural products. And one way to do this, the report suggested, would be to make other industries in the central economy more competitive in foreign markets.

> . . . the so-called "voluntary quotas" on Japanese textiles and other manufactures adversely affect the willingness and ability of the Japanese to purchase Canadian grains and meat. If other sectors of the Canadian economy have not made the adjustments necessary to become competitive (as most of agriculture has), then it is time they were helped to do so by pressure of competition.[9]

Another example of the way in which the federal government's basic approach to economic policy worsens the terms of trade for the Maritimes is the St. Lawrence Seaway. This project completely wiped out any competitive advantage the Maritimes might have had in manufacturing for the European market.

Another important policy left out of regional-development planning is the problem of raising capital in the Maritimes and on the Prairies, where financial institutions are immature compared to those that exist in industrial eastern Canada.

The federal task force on agriculture studied this problem and pointed out that

> . . . management ability is of little value if the farmer does not have the necessary capital to finance his operations. The modern progressive lending institution should have the capacity to serv-

8. Task Force on Agriculture, *Report* (1969), p. 41.
9. Ibid, p. 59.

ice both capital and management needs of the commercial farmer.[10]

The capital now available to farmers through the Federal Farm Credit Corporation often comes through a complex and restrictive route.

> . . . there remain the problems of duplication, restrictive loan limits set by several of the provincial credit agencies, subsidization of interest rates, difficulty in mobilizing the necessary capital funds by many of the provinces, a lack of suitable credit facilities for sub-commercial farms, and the serious jurisdictional problem between the federal and provincial farm-credit agencies in providing farm management and supervisory credit services.[11]

As the report points out, no less than eleven federal government departments are involved in some way or another in the farm lending business.

> This multiplicity of federal credit agencies must inevitably result in confusion, conflict and inefficiency. If the federal government is to continue its involvement in these various fields, it would seem prudent to integrate and consolidate many of the agencies involved. Furthermore if the federal government is to have one credit policy for Canadian agriculture, it would seem prudent to have one department administer such a policy.[12]

Agriculture is not alone with the problem of securing capital. Small businesses, which characterize the economy of the less developed regions, have the same trouble. Their position is even worse than that of the small businesses of the central economy. There are no effective government measures to take care of these problems. This has an even more depressing effect upon the management ability and appropriate entrepreneurial skills that are already languishing in these areas.

10. Ibid, p. 356.
11. Ibid, p. 357.
12. Ibid.

The principal economic problem of the depressed areas of Canada revolves around the limited amount of capital available for investment and the overwhelming numbers of people looking for jobs.

The solution would then seem to lie in the direction of creating viable enterprises that would develop as many jobs as possible. The Department of Regional Economic Expansion uses capital incentives to attract industries to these areas in the hope that they will do just that.

But the capital grants are made in such a fashion that the money is used primarily to pay for installing machinery. The public subsidies are therefore being invested in machines, not people. Moreover, most of the capital that is being rewarded is Bay Street capital.

In Ontario, where the provincial government uses the same approach, there is a certain amount of evidence to suggest that firms are closing down old plants to open up new ones needing fewer workers because of this increased investment in machinery. The Swedes have considered the same problem.

> Whereas it is labour that is regarded as the abundant factor and capital as the scarce in northern parts of the country, the policy has chosen to subsidize capital rather than labour, thus stimulating capital-intensive production technique, and even the substitution of capital for labour in existing firms. This means that employment-creating effects will be smaller than if labour costs instead had been subsidized.[13]

During the decade of the 1960s, the federal and provincial governments were seized by the idea of industrial development for Canada's depressed areas. And during those years literally billions of dollars have been poured into private corporations to make regional industrial development a reality.

No doubt some of that investment has paid off in bringing industry to otherwise backward regions. But at very best this enormous expenditure of welfare payments to corporations can only be called a partial success. There are many sad lessons to be learned from this

13. A. Lindbeck, "Theories and Problems in Swedish Economic Policy in the Post-War Period," *American Economic Review* 58, no. 3, part 2, supplement (June 1968), p. 66.

period, of which the most important is the total lack of integrated economic planning. For example, local governments, in scrambling to attract industry through subsidies or tax concessions, can undermine federal development programs. Communities with financial strength, then, can attract more industry; poor communities cannot.[14]

Despite the fact that regional development is essentially a matter of balancing investment from one region to another, the federal government restricts its development efforts to the occasional provision of a carrot in depressed areas.

Pulp and paper mills sprang up in remote areas of Quebec, built to compete with mills in British Columbia, and overproduction was on its way. Provincial agencies to attract industry sprang up in ad hoc fashion:

> . . . the most controversial have been the Manitoba Development Fund (MDF) and Nova Scotia's Industrial Estates Ltd. (IEL). Both IEL and MDF were made responsible to a board of directors which, though appointed by the government, was not directly responsible for the activities of the corporation. The directors were all members of the business establishment. Both corporations were headed by drumbeating promoters . . . tough, hard-working salesmen who would travel around the world personally to persuade business tycoons to come to Nova Scotia or Manitoba. The style was the same; some critics called it "twanging the old-boy network," an activity facilitated by having leaders of the business community on the boards of directors. [These salesmen] would work out "deals" with companies they felt they could persuade to come to their province, offering income incentives that were often not made public.[15]

The Liberal Saskatchewan government of the late Ross Thatcher led the way in these "give-away" programs. In 1965 it made a deal with the US firm of Parsons and Whittemore to build a $65 million pulp-and-paper mill just north of Prince Albert. It worked this way:

14. See L. H. Klaassen, *Area Economic and Social Redevelopment* (Paris: OECD, 1965), p. 60.
15. Philip Mathias, *Forced Growth* (Toronto: James Lewis and Samuel, 1971), p. 7.

The federal government put up $5 million as an area development grant. Parsons and Whittemore put in $7 million, for which they received a seventy per cent equity in the plant. The Saskatchewan government put in $1.5 million and took the risk of guaranteeing the balance of the $50 million to be raised as a loan. So, for taking eighty per cent of the risk involved — concessions were also made in supplying wood — in a $65-million enterprise, the Saskatchewan government was rewarded with a paltry thirty per cent of ownership of the mill. Just to make the deal a little sweeter for Parsons and Whittemore, the contract guaranteed the firm a contractor's "turn-key" commission of ten per cent once the plant was built.

The firm would be permitted to make a further profit from machinery sold to the mill through one of its own subsidiaries. As a result, barring overruns in the construction costs, the turnkey commission and machinery profits would theoretically have made it possible for Parsons and Whittemore to get back their financial outlay just by building the mill. The seventy per cent ownership of the mill was pure gravy.

We are not suggesting that present DREE policies are working on this generous a scale. But there is no information as to where money and control is coming from in the kind of investment that is now being subsidized in these regions.

Before we can determine whether DREE is really only one more multimillion-dollar welfare vehicle to establish greater US ownership and control in this country, we will have to wait for the evaluation report that has been promised for the spring of 1972.

Another major problem in the depressed regions is the lower standard of education and skills — as compared to more successful areas of the country — and the difficulty local residents have in adjusting to industrial development and technological change.

In both of these areas the Department of Regional Economic Expansion is paying insufficient attention and not providing enough funds.

DREE has approached the problem obliquely. Education is under provincial jurisdiction, and it becomes constitutionally awkward for the federal government to become involved in paying for education. So it has instead built projects like roads, bridges, sewers and serviced land. The idea was that the provinces would be freed from having to spend money on these projects and would spend more money on education. However, there is no indication this has happened.

In fact, DREE has found a way around the constitutional problem. Under special area agreements they pumped some $4 million of direct federal aid into education for Nova Scotia, New Brunswick, Alberta, Manitoba and Saskatchewan over a two-year period. But the commitment has been haphazard, grudging and, it appears, temporary.

The department is compounding the basic problems of regional development by failing to utilize and train whatever managerial talent already exists in depressed areas. Grants and subsidies are increasingly going to companies and corporations from outside poor regions, often to US-owned firms or subsidiaries of Ontario companies. The results of this practice are predictable: the outside corporations import both their own managers and their own skilled workers, and nothing is done to encourage or develop vigorous managerial skills in the resident population. If depressed regions are ever going to stand on their own feet, development of local managers, as well as local workers, is essential. The final result of the present DREE program, however, is not the creation of more jobs for local workers, but merely the shuffling of jobs and workers from one province to another.

III.5 INDUSTRIAL-ORGANIZATION POLICY

The supposed value of a competitive economy stems from the benefits it yields to the nation. But many of these possible benefits have been undermined by powerful corporations, which can control the supply and demand of the market. The government has in no way effectively opposed their power, and in some areas has contributed to its greater concentration.

It has helped the monopolies out with:

Patent protection, which gives the patent owner monopoly power for seventeen years. The result is that a monopoly can be created and so control a whole industry or technology. In this way high profits can be obtained from raising prices on products that do not have to compete. Profits go to the wealthy, and the poor are ripped off as consumers.[1]

Almost all the profits obtained by such monopolies and patent holders go to foreigners. This is because almost ninety-five per cent of patent licences are held by foreigners or foreign corporations.

> There can be little advantage to Canadians in maintaining the system, particularly in the light of the other criticisms [high profits and less competition] discussed.[2]

The exemption of services and particular professional associations in both competition and public regulation.

Traditionally all services — banks, insurance companies, etc. — have been exempt from competition policies; but under new legislation they will have to observe regulations, at least for the sake of appearances. However, the government has continued to allow professionals — doctors, lawyers — to remain free of any restraints. This means that such professionals can do what nobody else is allowed to do — set their own fees, without any consultation with those people who ultimately have to pay them.

Moreover, these professions usually have complete control over their licensing, and the admission requirements to their schools. The professionals are allowed, as no other group is, to put the consumer in a position in which he has no alternative but to pay the price. Doctors, for example, are given complete freedom to charge whatever price they wish; it is not surprising they are the most highly paid professional group in the country.

The encouragement, through tax concessions, of corporations to increase their market control through advertising.

Advertising is used by corporations as a device to obtain market control by creating artificial differences between products that are essentially the same, thereby establishing what is known as "brand loyalty."

---

1. See L. A. Skeoch, *Restrictive Trade Practices in Canada* (Toronto: McClelland and Stewart, 1966), pp. 167-226; and Brewis, *Canadian Economic Policy*, pp. 91-94.
2. Brewis, *Canadian Economic Policy*, p. 94.

This loyalty means that it becomes extremely difficult for a competitor to enter the same area of production: so resources are wrongly allocated, which is counter to society's best interests.

Through the vehicle of advertising, corporations can also force demand for a product to artificial heights, and create further economic inefficiency.[3]

The tendency of government regulatory agencies to represent the interests of monopolies instead of consumers.

As the Economic Council of Canada has noted, agencies that are supposed to regulate monopolies often favour the monopoly instead of the consumer they are supposed to be protecting. This is not to suggest a conspiracy, but it can be attributed to:

> The absence of clear-cut objectives and the lack of public attention to the regulations themselves.[4]

Anti-merger policies

Mergers between companies can have two effects. The first can be in the public interest; two or more firms may come together and form a more efficient and productive industrial unit, then pass on the benefits to the consumer.

The negative effect occurs when two or more companies merge and create what is known as a real-cost disadvantage. This means that the larger unit has become less efficient than the smaller units, and passes on the higher costs of this inefficiency to the consumer and to other producers.[5]

Between 1910 and 1948, there were over eight hundred mergers involving over 1500 firms and, of course, since 1948 there have been many more.[6] But in all this time the government has attempted to prosecute only two corporations. It is hard to believe that more than ninety-nine per cent of mergers are in the public interest. The ECC concluded that:

3. See Ibid. p. 30; also H. C. Eastman and S. Stykholt, *The Tariff and Competition in Canada* (Toronto: Macmillan, 1967), pp. 54-58.
4. See ECC, *Interim Report on Competition Policy* (Ottawa, 1969), p. 154; also Brewis, *Canadian Economic Policy*, pp. 69-90.
5. W. Fellner, *Competition among the Few* (New York: Knopf, 1949), pp. 44-49, 282-328.
6. J. C. Weldon, "Concentrations in Canadian Industry 1900-1948," in Skeoch, *Restrictive Trade Practices,* table 1, p. 233.

In respect of corporation mergers, which are one of the more important means by which changes in industrial concentration and other dimensions of economic structure take place, the Act has been all but inoperative.[7]

Price fixing through information sharing
In some cases, information sharing between corporations can lead to informal price fixing. The government in 1960 changed the Combines Investigation Act to allow companies to share information about markets, and other helpful things. This amendment was made without any evaluation of its possible consequences, and was applied without regard to its effect. This provision has been carried over into the new 1970 legislation that covers this variety of collusion; again, without assessment of its consequences.

Government competition policy has been, both in ambition and in application, exceedingly timid, for several related reasons. The first is that those who shape both corporate and government policy are inevitably the same people. The second is that much of what goes on between government and corporations is kept quite secret. And, third, the public has been kept quite unaware of what is happening or what the alternatives might be.

III.6 GOVERNMENT HOUSING POLICY

In chapter II we pointed out that the housing needs of the poor are not being met. This is not surprising because current housing policy is almost totally directed at producing housing for the middle class.[1]

There is also some doubt as to whether or not a private housing market can ever meet by itself the housing needs of the poor. In 1970 the government tried to encourage the private sector with an allocation of $200 million in the CMHC budget. The money was intended to help the private sector find new ways of developing

7. ECC, *Interim Report,* p. 64.
1. The only exception is the peculiar form of economic segregation known as low-income housing. These units totalled only about 2.4 per cent of the total housing stock by the end of 1970. See CMHC, *Canadian Housing Statistics, 1969* (Ottawa, 1970), tables 40, 41.

low-income housing. But a recent evaluation of this program shows that nothing new was discovered.[2]

The government has not given the poor the financial power to obtain adequate housing; and it has generally not attempted to influence the housing market to satisfy those needs. (The housing market required that $200 million even to begin to think about helpful innovation.)

For example, the average family income in 1969 of all the borrowers under the National Housing Act was $10,810 — more than seventy-five per cent of all Canadian families earned less than that. In other words, the tax dollars of the working poor are being used up to help the most affluent group in our society to purchase equity in their homes. This subsequently worsens the inequalities and distribution of wealth.

If more low-income families were allowed NHA loans it would expand the demand for housing and, with an increase in the supply of housing, begin to meet the needs of the poor.

Low-income families tend to live in older housing, often in the worst conditions.[3] Canadian housing policies almost totally emphasize new housing. There is simply no money to fix up old houses. What little money does get through comes via the private market; section 24 of the National Housing Act enables CMHC to pay losses taken by private institutions when lending money for home improvements. Under this arrangement, 9,142 loans were made available in 1969 to cover both home improvement and extensions. Most of these represented rumpus-room conversions — party rooms for the bourgeoisie.

2. Canadian Council on Social Development, *Where the $200 Million Went* (Ottawa, 1971), pp. 9, 19.
3. In all urban Canada in 1961, twenty-four per cent of all dwellings inhabited by wage-earning household heads were over forty years old. And sixty-four per cent of the inhabitants of those dwellings earned less than $4,000 per year. (DBS census bulletin 2.2-11.)
    Some twenty-two per cent of non-farm family households had a family income of less than $3,000. Yet they occupied half of all single detached non-farm dwellings in need of major repair. Moreover, more than a third of this lower-income group lived in houses requiring major and minor repair. While the overall proportion of houses in major need of repair has improved, relatively the same number of the poor are stuck with living in them. (DBS census bulletin 4.1-8.)
    The proportion of houses over forty years old in need of major repair is four times as great as the proportion less than forty years old. (DBS census bulletin 2.2-7.)
    This data is not cross-classified by family size.

In a good year the housing market will produce housing starts equal to only three per cent of the existing housing stock. So, apart from the minimal home-improvement loans, CMHC policy ignores the problem of the ninety-seven per cent of the houses that were not built in that year. The CMHC, then, does not concern itself with the housing problems of all Canadians, but only with the problems of those who can afford new homes.

III.7 SUMMARY

The economy is most obviously not planned; governments merely react to crises. The little planning that is undertaken is unrelated to any ideal of equality.

Most current economic policies only increase the gap between the poor and the rich; they reinforce the position of those with power and privilege, and exacerbate the wretchedness of the poor. We find the government irresponsible because it refuses to deal with the fact that, in most essential aspects, the purposes of the modern corporate structure are in opposition to the collective good of society. Business behaviour, to be clearly in the public interest, depends upon the presence of the regulating forces of the market in a framework of pure competition. Canadian business constantly stifles competition; and the only remedy is government regulation.

Canadian government must stop using crude monetary and fiscal policies in its reaction to the structural problems in the economy. It must instead intervene in the economic arena with an array of selective and discriminating economic policies, in a planned economic attack that has, as its first objectives, equality and social development. No large business can afford merely to react to changes in the environment; neither can any government. And that is what the next chapter is all about.

IV

Towards Full Employment

V.1 THE IDEAL OF EQUALITY

Equality of opportunity, in Canada, is an ideal restricted to high-school civics textbooks. Equality of *reward* is not even found there; very few people have challenged the idea that the rich, the talented and the ruthless deserve more in wages and praise than the disadvantaged.

The argument for rewarding some people more than others, because they are more talented than others, is not as conclusive as it seems:

> To convert a phenomenon, however interesting, into a principle, however respectable, is an error of logic. It is the confusion of a judgement of fact with a judgement of value. . . .[1]

Talent is a nice thing to have. But it should not necessarily make its possessor rich. There is no reason why people should have to be rewarded with enormous affluence in order for them to make full use of their talents. Nor, for that matter, should wide inequality in wage differentials be maintained, so that people need to save to adjust to changing economic conditions.

Absolute equality of income is probably unattainable. Long years of training will have to be rewarded. Furthermore, there will always be dirty jobs; someone will always have to do them, and they will have to be compensated for undertaking them.

Various people have objected that increased equality of wages will

1. Tawney, *Equality*, p. 50.

remove workers' will to work, affect the nation's moral fibre and destroy the economy. There is less than no reason to go along with this. Britain, it is true, has a better income distribution than Canada, and a slower growth rate. But Sweden has both more wage equality and an economy that grows faster than ours. Efficiency does not depend on inequality, unless the Swedes are cooking their books.[2]

Increased equality, then, will do no harm to the economy, and will probably do a lot of good. To bring increased equality about, the federal government should go after inequality of incomes with a comprehensive earnings policy.

This will horrify those policy makers who consider that government planning should restrict itself to ensuring efficiency, stability and growth, in narrow terms, and that redistribution of income (not, emphatically, of wealth) should be handled exclusively through the tax and transfer systems.

The tax and transfer systems, however, are inadequate vehicles for the redistribution of income and wealth. For one thing, they are absolutely obvious; income from welfare systems, for example, is publicly defined as "easy money," reserved for the worthless and the lazy. Income from work (and, curiously, from coupon clipping) is

2. On the one hand, Britain has a more equal income distribution than Canada but also a lower growth rate. Using as a measure of income distribution the ratio of the top of the lowest income quintile to the bottom of the highest income quintile in 1960-61, Canada's ratio must be about .30 to .35,[a] while Britain's has been estimated to be .48.[b] The annual growth rate of Britain's per capita GNP in 1961-68 was 2.0 per cent, compared with Canada's 2.8.[c] On the other hand, Sweden has a still more equal distribution of income than Britain but has had a higher per capita GNP growth rate than Canada. Sweden's ratio of the top of the bottom income quintile to the bottom of the top income quintile has been estimated to be .57,[d] and its per capita GNP growth rate in 1961-68 was 3.2 per cent.[e] The available evidence certainly does not suggest any clear-cut relationship between income distribution and the rate of economic growth.

a. Canada's income distribution is similar to that of the United States. See J. R. Podoluk, "Some Comparisons of the Canadian-US Income Distributions," paper presented to the 11th General Conference of the International Association for Research in Income and Wealth, Tel Aviv (Aug.-Sept. 1969). The ratio for the US was .30; see John H. Chandler, "An International Comparison," Perspectives on Poverty, Dorothy K. Newman et al (University of Wisconsin: Institute for Research on Poverty, 1969), reprint no. 32; reprinted in Monthly Labour Review 92 (Dec. 1969): 55-56.

b. Chandler, "An International Comparison," p. 56.

c. International Bank for Reconstruction and Development, World Bank Atlas (Sept. 1970).

d. Chandler, "An International Comparison," p. 56.

e. IBRD, World Bank Atlas.

considered to be deserved; income from government — even from social-insurance programs — is, in the same way, considered to be unearned.

An earnings policy that equalizes wages, and so attacks lack of income at the source, is obviously a much better device. Work disincentives are avoided (an exclusive reliance on the transfer system could produce crippling ones). Nobody is stigmatized. And the dole, at long last, disappears into the limbo it richly deserves. There will still be the need for a transfer system, as many people will still be outside the labour force; and nobody expects an earnings policy to work with absolute perfection.

There is nothing particularly wide eyed about this proposal; increased equality can pay off in increased efficiency. If wages in one industry are higher than in another, for example, and if there is encouragement to workers moving from one to another, employers in the low-paying industry will have to start paying decent wages (especially as wage differentials are compressed) — and increasing the productivity of their firms.

This is the way things ought to work, of course; things do not work this way because corporations are allowed to do as they please, and union leaders in high-wage industries tend to go along with them. Anyone setting out to plan an economy, then, in terms of prices, wages, distributions of employment and levels of production, must be prepared to tackle corporate autonomy. The corporations, which plan everything down to the colour schemes of their washrooms, must be forced to put up with a little planning from other people.

IV.2 CENTRALIZED COLLECTIVE BARGAINING

Existing unions can, and should, turn their attention to the organization of low-income workers. But that is not enough.

Collective bargaining in Canada is paying off for the powerful, not for the powerless; for bargaining is scattered all over the lot, with no co-ordination within or between industries. This produces vast differences in wages and incomes. The way to eliminate these differences is to centralize the collective-bargaining process itself.

First, bargaining can be centralized within industries. For example, all textile workers should be organized, and bargain with all textile employers, simultaneously, so that unions can deal with any objection from individual manufacturers that they are being put at an unfair and non-competitive disadvantage.

This is a beginning. But it leads logically to a second step: centralized collective bargaining *across* industries, to consolidate workers in one industry with workers in others. This would prevent unions and corporations in high-wage industries from boosting wages faster than or as fast as unions and corporations in low-wage industries, a prevention that is necessary if wage differentials are to be narrowed.

This is not utopian. It is European. In Sweden, for example, through government pressure on labour unions and employers' associations, bargaining at the national level was put into practice, and that bargaining now sets precise guidelines for local bargaining. If Canadian labour and business cannot find the gumption to do this for themselves, and if government cannot force them to do it, there is the alternative used in Holland, where the government assumes final responsibility for wage policies. This is obviously less desirable; the co-operation of labour and business becomes more difficult to obtain when government habitually resorts to a blackjack to ensure it. It is also probably more sensible for Canadian labour and business to push for centralized bargaining unilaterally, than to wait for the provincial and federal levels of government to wrangle through their jurisdictional and constitutional problems, of which they may be counted upon to discover many.

This does not mean that corporations will automatically jump for an economic policy that is aimed primarily at the redistribution of income. But the neatness of centralized collective bargaining should appeal to the corporate mind, for it centralizes disputes, and makes prediction of both problems and costs more accurate.[1] Corporations have, in fact, discovered this for themselves; some of the most advanced industries in the country are already employing industry-

---

1. After normal grievance procedures have been exhausted, the Swedes refer disputes during the life of each collective agreement to a labour court that has final jurisdiction. Strikes can take place during bargaining; but the courts and centralized negotiations have cut man-days lost due to labour disputes almost to the vanishing point.

wide agreements or their equivalent in the form of "pattern bargaining" in union contracts. This is the collective-bargaining counterpart to the price-leader system: one agreement sets a wage rate, and the others follow.

Access to collective bargaining, then, should be a right of citizenship, extended by law to all workers.[2] And the bargaining should involve not only a general equalization of wages, but should also determine the size and extent of those wage differentials required for unpleasant or difficult jobs.[3] This can be done on a national basis, as it has been in Holland, where

> . . . after the war, all workers were divided into three skill classes. The unskilled wage was based on what was regarded as a social minimum. The semi-skilled wage was fixed at 110 per cent, and the skilled wage at 120 per cent of the unskilled wage. This rigid structure was later modified by an important, though not fully adopted, nation-wide job evaluation scheme in which jobs were assigned points according to the technical characteristics of the job, such as knowledge required and self-reliance, and wage differentials were related to the ranking of jobs. Acceptance of the social desirability of such an approach to determining relative incomes from work removed much of the economic competition for higher wages and made a stronger form of incomes policy easier to administer.[4]

Some economists argue that large wage differentials are necessary

2. Collective bargaining must be extended to cover the whole labour force, specifically to include the large number of low-wage workers that at present have no representation. This means changing some of the present rules. As a minimum, the following recommendations on the Woods Task Force on Labour Relations should be implemented:
    — Agriculture workers and domestic servants should no longer be excluded from the collective-bargaining process.
    — Only thirty-five per cent membership should be required to initiate the procedure that leads to the certification of unions.
    — A simple majority of voting employees only should be required for certification.
    — The certification procedure should be accelerated in high-turnover industries where the employers at present count upon being unable to organize transient labour.
3. "Wage Negotiations and Wage Policies in Sweden," *International Labour Review* 83 (Nov. 1959): 405; cited by D. C. Smith, *Incomes Policy* (Ottawa: ECC, 1966).
4. Smith, *Incomes Policy*, p. 131.

to get workers to move from one area or job to another. The Swedes, however, have discovered that there are other ways to attract workers than by bribing them; they argue that large wage differentials can be inflationary, and are in any case inequitable. The Swedes argue, furthermore, that general equality of wages, natural justice aside, tends to squeeze inefficient firms out of business and makes the economy more efficient; considering that the Swedish economy is a lot more efficient than ours, it is difficult to argue against them.[5]

Occasionally wage differentials can be used to deal with critical shortages and surpluses of labour:

> *But a case would have to be made for them.* That alone would constitute a remarkable difference from the present situation in which no case of any kind need ever be made for any wage bargain — at least not in terms of consistent and intelligent principles. Under the kind of arrangements proposed, wage rates out of line with the general pattern of social policy would be justified on one ground and one only: *viz.* inability to maintain recruitment. General policy, in fact, would be framed in terms of ethical and social policy; but these exceptions would represent unavoidable concessions to economic necessity.[6]

The government, as noted above, should generally stay out of the act as far as bargaining itself is concerned, unless labour and business demonstrate that they will negotiate nothing worthwhile on their own. But the process of centralized collective bargaining will require time to take hold; and to make sure that low-wage workers do not starve before it does, provincial governments should *immediately* establish a minimum wage, without exemptions, at sixty per cent of the average wage. (The only province in Canada with a minimum wage now set at this level is Prince Edward Island. One minimum wage for all of Canada, at the moment, is probably unworkable, because of wage disparities between provinces.[7])

5. Smith, *Incomes Policy,* p. 157.
6. B. Wootton, *The Social Foundations of Wage Policy* (London: George Allen and Unwin, 1962), p. 178.
7. In 1970 the ratios of minimum to average wages varied from forty per cent in rural Saskatchewan to sixty per cent in Prince Edward Island. It is proposed

This proposal is directly related to the establishment of the guaranteed annual income; for an increased minimum wage will make workers more self-reliant and less dependent on the guaranteed income, and that will help to bring down the costs of the program.

It is true that hiking the minimum wage will force some employers to modernize and to close down marginally efficient operations; and this will put some people out of work. But a tight labour market, along with policies to create more high-wage jobs, would ensure that most of these people got work again immediately, and skill training and other programs should be mounted to help those who did not.

Centralized collective bargaining will do a great deal to reduce income inequality; but barriers between low-wage and high-wage industries must be tackled in other ways.

Many apprenticeship programs, at the moment, are not as much training courses as screens used by unions to keep workers away from skilled jobs and so to protect high wages. This is inexcusable and must be stopped, even — or especially — in professional areas like medicine and the law. Medical schools should start training enough doctors to meet the needs of society, whether that drives medical salaries down or not. And the other barriers between low-wage workers and high-wage jobs — union entrance requirements, initiation fees, and so on — should be reviewed.

Similarly, unions and employers must work out agreements to allow mothers to work half-day shifts, and integrate those shifts with a systematic provision of day-care centres. These could be run commercially or publicly, with the employer making facilities available. And company pension plans should be made portable by law, and backed up with a decent public pension scheme that would diminish their importance.

Centralized collective bargaining is an absolutely crucial tool in the equalization of wages; but it will inevitably contribute to the

that in all jurisdictions the minimum wage be raised to sixty per cent of the average wage level. This would have meant in 1970 about $1.90 in federal-jurisdiction industries and about $2.05 in British Columbia. The negative consequences are not likely to outweigh the positive consequences until a higher ratio of minimum to average wages is reached. This would probably apply even before a guaranteed income was instituted, although in that case it would be necessary to proceed more cautiously because persons that are displaced are not so well protected. Beyond the sixty per cent level an experimental approach has to be adopted.

alienation of individual workers, who will be less involved in wage negotiations than they were before. This can be overcome if workers are allowed to participate in the production decisions themselves; the caste systems within plants are at the root of alienation, and their removal will alleviate it. At the same time, government should make sure that union leaders and negotiators are elected in a democratic way. If representatives have the power to negotiate a binding contract, it is essential that they represent the people who will be bound by it.

None of this can be accomplished by rhetoric alone. We do not expect altruism on the part of the business community to play a great part in the creation of an egalitarian society. Corporations, as they have amply demonstrated, have no conscience, and no consciousness of social priorities. Government, then, must assume more control over economic activity. If corporations insist on behaving in irresponsible ways, they must be brought to heel.

IV.3 FULL EMPLOYMENT

The policies just described will fail completely if they are not backed up with full employment. Training, regional development, centralized collective bargaining and the rest depend on a tight labour market. Without it, they will flounder.

It is absolutely essential, then, that the federal government abandon its practice of fighting inflation by creating unemployment. This procedure is stupid to the point of being criminal, and it should be forbidden, as other criminal activities are, by law: economic emergency-measures legislation should be enacted that would trigger automatic tax cuts and increased government spending when unemployment exceeded 3.5 per cent.

Inflation, to the extent that it is evil, can be fought with a whole array of precise economic instruments that deal with specific problems and do not flatten the entire economy in the process.

Stabilization policy should be specific. It makes no sense to use the same measures in depressed regional areas and in the thriving centre economy. Instead, as one recent Canadian study proposed, the government should introduce

. . . regional tax or expenditure policies into those regions where an excessive rate of total spending was contributing to inflation while simultaneously pursuing expansionary policies in regions of high unemployment. That such a policy would be effectively applied in Canada is once again confirmed by our empirical results.[1]

Quebec Premier Robert Bourassa has sensibly proposed a regional stabilization fund that would give depressed regions easy access to low-cost loans. This fund would channel spending into areas where it was needed, in order to get depressed regions out of difficulty, and stop developing trouble in regions that showed signs of slowing down.

Other policies are useful in regulating demand for goods and services, in controlling investment and in balancing foreign trade. These are specific areas in the economy, and specific techniques are required to deal with them; it makes no sense to knock one on the head and expect the other to blink.

At the moment, the federal government evidently considers that the only way to control rising prices is to attack demand; this also tends to suppress supply, which in many cases only aggravates the problem. For example, this technique can, and has, strangled credit for housing. This, in turn, has produced drastic rent inflation, towards which the government has adopted a hurt expression, but done nothing worthwhile.

This, of course, is nonsense. The intelligent alternative is to *increase* the availability of those goods and services that are in short supply, and drive down prices that way. The government, then, should pour funds into low-income housing and increase the supply of housing, which will not only benefit the poor quite directly, but also stop that particular kind of inflation in its tracks.

Once again, the specific nature of stabilization policy is important. For government must make sure that industries that increase the productive capacity of the economy — machine-tool firms, for

1. F. C. Miller, "The Case for Regional Fiscal Policy in Canada," paper read to the Canadian Economics Association, Memorial University, St. John's, Nfld. (4 June 1971), p. 10.

example — are not treated in the same way as other industries.[2]

Investment is a highly volatile component of national spending, and should be dealt with carefully, by timing investment to fit the needs of the economy. Sweden has developed a stabilization investment fund that does precisely that:

> In general, both business and government regard the investment reserves as a useful and flexible anti-recession device, as well as being of assistance in promoting the re-equipment of industry.[3]

At the moment, the federal government provides investment subsidies to stimulate industry in depressed areas. This is, in principle, reasonable, and would be more so if government concentrated on subsidizing healthy labour-intensive industries. But subsidies are only one side of the coin; the government should crack down on individuals and corporations that insist on investment in high-growth, full-employment regions, with surtaxes and punitive taxes (see IV.5).

The government should give warning of its intentions by making public a comprehensive plan that would mark the country off into areas, so making it quite clear to investors where investment is appropriate and where investment will cost them money.

Companies can be given tax incentives during inflationary periods to save their profits, by putting money into the stabilization fund; and, of course, companies that reinvested them right away would be slapped with tax penalties. In times of recession, the saved profits could be invested, and the co-operating companies rewarded with a tax advantage.

The government is evidently quite upset about the effect of inflation on the cost of Canadian goods produced for foreign markets, which has apparently made us less competitive with other countries and impaired our balance of payments. This has been used to justify the idiot practice of keeping inflation down with unemployment. That

2. See Arthur Smithies, "Fighting Inflation," *American Economic Review* 47 (1957).
3. L. A. Skeoch and D. C. Smith, *Economic Planning: The Relevance of West European Experience for Canada* (Montreal: Private Planning Association of Canada, 1963). For a more detailed discussion, see Lindbeck, "Swedish Economic Policy," ch. 6.

policy is unnecessary, for a basic and simple remedy is available to deal with foreign trade, and that is to float the dollar at a flexible exchange rate and let it look after itself.

The broad lines of a rational stablization policy are clear. The next sections contain a discussion of policies dealing with more specific imbalances in supply and demand.

IV.4 MANPOWER

When centralized collective bargaining begins to raise low incomes, some workers will lose their jobs. Manpower programs should be ready to make sure that they get new and better ones.

To a great extent, a full-employment policy will ensure that most available workers get snapped up as soon as they are laid off. As this demand for workers increases, only the unskilled or handicapped workers who have the most trouble finding jobs will be left unemployed. In conditions of full employment, then, manpower programs can begin to concentrate on their main job: to help disadvantaged workers fit into the labour market.

Centralized collective bargaining, for example, is likely to hit firms in the textile industry quite hard; there are a great many female workers in this business, and they tend to be badly paid and unskilled. Manpower programs should catch them as the textile industry is shaken up and some lose their jobs to mechanization. Those who become unemployed should be moved into other trades, or para-professional occupations, where the pay and working conditions are much better. This process will directly attack wage inequalities.

If the Manpower Department is to carry out its new responsibilities, it will itself need a shaking up. For it must be made responsive to the needs of individuals. As a start, personnel from the Manpower Department should be assigned to clients as their "advocates." Those who need such advocates most are the disadvantaged, the workers who get shuffled aside when employment is slack and need special assistance even when demand is so high that there are general worker shortages.

These disadvantaged workers, moreover, should be identified and given help right away. If the department discovers that people are likely to be unemployed for a long time without help only when they have already *been* unemployed for a long time without help, it will have to cope with large numbers of people who have been thoroughly demoralized. In addition, these workers should be helped in the period immediately after they have got jobs; advocates should stick with their clients until they are quite sure that the clients are secure in their new employment.

Obviously, the department will have to begin branching out from its glass palaces in the centres of cities, which intimidate workers before they walk through the front door, and establish store-front offices in the slums, where their clients live. And the department should make sure that its advocates are working in the interests of their clients, not in the interests of bureaucracy; American officials have discovered that field workers in outreach programs must be replaced every six months or so, before they begin to identify too heavily with the bureaucracy and lose their effectiveness in the community.

The Americans have also developed a system of paying subsidies to employers who will take disadvantaged workers and train them for jobs that will become available on completion of the training period. This ensures that the training is right for the job, and that a newly trained worker does not lose heart when he does not land a job immediately. (Some American programs use the "buddy system"; an experienced worker is assigned to every worker-trainee, to see him through the adjustment period and look after him when he runs into trouble.)

These employment subsidies, obviously, will have to be watched with great care; they must not become new openings for corporate rip-offs. There is also a danger that disadvantaged workers will be trained only for the dead-end jobs nobody else wants, with the result that the trainees become demoralized and drop out of the system entirely.

The Manpower Department should also launch a decent medical-rehabilitation and vocational-training program for disabled workers. If employers resist hiring such workers even after vocational training, they might be required to submit to the British system, which keeps a certain percentage of jobs open to disabled workers by law.

It is also high time the department interested itself in job development. This does not mean merely the creation of new jobs, but the creation of new and socially useful jobs. This approach has been tried in the United States under the title "new careers for the poor":

> The new career concept has as a point of departure the creation of jobs normally allotted to highly trained professionals or technicians, but which could be performed by the unskilled, inexperienced, and relatively untrained worker; or the development of activities not currently performed by anyone, but for which there is a readily acknowledged need and which can also be satisfactorily accomplished by the unskilled worker.[1]

Finally, the government should make an effort to enforce the legislation prohibiting hiring practices that discriminate against minority groups and women. Government officials should develop a process of complaint, investigation and enforcement that does not put the entire burden and risk on the individual being victimized.[2]

The main thrust of a manpower policy is to help those who most need help. But that is not sufficient. Manpower systems should be used to fill jobs as quickly as possible, and so ensure a tight labour market.

Employers must be required to register all vacancies with the Manpower employment office. In this way, Manpower offices can become true referral services, supplying information not only about jobs that employers cannot fill any other way, but about all jobs, right across the country. As things stand now, employers often ignore the public employment service because workers looking for jobs go directly to company employment offices. This confirms the employers' suspicions that a public employment service is unnecessary, and also puts the worker seeking employment at a disadvantage; for he has to spend the little money he has in running around from office to office when, with proper organization, he could get all the information he wanted at one centralized public labour exchange. The current system also creates discriminatory practices; employers

1. L. A. Ferman et al, *Poverty in America* (Ann Arbor: University of Michigan Press, 1968), p. 613.
2. For further reading, see proposals of the Royal Commission on the Status of Women, *Report,* ch. 2, part c.

tend to hire people through the grapevine and minor systems of privilege and patronage begin to develop.

Training to meet labour shortages can be left to industry much more than it is now. The British have developed industrial training boards, composed of employers and union representatives. The boards are empowered to tax companies in an industry to pay for the costs of training new workers. This procedure relieves the government of the costs of training workers for specialized jobs, and also releases funds for training the hard-core unemployed. The British have also organized a training system involving "skill clusters" that is designed to give workers more flexibility. If a worker is knocked out of a job, he can move into a closely related one in the same "skill cluster" with a minimum amount of retraining.

The Manpower Department should make mobility assistance and training a package deal. Workers must be able to get financial assistance to move to areas where employment prospects are more promising, and also obtain training in the locations they have moved to.

Manpower policies, in short, are crucial in an earnings policy; and the current practices of the Department of Manpower will not do.

IV.5 PLANNING OUR INDUSTRIAL STRUCTURE

Leaving stabilization aside, an investment policy should do three things. It should expand employment in high-wage industries; it should increase productivity in low-wage industries; and it should help to balance investment out by region. These procedures all tend to equalize wages; so, while manpower policies can be used to reduce wage differentials, investment policies can be pushing for the same goal at the other end.

If workers are to be helped to get at jobs in the high-wage industries, obviously companies should be helped to get themselves established in high-wage industries so that there will be jobs for the workers to go after. At the moment, corporations are permitted, or even encouraged, to retain their profits in the form of earnings and plough them back into the corporate structure; this procedure dries up the money market, and makes an attempt to break into high-wage industries difficult to finance. A surtax on retained earnings would pry a lot of this money loose in the form of dividends distributed to shareholders. This would quickly get the money market looking a lot healthier, and allow smaller companies to compete for the increased cash.

Some industries may still resist competition; if necessary, firms proposing to buck that kind of opposition should be underwritten by government, through low-cost credit and government support in the event of a price war aimed at eliminating competition. And, in the final analysis, government should be prepared to enter directly into competition with tough oligopolies, like the drug industry, through crown corporations.

One of the main weapons large corporations have is patents; for patent pooling will permit one consortium to take control of an entire industry.[1] Patent protection, therefore, should be reduced to a much shorter period; complicated innovations, which cost more, take longer to introduce and therefore require more protection, could be exempted on a case-by-case basis.

The American plundering of our natural resources must be stopped; increasingly, Canada should require that resources be processed here, rather than being shipped out in their raw form. This can be done through export surcharges on raw materials, or through flat bans on such exports by foreign-owned firms; in any case, it should be made expensive enough to ship unprocessed ore, for example, out of the country to ensure that high-paying secondary manufacturing jobs stay here.

All this will produce an expansion of jobs in high-wage industries; and that, combined with a high level of aggregate demand, will attract workers from low-wage industries. This, of course, will produce labour shortages in the low-wage industries, and they will require government assistance in boosting their productivity in order to cope; when the productivity rises, of course, the wages will rise as well.

Competition is not always a good thing; untrammelled competition can splinter industries, and hold down advances in technology because no one firm can grow enough to afford research and innovation.

1. These are discussed in more detail in Skeoch, *Restrictive Trade Practices,* pp. 167-226.

In certain industries, consolidation should be encouraged; and so, in some cases, information sharing, co-operation in research and development, combined training programs and modified collective agreements should all be permitted. In the same way, government might encourage mergers (of production facilities, sales organizations or companies themselves) and the discontinuation of redundant products.[2] After an industry has been organized in this way — or "rationalized" — it should be made to compete internationally, in order to make sure that the benefits of increased productivity are passed along to the consumers.

These measures, however, should be permitted only when they can be proven to be in the public interest, and otherwise forbidden; mergers should be allowed only when the hopeful companies can prove to a public agency that increased efficiency will result, and those mergers should be continuously reviewed to make sure that the increase has come about, and that the benefits are being passed on to the public.

Investment policy can also balance the regional placement of capital, to make sure that new capital gets to places where it will do the most good. Industries can be discouraged from locating new plants in the centre economy through investment surtaxes; and subsidies can be made available to companies that can prove that investment in depressed regions would be substantially more expensive.

If all this control is necessary, it follows that public ownership of all capital and industry might make a lot of sense. But in terms of political energy expended on change, the government can get more mileage out of manipulation than it can through outright ownership. The weakness of public ownership is that it tends to foster smug bureaucracies, without any market pressures to make them look alive. Still, if public control is not sufficient to make private capital perform responsibly, public ownership will be necessary.

IV.6 PRICE CONTROLS

A just earnings policy, of course, must cover all forms of income,

2. These are from Skeoch and Smith, *Economic Planning,* p. 66. The authors describe the Swedish use of structural rationalization.

including money from self-employment, personal income from property — rent, dividends and interest — and income from capital gains, and from corporate profits that are reinvested in the corporations.

The best way to do this is to cut down on the return on investment. Capital is concentrated among the rich; and the more profitable it is, the more it is concentrated. Correcting this involves the establishment of an easy-money policy that would make money readily available and easy to borrow. That cuts down interest and profits, and works along with the other policies proposed to increase investment and control inflation by increasing productive capacity and growth. It also helps to raise the productivity of low-wage industries, by making credit more available to low-wage industries for modernization.

The aim of price regulation should be, once again, to equalize incomes. Oligopolistic industries, which pay high wages and grab off large profits, should have their prices set for them. Similarly, price floors should be set for other producers whose products are doing badly in relation to average earnings — certain types of farming might be saved from liquidation this way. Government would have to avoid going too far along this line, and be careful not to get involved in a permanent subsidy to inefficiency and/or overproduction. There are ways around this, and they have been described in the preceding section.

Canadian politicians don't like price controls, and don't think they will work. This has not stopped the French, the Norwegians, the Dutch and the Austrians from using them extensively, and the Danes and the Belgians substantially.[1]

It is not always necessary, of course, to use the axe; occasionally the rapier will do. Government may find it useful (and pleasant) to keep the public informed about which corporations are doing what, and what the government might be forced to do unless they stop. This would be a practical assignment for the Prices and Incomes Commission, which certainly needs one.

Certainly the housing market needs scrupulous supervision — not only in terms of voluntary guidelines, but also mandatory controls.

1. This was the situation in the mid-sixties. See *Policies for Prices, Profits and Other Non-Wage Incomes,* no. 17451 (Paris: OECD, 1964); and *Non-Wage Incomes and Prices Policy,* no. 20483 (Paris: OECD, 1966).

Credit policies should stimulate the right kind of demand — that is, credit should be extended to low-income families at rates they can afford, even if that means subsidizing interest rates that are high enough already. Similarly, home-improvement loans should be expanded to make them available to low-income people. Rent control on existing housing should be applied in cities in which the vacancy rate is intermittently or permanently below 2.5 per cent. And public housing authorities should take advantage of existing CMHC legislation that permits them to build, buy or rent housing in any area, and should expand their operations so that no family at or below the Relative Poverty Line lacks decent housing.

There is probably no general housing shortage in Canada; but there is most definitely one for the poor. In other words, shortages of supply are sometimes specific. A prices and incomes commission should smoke them out, and recommend *when* price controls are needed, *where* and for *how long,* and so deal with specific problems in the economy without strangling the whole.

Prices and fees for personal and professional services should be made subject to either collective bargaining or competition policy. When for any reason they still fall outside these two jurisdictions, fees should be set by public supervision and regulation.

The effect of all these policies, from centralized collective bargaining on down, will be to create full employment, with equal or almost-equal incomes for workers, and, at last, equal opportunity for all Canadians.

V

Taxes and Transfers

If corporations restrict competition; if their independence goes un-challenged by government; if certain parts of the country are more favoured than others; and if political intervention in the economy generally protects the wealthy; then the gap between the rich and the poor will be wide.

The Canadian government has responded to that gap by instituting methods of taxation that act to maintain it. And government has dealt with the resulting poverty through programs of welfare and subsidy that are not only inadequate, but are also oppressive.

The result is a system that does very little for the poor. For

TABLE V.0.i
The distribution of income among families and unattached individ-uals before and after transfer payments, 1967

INCOME GROUP	Before transfer payments		After transfer payments	
	Income shares	Average income [a]	Income shares	Average income [a]
Lowest fifth	2.4%	730	4.2%	1,360
Second fifth	10.3	3,140	11.4	3,730
Middle fifth	18.0	5,480	17.8	5,810
Fourth fifth	25.4	7,730	24.6	8,030
Highest fifth	43.9	13,370	41.9	13,660
Total	100.0%	$6,090	100.0%	$6,520

a. Rounded to the closest multiple of $10.
Source: DBS, *Income Distributions by Size in Canada, 1967*, cat. no. 13-534 (Dec 1970), tables 31, 33.

Canada's tax and transfer machinery does not reduce inequality by very much.

Estimates of the effect of taxes and transfers on the national Gini ratio (a complex measure of economic inequality that is based on a numerical order in which 0 represents complete equality, and 1 complete inequality) have determined that before either taxes or transfer payments, the Gini ratio is .42; after transfer payments are added, it drops to .39; after personal taxes, it becomes .37 — not an overwhelming change.

In other words, on a national basis, taxes and transfer payments don't affect the ownership of money very much. The point is made in table V.O.i.

V.1 NO CHANGE

When the government's white paper on tax reform was made public, there were mournful cries from the wealthy; if Finance Minister Benson's proposals were put into effect, life for the rich, according to the rich, would become extremely hard in Canada. The economy of the country would suffer. The lifeblood of the successful would be drained away. It was all very depressing.

They need not have been concerned. The white paper was a dilution of the recommendations of the Royal Commission on Taxation, and the legislation that eventually emerged was a dilution of the white paper. If Mr. Benson ever felt any desire to change Canada's tax laws in any fundamental way, that desire had evidently vanished. Canada's taxes would remain almost as regressive as they had been before.

Taxes are collected to finance government programs, and manipulated to help stabilize the economy; they can also be used to redistribute income and wealth from the rich to the poor, and so to inject an element of equality into the life of the nation. But wealth in this country is largely and securely concentrated in the hands of a minority. Canada's system of taxation does very little to dislodge it. There has been no narrowing of the gap between the rich and the poor for twenty years; and if the new legislation is anything to go by, there will be no such narrowing over the next twenty.

Canadian government programs are financed with taxes that bear heavily on the poor. The rich are provided with loopholes, evasions, exemptions and dodges; and, in many cases, the rich are provided with explicit subsidies.

The poor are paying a high price for the privilege of continuing in poverty.

V.2 THE TAX SYSTEM

On the second page of the white paper on tax reform, beneath a list (in boldface type) of the various defects of the Canadian tax system, the federal government proclaimed its commitment to "a fair distribution of the tax burden based upon ability to pay."[1]

An analysis of Canadian methods of taxation, present and contemplated, indicates that that statement was, at best, cynical. Rates of taxation in this country have very little to do with ability to pay or with any equitable measurement of spending power.

The proofs are simple. The poor in Canada (say, those with incomes, before government transfer payments, of $2000 or less) pay, on the average, an overwhelming fifty-seven per cent of their income in taxation. People with incomes over $10,000 per year, on the other hand, pay only about thirty-eight per cent of their incomes in taxation. Table V.2.i makes the point. It is drawn from an analysis undertaken by economist W. I. Gillespie for the Royal Commission on Taxation.

The total tax system is regressive — that is, it taxes lower incomes more than higher ones — up to about the level of the average living standard. Above that level, the total tax system seems to become slightly progressive, at least for the lower brackets of the affluent.[2]

Very little is known about the taxation of people in the top income brackets, but the Royal Commission on Taxation expressed a sneaking suspicion that the very rich paid a lower percentage of their

1. Canada Department of Finance, *Proposals for Tax Reform* (Ottawa, 1969), p. 2.
2. See W. I. Gillespie, *The Incidence of Taxes and Public Expenditure in the Canadian Economy* (Ottawa, 1966), table A-9, p. 207.

TABLE V.2.i
Estimates of effective total tax incidence for the total tax structure, 1961

	FAMILY MONEY INCOME CLASS [a]							Total
	Under $2,000	$2,000 -2,999	$3,000 -3,999	$4,000 -4,999	$5,000 -6,999	$7,000 -9,999	$10,000 and over	
Income class as % of 1961 poverty-income line for average family size [b]	87-	87- 131	131- 175	175- 218	218- 306	306- 437	437+	
% distribution of families	22.0	12.1	13.5	14.5	21.2	11.6	5.1	100.0
Tax sources	%	%	%	%	%	%	%	%
Direct taxes (total)	1.2	2.2	3.8	5.2	8.3	10.2	14.9	8.6
-Personal income tax (fed)	1.1	1.9	3.3	4.5	7.2	8.8	10.4	6.9
-Personal income tax (prov)	0.1	0.3	0.5	0.7	1.1	1.4	1.6	1.1
-Estate duties (fed)	-	-	-	-	-	-	1.4	0.3
-Succession duties (prov)	-	-	-	-	-	-	1.5	0.3
Social security contributions	6.1	4.1	4.4	3.9	2.5	1.9	1.1	2.8
-Hospital insurance (prov)	2.6	0.9	0.7	0.5	0.4	0.3	0.1	0.5
-Others (fed)	2.7	2.5	2.9	2.6	1.2	0.7	0.5	1.5
-Others (prov)	0.8	0.7	0.8	0.8	0.9	0.9	0.5	0.8
Partly direct taxes (total)	27.5	12.9	10.5	9.1	8.8	9.0	14.0	10.8
-Corporation income tax (fed)	6.5	3.4	2.8	2.3	2.4	2.7	6.1	3.4
-Corporation income tax (prov)	2.0	1.1	0.9	0.7	0.7	0.8	1.9	1.0
-Property tax (local)	16.3	6.8	5.4	4.8	4.3	4.0	3.8	4.8
-Other taxes (prov & local)	2.7	1.6	1.4	1.3	1.4	1.5	2.2	1.6

indirect taxes (total)	25.2	13.6	13.6	12.2	13.2	13.0	8.5	10.6
-Sales tax (fed)	8.0	4.2	4.2	3.7	4.0	4.1	2.7	3.9
-Selective excises (fed)	4.3	2.6	2.6	2.3	2.5	2.4	1.5	2.3
-Import duties (fed)	4.7	2.3	2.2	1.9	2.0	2.0	1.3	2.0
-Sales^c & excises (prov)	8.2	4.5	4.6	4.3	4.7	4.5	3.0	4.4
Total taxes								
-Incl.} social security	60.0	32.9	32.2	30.5	32.8	34.2	38.4	34.7
-Excl.} (non-hospital)	56.5	29.7	28.5	27.1	30.7	32.6	37.4	32.4
Federal Taxes								
-Incl.} social security	27.3	16.9	18.0	17.3	19.3	20.7	23.8	20.2
-Excl.} contributions	24.6	14.4	15.1	14.7	18.1	20.0	23.3	18.7
Provincial & local taxes								
-Incl.} social security	32.7	16.0	14.2	13.1	13.5	13.5	14.6	14.5
-Excl.} (non-hospital)	31.9	15.3	13.4	12.3	12.6	12.6	14.1	13.7
Total taxes as % of family income (incl. transfer payments)								
-Incl.} social security	39.0	29.0	32.0	31.0	33.4	35.3	45.8	35.3
-Excl.} contributions	35.0	26.2	28.4	27.5	31.3	33.7	46.9	33.1

a. While the income classes refer to all money income before taxes, ie. including transfer payments, the percentages indicating the rate of incidence use as denominator the "broad income" concept, ie. excluding transfer payments but including imputed income in kind and interest, retained corporate earnings, the unshifted portion of the corporate income tax and that portion of social-security contributions that is either paid by or shifted to the employee. The last rows in the table give the overall tax incidence based on family income.

b. The average size of economic family units (including unattached individuals) in 1961 is estimated to be 3.24. The poverty-income line per living-standard equivalence point in 1961 was $367. Therefore, the poverty-income line for the average family size was $2290 (6.24 living-standard equivalence points).

c. From a legal perspective, provincial sales taxes may be considered direct taxes, but from an economic perspective they are indirect because they are really paid to the government by the retailer but borne by the customer.

Source: Royal Commission on Taxation, *Report*, vol 2, *The Use of the Tax System to Achieve Economic and Social Objectives* (Ottawa, 1966), table 6-2, p 246; and W. I. Gillespie, *The Incidence of Taxes and Public Expenditures in the Canadian Economy* (Ottawa, 1966), pp 18-21, and tables A4 and A5, pp 201-202, and statistical appendix to table I.A.3, paras 3, 7.

incomes in taxes than people at the bottom end of the over-$10,000 bracket:

> The lack of available data makes it impossible to estimate on a comparable basis the progressiveness of the tax system for those with above $10,000, except as a group. However, an examination of the personal income taxes paid by families and individuals within the "$10,000 and over" class shows that the average effective rate of tax, based on a comprehensive definition of income, is less for families and individuals at the upper end of the class than it is for those at the lower end of the class.[3]

The very rich, then, demurely concealed behind a screen of "lack of available data," are probably getting away with murder. The poor, on the other hand, are taxed at a rate that amounts to confiscation. The Royal Commission summed it up:

> . . . the present tax system is inequitable in many important respects. The combined effect of sales taxes, corporate income taxes, property taxes, and the present personal income tax and base, is such that low-income individuals and families pay higher taxes than is equitable when compared to middle- and upper-income individuals and families.
> Sales taxes and corporate income taxes are inequitable because they apply without regard to the ability to pay of the taxpayer.[4]

These inequalities are even more vicious than they seem to be at first. For the wealthy are in the happy position of paying very little tax on their wealth; they are taxed — benevolently — on their income. The poor, on the other hand, are taxed considerably beyond their ability to pay; for their incomes are reckoned with very little attention to their needs. There are no adjustments, and only token exemptions, for family size, although the number of people depending on an individual income greatly determines just how far that income will go.

3. Royal Commission on Taxation, *Report* 2 (Ottawa, 1966): 270.
4. Ibid, 2:11.

These inequalities reflect the political power of the wealthy. Canadian governments, at all levels, rely heavily on regressive taxes, which take a higher proportion of the income of the poor than of the wealthy.

Taxes that are totally regressive include taxes on property and sales, and import duties and excise taxes. For they are tacked directly on to the cost of products, and raise their prices; they hit everybody for exactly the same amount, regardless of ability to pay, and become, in effect, taxes on consumption — or taxes on need. (Property taxes tend to be shifted on to tenants, in higher rents; and a lot of real estate is owned by people with low incomes, particularly the aged, many of whom have most of their life savings invested in their homes. No taxes of this kind are assessed on savings, or on services, many of which are used disproportionately by the wealthy. And sales taxes on used cars and appliances mean that the poor pay again and again for the same objects.)

These completely regressive taxes made up in 1961 more than half of all the taxes collected in the country.[5] (That figure excludes social-security contributions.)

A great part of the rest of the money raised in the country comes from partly, or mostly, regressive taxes: corporation income tax, and other provincial and local business taxes. These are only partly regressive, because as a rule only part of their cost gets passed along to the consumer.

These partly regressive taxes amounted to one-fifth of the total collected in the country in 1961. The progressive taxes (personal income taxes, and estate and succession duties), which get stiffer as the amount to be taxed gets larger, amounted only to about a quarter of the total.[6]

This reliance on regressive taxes is out of line with the practice of most nations, as table V.2.ii shows. (Direct taxes are usually progressive, corporate direct taxes partly regressive and indirect taxes regressive.) We are doing a little better than Greece. And things do not seem to be getting much better. During the 1960s, there has been little significant change in the way Canadian taxes have been raised;

5. Gillespie, *Incidence of Taxes and Public Expenditure*, table w.1, p. 32.
6. Ibid.

TABLE V.2.ii
Percentage composition of taxes

COUNTRY	Direct tax on household	Direct taxes on corporations	Indirect taxes	Total
Austria	48	7	45	100
Belgium	52	6	42	100
Canada	30	16	54	100
Denmark	47	4	49	100
France	48	5	47	100
Germany	51	8	41	100
Greece [a]	36	2	62	100
Iceland [a]	29 [b]	—	71	100
Ireland [a]	23	9	68	100
Italy	57 [b]	—	43	100
Japan	38	21	41	100
Luxemburg [c]	58	10	32	100
Netherlands	62	8	30	100
Norway	53	4	43	100
Sweden	60	6	34	100
Switzerland	56	10	34	100
United Kingdom	45	8	47	100
United States	50	16	34	100

a. 1963—64.
b. Includes direct taxes on corporations.
c. 1963.
Source: Statistics of the Organization for Economic Co-operation and Development.

and provincial changes in taxation — at least in Ontario — have tended to be regressive.[7]

Governments distort the personal income tax from progressive, in theory, to regressive, in practice, by keeping exemption levels low. The levels, in fact, are considerably below the Relative Poverty Line — and the poor pay taxes on anything they make beyond the exemption. Until the recent changes, exemption levels had not been raised since 1919, although average incomes had risen many times over.

In 1967, the Relative Poverty Line for a single person was $2200; the income-tax exemption, $1100. So a single person at the poverty line paid tax on half of his poverty-level income, to the tune of $170.

7. W. I. Gillespie, "An Examination of Tax-Burden Changes in Ontario, 1960-69," *Canadian Tax Journal* 19, no. 4 (July-Aug. 1971): 340-379.

The 1971 Relative Poverty Line for a family of four was $5100; the exemption, about $2700; the tax about $400.

The same line for a family of ten was $9400; the exemption, about $4500; the tax (after deductions for tax-free Family Allowance)$2200. So large families are directly hurt by low tax-exemption levels; a large family needs more income than a small one to pull itself above the poverty line — and that higher income is taxed at stiffer rates.

Any use of exemptions, high or low, rather than transferring money directly to people with low incomes, usually pays off better for the affluent than for the poor.

A man who earns $2000, for example, and who is taxed on all of it at the rate of ten per cent, pays a tax of $200; if he is granted an exemption of $1000, he pays ten per cent of the remaining, non-exempt $1000 for a tax of $100. The exemption saves him $100.

A man who earns $101,000, on the other hand, and who is taxed without exemption at a rate of fifty per cent, pays a tax of $50,500; if he is granted an exemption of $1000, he is taxed at a rate of fifty per cent on his remaining $100,000 worth of income, and pays a tax of $50,000. He saves $500.

The Royal Commission on Taxation commented:

> The basic problem, of course, is that an exemption is a very inadequate basis for a good welfare scheme. The way to help the most underprivileged is by positive assistance, not by income tax concessions that fail to discriminate between the needy and the affluent, that give no benefit where it is needed, but do give a benefit where it is not needed.[8]

The new "tax-reform" legislation has chosen to raise exemptions for the aged from $500 at seventy years of age to $650 at sixty-five; and to introduce exemptions for child care to a maximum of $500 per child under fourteen (unless the child is disabled), with a top exemption of $2000, usually to be claimed by the mother. These exemptions give more comfort to the affluent than the needy.

The government has consistently refused to substitute a system of

8. See Ibid, 3:60.

tax credits, which might be used instead of some of these exemptions, and which could be substantial enough to compensate the poor for the income they lose to regressive taxation. Tax credits are, quite simply, statutory amounts to be knocked off income *taxes,* rather than taxable *income;* and the rich get precisely the same dollar allowance — say, $300 per child — as do the poor.

The wealthy, then, are in a comfortable position to take advantage of inequities in the personal income-tax system. They have nothing much to complain of in the rest of the tax structure, either. Until now, capital gains have gone scot-free, a policy that resulted, not from legislation, but from a series of court decisions.[9] Now one-half of all capital gains will be taxed as income. Deductions for various business expenses are still viewed more charitably than deductions for work expenses.[10]

Shareholders are the fortunate recipients of a one-third tax credit on their dividends. The rationale for this concession, as for the half-exemption on capital gains, is that corporate income has already been taxed, and it's not fair to assess all of it again on the shareholders. Corporations may happily pass the corporate tax along to their customers, and allow their shareholders to take in the profits.

These fiddles indicate that the idea of progressive taxation is fighting a losing battle in Canada, and a look at the new tax rates confirms that suspicion. The first taxable dollar is taxed at twenty-two per cent, and the highest tax rate is sixty-one per cent; the old rates, at sixteen and eighty-one per cent respectively, were more progressive at either end.

And wealth is still benignly ignored.[11] At least those aspects of wealth that are associated with the rich; for there are in fact two wealth taxes in Canada and, ironically, the largest of them is consistently assessed against the poor. These two wealth levies are taxes on property, and the taxation of bequests and gifts.

The property tax is substantial; and it is largely shifted to tenants, or falls on elderly low-income home-owners whose houses represent their sole wealth. The point shows up clearly in table V.2.i.

Inheritance taxes, under the new tax legislation, have largely been

9. See Ibid, 4:77.
10. See VI.2.
11. See Canada Department of Finance, *Highlights of the Budget Measures and Tax Reform Legislation* (Ottawa, 1971).

scuttled. Not that they were of much use in the first place; the old legislation was so openly avoidable that the government may simply have abandoned it in embarrassment. Inheritances were exempt from taxation on the first $50,000, with further exemptions of around $15,000 to $20,000 per head for dependents. The maximum rate of taxation was fifty per cent, which was not reached until the $300,000 level. There was no tax on transfers to husbands or wives; tax credits were given to citizens of provinces that levied death duties, and two provinces were generous enough not only to refuse to levy such duties, but to return to beneficiaries the seventy-five per cent provincial share of the inheritance tax collected by the federal government.[12]

Theoretically, the wealthy were prevented from transferring their assets to their sons and daughters as tax-exempt gifts before their deaths through the imposition of a gift tax, but this tax was set at a soothingly low level,[13] and had an annual exemption level high enough to allow a gradual transfer of wealth over time without shrinking it by a nickel.[14]

The federal government responded to the defects in the inheritance- and gift-tax legislation by abolishing it. Now, the government proposes to tax only those parts of estates that can be considered capital gains (with that fifty per cent exemption). This is an inadequate substitute; estates are not capital gains, or income, but *wealth*, and should be taxed as wealth. Capital gains, on the other hand, should be taxed regularly, not merely at the death of their proprietor.

There are, unsurprisingly, a number of other little kinks and gaps in the tax laws, each of which pays off for the affluent; and these provide enough elbow room to have set up a booming industry in creative tax avoidance.[15] The Royal Commission on Taxation has described various colourful methods of tax avoidance, such as "stock-stripping."[16]

12. Canada Department of Finance, *Summary of 1971 Tax Reform Legislation* (Ottawa, 1971), p. 33.
13. E. J. Mockler and Donald B. Fields, *Gift Tax*, Studies of the Royal Commission on Taxation no. 13 (Ottawa, 1966), pp. 2, 36-37.
14. Royal Commission on Taxation, *Report* 3:473.
15. There are very few Canadian surveys in this field, which is suggestive. For an analogous survey of the British scene, see Paul Streeten, "Taxation and Enterprise," in *Economics: Canada*, Melville H. Watkins and D. F. Forster eds. (Toronto: McGraw-Hill, 1963), pp. 57-65.
16. See Royal Commission on Taxation, *Report* 4:18.

The new capital-gains tax will certainly allow room for manoeuvre.[17]

And, as the royal commission noted, certain kinds of corporations offer ample opportunity for imaginative broken-field running:

> Shareholders controlling closely held corporations have had a tax advantage over other shareholders because they could limit the dividends of the corporations so as to minimize personal taxes.[18]

The royal commission, moreover, expressed considerable suspicion of the disinterested quality of public benevolence:

> The major practical problem relating to charitable donations is to ensure that the receipts issued by a charitable body are matched by actual contributions to it.[19]

The royal commission, perhaps apprehensive of complaints from charitable organizations, left it at that.

It is not always necessary, however, for the wealthy to patronize slick accountants or to give a lot of money to the United Appeal in order to avoid taxation. Often it is enough to be in the right business. For certain industries are, year after year, given huge tax concessions by government, concessions that amount to outright subsidies, but are made through the tax system for the sake of appearances.

The mining and petroleum industries, according to the royal commission, were in 1964 getting away with some $320 million worth of unjustified income exemptions — about eight per cent of *all* taxable corporate income.[20] By 1970, the tax gift to the mining, oil and gas industries had risen to $300 million, and the pulp-and-paper, refining, printing-and-publishing, transportation, electrical-products and textile-mills industries were also basking in the warm light of sizeable exemption.[21] (More than occasionally large companies are

17. See Gabriel Kolko, *Wealth and Power in America* (New York: Praeger, 1962).
18. Royal Commission on Taxation, *Report* 4:19.
19. Ibid, 6:9.
20. Ibid.
21. *New Democrat* 9 (May-June 1971): 4.

forgiven taxes — Ford recently got away with over $75 million.)

In 1970, outright subsidies by all governments to businesses — free, no-strings-attached gifts — amounted to some $724 million.[22] The National Council on Welfare attacked this kind of boondoggle, these

> . . . payments to the real beneficiaries of government welfare programs, the corporate rich. Only these aren't called welfare programs. They are called things like "economic growth incentives." These payments — mining subsidies, tariff supports, tax incentives — represent regressive income transfer programs, money taxed from the poor and near-poor and given to the rich.[23]

In this context, the highly touted new tax legislation is a travesty of the idea of reform. Exemptions have been raised, but deductions for family dependents remain the same;[24] the wealthy have had their taxes reduced, and taxes on high incomes level off, at the new low rate, at $60,000; tax credits have not been introduced except for stockholders; charity deductions have been raised to twenty per cent of income; estate and gift taxes have been junked; and sales of homes are entirely exempt from taxation.

And nothing has been done to reduce the heavy emphasis in Canada on the use of regressive taxes. The government did say something about that, in the white paper on tax reform, back in 1969:

> Reform of the sales tax is less urgent and can be undertaken after action on the proposals in this paper.[25]

True to form, sales taxes go untouched in the new reform legislation. The government's sense of social priorities is still intact.

22. DBS, *National Income and Expenditure Accounts,* cat no. 13-201 (Ottawa, 1970).

23. National Council on Welfare, *Statement on Income Security* (Ottawa, 1971), pp. 15-16.

24. The new tax rates are *less* progressive than the old ones; and so those increased exemptions benefit the wealthy more than the poor.

25. Canada Department of Finance, *Proposals for Tax Reform,* p. 8.

V.3 DIRECT GOVERNMENT PROGRAMS

In Canada, the most successful demands for financial support and subsidies have come from the business community and corporations. Other groups, notably the workers, have been less lucky in stimulating the charitable impulses of government.

The poor, in particular, have been badly done by. Aid to the specifically needy is administered through an appallingly inhumane and messy network of welfare systems, which will be discussed in the next section. Certain other payments are made directly to certain groups of people, *some* of whom are poor; and so the poor benefit from them, in a rather indirect and insufficient way.

These direct payments come in a mixed lot: Old-Age-Security pensions, the Canada and Quebec Pension Plans, Youth and Family Allowances, Workmen's Compensation and Unemployment Insurance. None of them, obviously, is directed exclusively at the poor; no categorical program (that is, a program that pays off for everyone in a certain category, like parents or the aged, regardless of need) can be. But, in each categorical program, some poor people are receiving some benefit. And some of these people (in the case of the aged, a clear majority) are living on just those benefits, and nothing else. So the tangential effects of these programs on the lives of the poor are important.

Old-Age Security is the one categorical program that most obviously bears on the problem of poverty in this country, for it is responsible — at least by default — for keeping a lot of old people in poverty. At least half of all Canadians over the age of sixty-five, and probably significantly more, are now living on less than fifty dollars per week, and a sizeable percentage of that majority is restricted to less.[1]

OAS payments — old-age pensions — are now worth a splendid $80 per month. This cheque goes out to all citizens over the age of sixty-five who apply for it; almost all old people (including some

---

1. Calculated from figures included in the brief of the Department of National Health and Welfare to the Special Senate Committee on Poverty (Feb. 1970) 23:91. About half of all Canadians who are now receiving Old-Age-Security payments are also receiving some part of the Guaranteed-Income Supplement; eligibility for any part of the supplement stops when income — benefits and outside income combined — exceeds approximately fifty dollars per week.

members of the Senate) do apply for it, whether they need it or not.

Old people with no other sources of income are also entitled to the Guaranteed-Income Supplement, for a total package of $135 per month ($1600 per year); eligible married couples receive $255 per month (about $3100 per year). The Guaranteed-Income-Supplement payments decrease at a rate of one dollar for every two dollars of outside income the individual or couple reports.

The Department of Health and Welfare's brief to the Senate Committee on Poverty explained that Old-Age Security, all by itself, is not intended to be adequate; instead, it is meant "to provide a basic pension as a floor on which Canadians could build a retirement income."[2] Old-Age Security with the Guaranteed-Income Supplement presumably *is* intended to be adequate, and provides an index of the federal government's estimation of "adequacy," for a lot of Canadians are living on just that, and no more — 475,110 of them (twenty-eight per cent of all pensioners) in August 1970. Another twenty-one per cent were receiving part of the Guaranteed-Income Supplement — or, in other words, had an outside income of less than $64 per month.[3]

Canadian governments have consistently refused to consider building an adequate escalator clause into the Old-Age-Security program. The tiny cost-of-living annual hike is restricted to two per cent, which is infuriating; the minister of Finance was recently treated to a shower of small change, as enraged pensioners mailed back their adjustments to him. Instead, the basic pensions are raised whenever the government gets around to it, an eventuality, as cynics have observed, that is more likely to be eventuated when an election is in the breeze. Between times, the relative position of the old-age pensioner in the Canadian economy slips badly.

This relative deterioration — which is, ironically, faster and harder in boom years — has been documented by the Canadian Welfare Council (now the Canadian Council on Social Development):

> During 1968 wages and prices went up by 8.8 per cent. Rising costs of around 4 per cent eroded about half the increase in wages and incomes, but one can talk in terms of an *increase* in

2. "A Review of the Role of the Department of Health and Welfare in Relation to Poverty," brief presented to the Special Senate Committee on Poverty (Feb. 1970) 23:88.
3. For similar figures in August 1969, see Ibid, 23:91.

the standard of living by over 4 per cent for those who were employed. At the same time those aged who depend on their almost fixed old age security income had a *decline* in their purchasing power of 2 per cent. This is because the increase in old age security benefits is limited to only 2 per cent, whereas as indicated, the consumer price index went up over 4 per cent. The net result was that the gap in the standard of living between the aged depending on the old age security and the guaranteed income supplement and the average person in the labour force grew during this good year by over 6 per cent.[4]

Old-Age-Security and Guaranteed-Income-Supplement rates are now delivering only about three-quarters of a Relative Poverty-Line income for a single person, and less than ninety per cent of a poverty-line income for a married couple. This gap, of course, will grow until the next hike in the OAS-GIS benefit. Every year the average standard of living in Canada grows more than the two per cent pension escalator. (The rise in the standard of living has not been under three per cent annually since 1954.)

The pensions, then, are inadequate; and, in one sense, the governments of Canada are turning a nice profit on that inadequacy. A report by the National Council of Welfare points out:

The Old Age Security and Guaranteed Income Supplement Programs are financed by specially earmarked taxes — a 4% tax on personal income (with the regressive feature that the maximum tax is $240), a 3% tax on corporate taxable income, and a 3% sales tax. In the fiscal year ending March 1970 revenues received from these three taxes exceeded total expenditures on Old Age pensions by $100 million. The picture for the 1970-71 fiscal year was almost the same before the White Paper changes. The total credit balance in the Old Age Security Fund constituted by law is now over $700 million.[5]

The money, then, is in the bank. But it is staying there. For just

4. Brief of the Canadian Welfare Council to the Special Senate Committee on Poverty (19 June 1969) 12:46.
5. National Council on Welfare, *Income Security*, p. 17.

about half of our old people, who have invested their sweat and convictions in the building of this country, there is no such thing as a "boom-or-bust" economic cycle; it is all bust, and their poverty becomes more oppressive with each passing year.

The Canada Pension Plan, which is slowly being introduced into service, is a slight move away from the Old-Age-Security concept of a flat-rate pension for the old. It is also a move away from the Guaranteed-Income-Supplement principle of a pension tailored to the needs of its recipient. The Canada Pension Plan (in Quebec, a similar Quebec Pension Plan) is a contributory scheme — you pay half, your employer pays half — and is designed to ensure continuity of income into retirement. If you were poor before you retired, the Canada Pension Plan keeps you poor. If you were rich, the CPP will do you a little better.

Like the Old-Age-Security fund, the CPP is at least partly designed to give. Canadian governments a little cash in hand. The National Council on Welfare notes:

> The single most important feature of the Canada Pension Plan (and the Quebec Pension Plan) from the present point of view is the very large excess of contributions over expenditures: in 1970 the surplus generated in this fashion was over $800 million. The bulk of this money is made available monthly to the provinces by the purchase of provincial securities with these funds. Up to the 1970 fiscal year the amount of surplus lent to the provinces in this way came to $2.8 billion. Even with the proposed revision, it is estimated that the fund will continue in surplus until at least 1985 and perhaps 1995, because the increased benefits are to be offset in part by the increase in contributions as a result of raising the ceiling while freezing the basic exemption of $600.
>
> Setting aside the quite misleading insurance terminology, the Canada Pension Plan is thus, at the present time, primarily a means of financing provincial investment expenditures through a regressive payroll tax. In a real sense, what the average taxpayer probably considers to be a purchase of a pension for himself — or perhaps a payment tax helping to finance the

pensions currently being paid to others — is substantially financing not income security but highways and other provincial government activities.[6]

The surplus of contributions over expenditures comes about because the plan is not yet paying off in full to those unlucky enough to be in need of it *now*. The plan is, according to the government's white paper on income security,

> . . . designed to provide an earnings-related pension for members of the labour force. . . . It also provides benefits to contributors who become severely disabled, and to their children. When a contributor dies, a lump sum death benefit becomes payable, together with monthly benefits for the widow and children, or for the disabled widower and children if they had been dependent on the contributor. The Canada and Quebec Pension Plans are closely co-ordinated and operate together to provide one nation-wide system.[7]

But, as the white paper noted, the 1970 rates were not very high. The death benefit, for example, was a miserable $530; the maximum rate for a disabled person, $106 monthly; the rate for a disabled person's child, $26.53 monthly. All these will rise as the CPP grows towards maturity in 1976, and, when the white paper proposals are put into effect, they will rise a little faster. But they will not rise enough to keep many people out of poverty. In 1976, the *maximum* combined benefit from Old-Age Security and the Canada Pension Plan for an individual will be $2600, below the Relative Poverty Line — and a couple, both of whom are eligible for maximum benefits, won't do much better.

There are a number of people, furthermore, who will get no benefit from the Canada Pension Plan at all. Anyone born before 1895 is ineligible; anyone disabled before 31 December 1969 is ineligible; anyone widowed before 31 December 1967, and who has not

6. Ibid, pp. 19-20.
7. Canada Department of National Health and Welfare, *Income Security for Canadians* (Ottawa, 1970), p. 47. The rates indicated for 1970 should be kept in the perspective of the estimated 1976 poverty line, which will, for an individual, approximate $3200.

arranged to be widowed again, is ineligible as well. Taken together, this amounts to a considerable number of people, many of whom cannot be expected to die in the near future. Some 1,812,000 people (the old, disabled, widowed or orphaned) needed immediate help from the plan in October 1967, and only 45,000 were eligible for it.[8]

Furthermore, as actuary James Clare points out, the plan is remarkably liberal towards the affluent:

> Take a Canadian, age 55 at the start of CPP/QPP, earning $5,000 or more a year. His CPP/QPP tax payable initially totalled $158.40 a year. If he is self-employed he pays the entire amount; if he is an employee, his employer pays at least half. If this man works for ten years until age 65 and then applies for the CPP/QPP age retirement pension, a total of at least $1,584 in CPP/QPP taxes will have been paid in for him.
>
> This man's annual CPP/QPP pension payments will be at least $1,250 a year (payable monthly). In the first two years of his retirement the CPP/QPP pension payments will total $2,500. This will more than return his CPP/QPP taxes of $1,584, even allowing generously for interest. If he is a single male, he can expect to live, on average, about a further 12 years in retirement. He can, therefore, expect to receive a "gift" of at least about $15,000 (12 x $1,250) in excess of what his CPP/QPP taxes should have paid for.
>
> Now consider a man with everything as above, except that his earnings are only $2,500 a year instead of $5,000. This man may expect to receive a "gift" of only about half, or about $7,500.[9]

The real difficulty with this windfall is not so much that it *is* a windfall — most new public pension schemes of any size must provide one — but that the windfall, like the plan itself, is based on keeping the differences between the poor and the affluent fairly broad. The plan is not based on need, but on economic position. And the "escalator" built into the plan will do nothing very much to narrow the gap — for, like most government escalators, it is calcu-

8. James Clare, "The Canada Pension Plan Must Be Changed — Now," *Canadian Business* reprint no. 713 (October 1967), p. 1.
9. Ibid, p. 2.

lated not on the standard of living, but on the *cost* of living. A cost-of-living escalator does nothing to narrow the spread between incomes (and pensions), and, in fact, tends to increase it.

Finally, the Canada Pension Plan and the Quebec Pension Plan both serenely ignore one of the largest classes of workers in the country: housewives. The Report of the Royal Commission on the Status of Women notes:

> The housewife who remains at home is just as much a producer of goods and services as the paid worker, and in our view she should also have the opportunity to provide for a more financially secure future. Canada has given some of its workers an opportunity to do this through the Canada and the Quebec Pension Plans. To neglect to do the same for some three and one-half million other workers in the home is to ignore the essential nature of their work.[10]

Furthermore, the plans make no provision for the transition of a housewife into the "official" labour force; if she makes that transition late in life, her pension suffers. And a wife who divorces or is divorced by her husband loses all rights to the widow's pension — which may, in fact, go to a second wife.

This may well leave an unskilled, newly separated, middle-aged or older woman to scuffle in a harsh and low-paying job for the last few years — the first few recognized years — of her work life, and then to spend her retirement on the abysmal level provided by the Old-Age-Security/Guaranteed-Income-Supplement package — which by that time will likely have been "escalated" into insignificance. For her, and for many other Canadians, the Canada Pension Plan and the Quebec Pension Plan are worthless.

Family Allowances, or "baby bonuses," are worth $6 per month for every child below the age of ten, and $8 per month for every child between ten and sixteen. (In 1948, the rates were $5 and $6 respectively.)

They are inadequate, and the government admits they're inadequate. The Department of National Health and Welfare's brief to

10. Royal Commission on the Status of Women, *Report,* p. 38.

the Senate Committee on Poverty noted that "family allowances have not kept pace with the growth in national income and the purchasing power of Canadian families."[11]

They are, moreover, overwhelmingly going to the wrong people, and are not being recovered in taxes. The government's white paper on income security admitted with some embarrassment:

> It is estimated that in 1971, 24 per cent of family and youth allowances will be paid to families with less than $5,000 income, and 76 per cent to families with incomes above this level.[12]

The white paper proposed that the allowances be taken away from families that don't need them, and somewhat increased (in some cases, doubled, to a rousing $16 per month) for families that do — although the government had to be crossfired into admitting that family size should make any difference in determining the categories of need.

The proposals evoked a hostile reaction from some citizens who attacked the whole idea of paying people to support children, arguing that more generous allowances to the needy would encourage the sudden production of a swarm of poor infants.[13] This criticism was so widespread that Reuben C. Baetz, the executive director of the Canadian Council on Social Development, was moved to knock it on the head once and for all:

> I have no empirical evidence to prove that allowances are not an inducement to larger families. But I know of none that proves they are. And I do wonder how the critics can reconcile their views with the following facts.
>
> Quebec is the only province that has augmented (in 1967) the federal family allowances through a provincial supplement which pays higher allowances per child up to the sixth. This apparently was partly intended as an inducement to a higher birth rate. Yet Quebec since then has consistently had the lowest birth rates in Canada.

11. Canada Department of National Health and Welfare, brief, 23:92.
12. Canada Department of National Health and Welfare, *Income Security,* p. 44.
13. See p. 197.

France has the most generous family allowances program in Western Europe, but also has one of the lowest birth rates. The highest in the world are in those countries that have no family allowance programs.[14]

Family allowances, then, don't do what their detractors claim, which is to stimulate the birth rate. Nor do they help much in defraying the costs of raising children (as the National Council on Welfare has pointed out,[15] a mother on welfare may be given $20 to $25 per child, per month, and another $8 to $10 on Family Allowances — and a foster mother will be given $80 or more a month to raise the same child). And they don't yet do more for the low-income family than for the affluent one. They may, under the new legislation, become a little more valuable; but unless the new rates are raised spectacularly, they will continue just about to defray the costs of keeping a cat.

Youth Allowances are intended to keep children of sixteen and seventeen in school; they're worth $10 per month (except as noted, in Quebec), and they stop when the child drops his education or passes the age limit. $10 per month, of course, does not cover even the peripheral costs of education, and does not approach the financial burden involved in staying in school as opposed to dropping out to take a job, even at the minimum wage. As an incentive to secondary education, it's insubstantial.

Unemployment Insurance is usually considered the first line of defence for the Canadian worker; if he loses his job, he does not immediately lose all income, but instead is entitled to benefits from the Unemployment-Insurance fund, to which he, his employer and the federal government have been contributing.

The program is not now, and never has been, an antipoverty program. J. M. DesRoches, the chief commissioner of the Unemployment Insurance Commission, told the Senate committee on poverty that at best, "the program can only have an indirect impact on poverty."[16] And until quite recently, the program could do

14. Letter to the Toronto *Globe and Mail* (27 July 1971), p. 6.
15. National Council on Welfare, *Income Security,* p. 14.
16. Proceedings (1969) 9:291.

very little for any unemployed person. It was purely and simply inadequate.

The benefits and procedures of the Unemployment Insurance Commission were apparently worked out to be useful when general unemployment was low, and when the loss of a job was not necessarily a calamity. There was very little provision made for periods of prolonged national unemployment. The insurance did not cover either illness or pregnancy, which both lead to a direct loss of income; the maximum benefit available was $53 per week, and benefits were arbitrarily cut off at the twenty-six-week mark, regardless of the prevailing demand for labour; finally, benefits were available only to people who had been working for some seven months or more. The benefits averaged about forty-three per cent of the earnings lost by the unemployed — for as long as the benefits lasted.[17]

This may have been good enough when unemployment was low; it was not good enough to pay for the crusade against inflation. The government noted, graciously, in its white paper:

> Like workers elsewhere in the highly developed post-industrial world, Canadians are realizing that they can no longer depend on seniority and good work performance alone to ensure that they remain indefinitely in the labour market.[18]

Certain changes were made to get the government off the hook. The insurance plan was extended to salaried workers who made more than $7,500 per year, a change that would bring more contributions into the kitty. Rates were raised to two-thirds of the worker's salary (in a few cases, three-quarters), up to a maximum benefit of $100 per week. Eligibility for part benefits was loosened a bit.

But the changes were not sufficient. Even the new benefit levels will not prevent some people from crossing the poverty line as soon as they are laid off. The head of a family of six, for example, who makes $150 per week or more, will fall immediately past the Relative Poverty Line level of $125 per week, to the maximum $100 per week. (The insurance scheme still grandly ignores the fact that six do not eat as cheaply as two; a wife, in terms of unemployment insur-

17. Canada Department of Labour, *Unemployment Insurance in the 70s* (Ottawa: 1970), p. 10.
18. Ibid, p. 5.

ance, will raise your benefits as much as a wife and any number of children.) The table facing, table V.3.i, makes the point clear.

Furthermore, the new legislation still withholds eligibility from many of those who need it most: the self-employed and casual, seasonal and part-time labourers. The reaction of the province of Quebec to this exclusion was swift and disapproving:

> People for whom the loss of income causes serious problems are not provided for: such people are the chronic unemployed, the young who have not yet begun to work, women who have returned to the work market, people on social assistance, certain unsuitable people and ineligible workers in the agricultural and industrial sectors.
>
> Now, Quebec has the largest groups of unemployed. We are, therefore, of the opinion that the reforms proposed in the White Paper do not provide a better protection for those who are in fact threatened by unemployment; on the contrary, the logical outcome of the suggested reform will, in the main, be a protection for those least in danger of loss of employment.[19]

These exclusions dismiss a great many of those who need unemployment insurance most — those who are most likely to be unemployed. The scheme does relatively little for the young worker, new to the labour force, who has not had time to build up insurance benefits, and is among the last to be hired. Males between the age of fourteen and twenty-five and females between the ages of fourteen and nineteen are hit harder by a slackening demand for labour than anyone else; of the more than 600,000 people unemployed during the winter of 1970-71, about forty per cent were between the ages of fourteen to twenty-four. The new scheme did relatively little for them.

(As a constitutional courtesy to fellow legislatures, the white paper proposed to allow provincial governments to opt out of the scheme on behalf of their employees, and the Quebec government, somewhat ominously, implied that it damn well might do just that.[20])

19. Quebec Department of Social Affairs, *Analysis of Federal Government White Paper on Unemployment Insurance* (Quebec, 1971), p. 2.
20. Ibid, pp. 9-10.

TABLE V.3.i
Comparison of unemployment insurance benefits with the poverty-income line (in $ per week)

FAMILY SIZE	1971 POVERTY-INCOME LINE	Persons earning $80/week UI benefits			Persons earning $100/week UI benefits			Persons earning $150/wk or more	
		Earnings	in first 20 wks b	after un-employ-ment of ½ year c	Earnings	in 1st 20 wks d	after un-employ-ment of ½ year e	Earnings	UI benefits f
1	$42	190%	126%	126%	238%	160%	160%	357% plus	238%
2	$70	114%	76%	86%	143%	96%	107%	214% plus	143%
3	$84	95%	63%	71%	119%	80%	89%	178% plus	119%
4	$97	82%	55%	62%	103%	69%	77%	155% plus	103%
5	$111	72%	48%	54%	90%	60%	68%	135% plus	90%
6	$125	64%	42%	48%	80%	54%	60%	120% plus	80%
..	..	..	..	..	..	..	..	..	..
10	$1,81	44%	29%	33%	55%	37%	41%	83% plus	55%

Notes: a. Derived from table I.1.ii. b. $53. c. $53 for a person without dependents and $60 for a person with dependents. d. $67. e. $67 for a person without dependents and $75 for a person with dependents. f. $100, which is the maximum benefit for any recipient.

Source: Canada Department of Labour, *Unemployment Insurance in the 70s* (Ottawa, 1970).

There were, of course, quite a few sensible and reasonable reforms contained in the white paper. The federal government was to pick up the burden of contributions when national unemployment levels rose above four per cent. (The Quebec government ungratefully pointed out that unemployment had to rise to 4.8 per cent before Ottawa began to pay more than it did under the previous scheme[21] and, in any case, four per cent is a dizzily high level for the federal government to begin to assume the cost of its own economic policies.) The government proposed to penalize industries that exhibited high rates of unemployment and lay-offs. And there was a gesture towards the beginning of a long-overdue co-ordination with the Department of Manpower.

But these sensible reforms are finally nullified by the one basically mistaken principle in the scheme: benefits are related, not to need, but to earnings alone. If you don't earn much, you don't get much. In other words, the scheme does nothing to raise the level of benefits due a low-income worker to the level he needs; instead it cuts the benefits of the high-income worker down to the same inadequate level. The head of a family of six, earning an *average* industrial wage, will be bounced by his unemployment insurance down to less than half his earnings when he loses his job — an income well below the poverty line.

Contributions are calculated on earnings. So are benefits. Both could easily be calculated on the basis of need. And the workers are left to pay for this mistake, particularly in periods of high unemployment. There is some evidence that many workers who become unemployed are forced to drain their savings, sell their cars, houses, and divest themselves of all personal assets, because their benefits have run out — and because no welfare system will touch them before they become indigent.

No records are kept of this process. But, from the evidence given by many of the poor, and from a look at some unco-ordinated data, it is necessary to conclude that this downward plunge takes place primarily in times of high and long unemployment. Evictions in the Toronto area more than doubled during 1970. More are expected

21. Ibid, p. 8. The government has also managed to finesse the administration costs of the act (in 1971, some $54 million) from its own accounts over to the contributors; see Budget Papers for 1971-72, in *Hansard* (18 June 1971): 189, part 2, table 25.

this year. For every new eviction, another family is shattered, and another group of inflation fighters is sacrificed to the shortcomings of an ungenerous government program.

Workmen's Compensation is a fund set up to protect some Canadian workers and their dependents from the financial consequences of injury or death on the job. It is provincially operated; the first fund was set up by Ontario decades ago (all provinces have had some form of Workmen's Compensation since 1951), and Ontario, at least, seems quite proud of it. That pride is not shared by many workers. One Toronto man told the Senate committee on poverty:

> The Workmen's Compensation Board has a reputation around the world for the efficiency and extent of coverage that it provides. It seems to me, however, that such a reputation has been built on the opinions of politicians and Workmen's Compensation Board administrators and certainly not by consulting those workers in Ontario who have had the misfortune of dealing with the Board.[22]

Consider one case, not hypothetical, but actual:

In the fall of 1970, a young business-machine serviceman, who earned $750 per month, was killed on an Ottawa street by planks thrown from the roof of a building under construction. Both the serviceman and the man who threw the planks — negligently, as it turned out — worked for employers who were covered by Workmen's Compensation.

The serviceman's widow and child are now living on a $175-per-month pension from the Workmen's Compensation Board. That pension is fixed, with no escalator clause. The widow has no right to sue the employer legally responsible for her husband's death. If she remarries, the pension will be stopped, and she will be provided with a lump-sum payment equivalent to two years' benefits. The $175 includes a handsome $50 per month for her child; and that stops on his eighteenth birthday.

The particularly nasty part of this case is the role played by sheer

22. Evidence of the Workmen's Compensation Committee of the Just Society to the Special Senate Committee on Poverty (12 Mar. 1970), 28:7.

blind misfortune; the husband was not killed on *his* job, but on somebody else's job, a job to which the act applied. But the major defect in Workmen's Compensation is the withdrawal of the protection of law; those injured, or the survivors of those killed, have *no* legal recourse against the employer. They must accept the benefit level set by the board. (Occasionally, the board succumbs to a fit of fair play and allows legal action against an employer, but in these rare and extraordinary circumstances the board revokes all rights to benefits, win or lose.)

Workmen's Compensation, then, is not an insurance fund for workers, but instead an insurance fund for employers — and premiums are paid as protection against the possibility of a major, expensive and legally justified suit for damages. It works very nicely for the employers. But the benefit levels for the employees are not quite as satisfactory.

In Ontario, benefits are theoretically set, for full disability, at three-quarters of a worker's earnings — but there is a ceiling on that level of about $100 per week. And so a worker earning more than $200 per week, as many do in the more dangerous trades of the construction industry, may not receive even half of his income as compensation — even if he is completely disabled.

"Disability" is interpreted by the board, and generally interpreted in the interests of the board, as the Just Society's John Neveu has discovered:

> Men who have worked for a lifetime to earn a living, provided for their families and generously paid their way through society, suddenly become suspect once they have been injured.[23]

In other words, honest workers, when injured, become malingerers, and batteries of physicians and lawyers are retained by the board to prove it. Death, of course, is simpler for everybody; the board pays $500 in a lump sum to the widow, and $400 for a funeral, and follows up with a pension of $125 per month, plus $50 per month for each child. The pension must not exceed the dead worker's average earnings, except in the case of a widow with three children, who receives an automatic minimum of $275 per month — well below the Relative Poverty Line.

23. Ibid, 28:8.

The Workmen's Compensation Committee of the Just Society in Toronto has taken on the board persistently and claims success in ninety per cent of its appeals. But, as the committee chairman noted before the Senate committee on poverty, the board is unimpressed by that batting average, and is apparently not convinced that there is anything much wrong with the system that produced all those appealable decisions. Instead, he discovered, the board has become somewhat protective about its procedures and principles, and is chary about handing out information:

> It is this type of silent wall of bureaucracy that faces not only the injured workman, but all the poor of Canada in their relations with the government and the government agencies of Canada.[24]

And the parallel is justified, for the injured and suddenly poor worker is treated by the board in much the same way as a welfare applicant is treated by the Ontario welfare system: as a potential, if not an actual, fraud. You do not, in Ontario, get something for nothing. Not even if you kill yourself to get it.

Canada's network of categorical programs — Old-Age Security, the Canada Pension Plan, Family and Youth Allowances, Unemployment Insurance and Workmen's Compensation — emerges as a frayed, ungenerous and contradictory patchwork of inadequacies. Those reduced to dependence on them are steadily falling behind the standard of living that prevails for other Canadians. The whole peculiar system badly needs an overhaul.

V.4 THE WELFARE SYSTEM

There is a public agreement in Canada that those who cannot work should not be allowed to starve. Dissenters from this opinion tend to keep a low public profile; advocates of the "are there no jails; are there no workhouses?" approach are not, at the moment, popular.

24. Ibid.

There is, however, a deep ambiguity hidden within the consensus. The same people who support the protection of the abject express a deep suspicion of the machinery that provides that protection: the welfare system, in the public mind, is letting a lot of widows and orphans get away with murder — or, rather, is doling out a lot of public money to people who are masquerading as widows and orphans, but who are in fact freaks, bandits and bums. On the one hand, Canada is a bountiful and generous nation that extends a sympathetic hand to the down-and-out; on the other, the down-and-out are a pack of worthless tramps, and are bleeding the country dry.

In other words, somebody is getting away with something.

There is a great deal of evidence to suggest that nobody is getting away with very much — so much evidence, in fact, that it is necessary to conclude that Canadians, or most of them, *need* to believe in the myth of the freeloader, for reasons that must be deeply embedded in the Canadian psyche. Some Canadians get so little joy out of working themselves that they are convinced a great many people, less virtuous than themselves, will lie and cheat to avoid it; others are confirmed believers in the natural larceny of the human spirit. In any case, the myth of the welfare bum has been indestructible.

There are, in reality, three major classes of welfare recipients, and neither of the first two meet the criteria of the myth.

A majority of the people who live on welfare in Canada have no resources of their own (welfare officials make quite sure that welfare recipients have no assets worth bothering about) and could not support themselves at any job, under any conceivable circumstances.[1] These are the penniless elderly, the physically and mentally handicapped, and single mothers with children — people who cannot and likely never will be able to earn a living without help.

The second large group of welfare recipients is composed of people who can work under some circumstances, but find it difficult to hold a job when times get tough — unskilled workers, for example, who get shaken out of the bottom of the labour market when unemployment levels rise. (During the last year, when unem-

1. Most professionals who have anything much to do with welfare systems in Canada would endorse these estimates without question. Statistical proof is made difficult by the general vagueness of statistical gathering in most welfare jurisdictions.

ployment figures in Canada climbed to the seven per cent mark, the number of welfare applications in many areas broke records.)[2]

Neither of these groups contain many people who are on welfare because they want to be; and the third group, which is composed of those who do not want to work and would not take a job if they could find one, is very small indeed.[3]

The reasons for this are fairly clear. First, life on welfare in most Canadian jurisdictions is so unpleasant that only the irrational would live on the dole if they could possibly avoid it. (Welfare recipients are publicly stigmatized; and rates tend to be kept at, or not too far above, the minimum wage, to fend off complaints from low-paying employers.) Second, Canadian welfare systems contain elaborate precautions — legal declarations of penury and snap inspections by welfare officials, for example — to eliminate the lay-abouts. And finally, the penalties for getting caught fiddling are severe enough to convince most people that the game is not worth the candle; one Toronto judge recently sentenced a sixty-nine-year-old widow to a six-month term in reformatory for having defrauded the local welfare department of $1127.[4]

As a result of these precautions— or, perhaps, in spite of them — the honesty of welfare recipients assays out at least as well as that of the general public. Thorough checks of welfare applications in the United States have turned up evidence of fraud in a mere three to five per cent of the cases examined, a level of integrity that compares favourably with the behaviour of more affluent income-tax payers. The city of New York, in fact, is considering the elimination of its routine security apparatus, which apparently costs more than it recovers, in favour of a system of random sampling.[5]

So the myth of the bum on relief bears little relation to reality; but the procedures of Canadian welfare systems are centred around that myth, and consequently tend to treat welfare recipients as potential, or actual, criminals.

2. Welfare loads in Metropolitan Toronto jumped about fifty per cent between December 1968 and December 1969. See brief of the Canadian Welfare Council to the Special Senate Committee on Poverty (5 Mar. 1970) 25:11.
3. Ibid notes: "In the Canadian Welfare Council's case studies of nearly 300 rural families and over 200 urban families, all described as 'poor,' the incidence of so-called 'shiftlessness' was practically nil."
4. See *Toronto Daily Star* (27 July 1971).
5. These procedures are both unpleasant and easily replaced. If the Department of National Revenue kept track of *all* income sources in this country, no such surveillance would be necessary.

There can be only one justification for this; and that is the assumption that welfare systems must act as their own deterrents—that there is a large army of potential lay-abouts who will run for the welfare offices if welfare systems are made even minimally humane. This assumption cannot be tested until the welfare systems *are* made minimally humane, a gamble that welfare officials resolutely refuse to take. The preferred policy, evidently, is to tyrannize the truly needy in order to discourage those who are not needy at all.

The argument is reduced, finally, to an estimation of the human character. Either you believe that human beings will take advantage of a free ride, any free ride, if it is offered; or you believe that human beings prefer, if it is possible, to stand on their two hind legs and work for their daily bread and their dignity.

The sections that follow are an examination of Canadian welfare systems, from the massive movement of public money at the federal level to the petty despotism of municipal welfare offices. The entire elephantine structure is shot through with an unspoken but absolute faith in the worthlessness of the human character — a faith that has no place in a Just Society, or in any other.

The Federal Structure

The federal government's transfer payments provide the backbone of Canada's social-assistance structure. Without Ottawa's co-opera-tion and financing, local administrations could not keep their programs in business, even at a bare subsistence level. In other words, the federal government has the power to overhaul Canada's welfare systems, by direct or indirect pressure on local authorities. That power has not yet been used.

Ottawa handles its transfer of money to the poor in two quite distinct ways: directly, through straight cash grants like the Old-Age-Security program and Children's and Youth Allowances, and indirectly, through federal contributions to provincial and municipal welfare schemes. These last payments, which form the underpin-nings of Canada's welfare system, are made through the Canada Assistance Plan, a piece of legislation that, more than any other single document, embodies the promises and failures of Canada's social policy towards the poor.

The Canada Assistance Plan (1966) arose out of an apparent

impulse to do something genuinely useful for low-income Canadians. It was designed, first, to straighten out a jumble of confused, contradictory and sloppy programs that were getting between the money and the recipients; and, second, to extend the whole idea of welfare beyond subsistence payments to the flat broke.

Essentially, the federal government promised to pick up fifty per cent of any provincial or municipal payment to the poor that could be called "assistance." And "assistance" was generously defined: "aid in any form to or in respect of persons in need for the purpose of providing . . . food, shelter, clothing, fuel, utilities, household supplies and personal requirements." This assistance, furthermore, was to be extended not only to those who were actually in need, but to those who were "about to become in need."

This last point was crucial; for it seemed to indicate that social planners in Canada were beginning to think not only about keeping the poverty-stricken limping along just above the subsistence level, but also about preventing people from falling to that level in the first place.

The hope died aborning. The CAP planners failed to confront the factors that had brought about the inadequacy and disparity of welfare programs in the first place.

The most obvious of these factors was the total control local politicians and administrators had over the services they would provide. This decentralization of control is traditional: in England, the Elizabethan Poor Laws quite specifically made local authorities responsible for relief administration, on the theory that only local authorities could separate the loafers from the truly needy.

This primacy of local authority in Britain went unchanged until 1948, when a Labour government abolished the Poor Law and the organization and financing of national assistance was centralized. The Canadian federal government, however, has refused to challenge Canadian local authorities;[6] provincial politicians (and, in some provinces, municipal politicians) are left to decide how much they can afford to pay in welfare allowances, how much they want to pay, and then to pay just that, and no more.

This local franchise had already led to a crazy quilt of welfare

6. Usually pleading a vague constitutional prohibition under the British North America Act.

programs, in which some provinces — Quebec, for example — posted welfare payments far below those offered in other provinces, like Alberta. In provinces that still extended financial discretion to regions, furthermore, welfare rates in some cities were well out of line with rates paid in rural areas ten miles away. In some provinces, medical care, drugs and other essential goods and services were provided to welfare recipients free of charge, as a matter of course; in others, they were emphatically denied.

The Canada Assistance Plan did not attempt to buck the local and provincial powers. For, finally, the Canada Assistance Plan was just that: a plan. CAP was a kind of shopping list for provincial and municipal welfare administrators, a schedule of approved expenditures for which they could get Ottawa to pick up half the bill. There was nothing in the plan that required local administrators to pay reasonable welfare rates, or really to do anything at all; the only hard stipulation was that the federal government would pay for half of what they did do.

So, if provincial welfare administrators decided, as a matter of public policy, not to give welfare cheques to anybody who had a job but extremely low wages, the provincial welfare administrators were quite free to do just that — and most of them did. (Alberta remains the only province in Canada that publicly helps working poor people in any systematic way.) The Canada Assistance Plan stated, quite specifically, that the federal government would pick up half the bill for welfare payments to the working poor; but if the provinces decided that they were not going to pick up the other half, and be damned to "those about to become in need," nobody could force them to do it. The initiative — and the power — remained at the local level.

There were, in fact, only two real requirements built into the Canada Assistance Plan. First, the provinces and cities were not to insist that people applying for welfare pass any kind of residence requirements before they got their benefits[7] — and, by and large, they did not, although single transient males still run into occasional trouble, and some local authorities are still beefing about this restriction on their freedom. Second, the welfare systems were

7. This requirement was restricted, of course, to persons applying for short-term welfare; long-term welfare recipients are required to be residents.

required to set up provincial appeal boards. After five years, the last of these appeal boards is now creaking into action; and the overall performance of welfare appeal boards has been oriented more towards the protection of welfare bureaucracies than welfare recipients.

The Canada Assistance Plan, moreover, has done little to overcome the disparities between various provincial and municipal schemes, simply because it extends the same fifty-fifty cost-sharing split to the poor provinces as it does to the rich ones. Either the CAP planners decided, mistakenly, that regional disparities could be left to the deliberations of others, or they decided that these regional disparities were beyond mending, or they decided that there was nothing much wrong with having great differences between one welfare scheme and another. This kind of cost-sharing split, appropriate or not, had become a kind of federal-provincial reflex.

Regional disparities are actually reinforced by the manner in which CAP controls the money flow. CAP requires that provinces pay the entire tab for their own welfare programs in advance, and then submit an accounting to Ottawa, which will, after due examination, reimburse the provincial treasury for half its expenditure. This procedure means one thing to a rich province, like Ontario, which can set up a reasonably adequate welfare system out of its own treasury — and quite another to a poorer province, like Newfoundland, which has difficulty raising even its eventual fifty per cent share of the final bill. In other words, rich provinces are given, under CAP, liberal assistance to set up relatively rich welfare schemes. Poor provinces are given little help of any kind. In poor provinces, then, there is less money to go around, and more people who will need it. And the gap between provincial welfare rates widens. Table V.4.i (December 1970) makes the point.

One ugly result of these disparities, by way of illustration, is that some unskilled workers, unable to get either jobs or welfare in depressed areas, migrate to relatively richer regions where welfare is more adequate and easier to obtain. This has resulted in a strong and growing contempt for low-income Maritimers in large central cities like Toronto.

The Canada Assistance Plan was unveiled in 1966 in a fair-sized burst of publicity. It has turned out to be merely a new accounting

TABLE V.4.i

Monthly and annual budget standards for items of basic welfare need, by province, December 1970 [a]

PROVINCE	Monthly	Annually
Newfoundland [b]	$230.00	$2,760
Prince Edward Island [c]	244.00	2,928
Nova Scotia [d]	263.00	3,156
New Brunswick [e]	187.66	2,251
Quebec [f]	218.00	2,616
Ontario [g]	271.00	3,252
Manitoba [h]	246.10	2,953
Saskatchewan [i]	215.15	2,581
Alberta [j]	335.00	4,020
British Columbia [k]	211.00	2,532

Source: *Monthly Budgets for Items of Basic Need under Provincial Assistance Programs (Revised December, 1970)* Welfare Research Division, Department National Health and Welfare (December 1970).

Note: Actual allowances granted may be subject to ceilings (*see footnotes*) and do not necessarily correspond to the budget standards. Municipalities that administer assistance may supplement provincial allowances.

Basic needs are defined as food, clothing, and shelter. Extra allowances for special diets, extra fuel or rent that may be given under special circumstances are not shown.

a. Allowing for a family of four: two parents and two children, a girl of eight years and a boy of thirteen years.
b. Urban rent, including fuel allowance.
c. Exclusive of fuel allowance, which may be paid on basis of actual cost, includes urban rent.
d. Including allowances for fuel, rent, and utilities, which together may not exceed $115. However, *provincial maximum monthly allowances are set as follows:* $75 for women 60-65 years who are single, widowed, deserted, divorced or unemployed; $100 for disabled persons and persons 65 or over, *$175 for families.*
e. Exclusive of fuel allowance which may be paid on the basis of actual cost. Amounts specified for the various items of basic need are maximum amounts and the total allowance may not exceed an amount considered to be a reasonable standard in the community. Rent at $60 per month for urban accommodation is included in the $188 shown on table. However, rent is usually paid at cost and $60 per month is only used as a guide.
f. Includes fuel and rent for Zone III (Montreal): Zones II and I are $5 and $15 less respectively.
g. Rent for heated premises.
h. Exclusive of fuel and utilities which are paid on the basis of actual cost.
i. Exclusive of fuel allowance which may be granted according to provincial schedule or on the basis of actual cost. Rent may also be paid on actual cost.
j. Amounts for provincial allowances are specified for food, and clothing only; other rates are set at community standards. Rates are not specified for municipal allowances. However, amounts shown are fair approximations, according to telephone conversation with the Department of Social Development, Province of Alberta.
k. Includes fuel.

procedure — improved bookkeeping, but not improved performance — for Canada's welfare systems. It may have been a mistake to believe that any apparently new system could succeed if it retained local welfare structures or, indeed, any "welfare" structure at all. But the belief was very nice, while it lasted.

Provincial and Municipal Systems
Under the broad and uncritical umbrella of the Canada Assistance Plan, provincial and municipal welfare administrators (and the politicians who control them) tend to call their own shots. And it is at this level — the "delivery" level — that the values and procedures of the welfare systems come into uncertain contact with the interests of the poor.

This, of course, leads to considerable differences in the way the poor are treated from one province to the next; so there is very little point in attempting to discuss specific aspects of the state of welfare in all of Canada. Instead, we have chosen to examine Ontario's welfare system, primarily because there is a lot on record about it. In many ways, however, a welfare system is a welfare system, and works according to certain prejudices and assumptions common to all such systems; and many of those we found in Ontario are no doubt at work in other provinces.

Ontario is rich. And it has a lot of poor people: about one million of them in 1969, broken up into some 400,000 individual and family units.[8]

This is a staggering number, and a staggering percentage of the population of Canada's most prosperous province; one-third of all unattached individuals, and about one in seven of all Ontario family units, are living below the poverty line.

Ontario spends an immense amount of money keeping the most deprived of these people afloat. Between the fiscal years 1959-60 and 1968-69, the budget of the Ontario Department of Social and Family Services rose from $68 million to $242 million, an average annual jump of some thirteen per cent. The gross per capita expen-

8. See brief of the Ontario Department of Social and Family Services to the Special Senate Committee on Poverty (25 May 1970) 43:51. Unless otherwise noted, all figures relating to and technical descriptions of the Ontario welfare system are drawn from this source. Ontario planners used a projection of the ECC poverty line to arrive at their estimates; in 1969, the poverty line was barely below the Relative Poverty Line, except for families of three or more.

diture — the amount extracted from each Ontario resident to finance the department — rose from $11 in 1959-60 to $33 nine years later.

Ontario taxpayers have been complaining, understandably, about the mammoth rise in public expenditure on welfare systems; for although the costs of the services provided for the Ontario poor are rising like a Bensonite dream of inflation, poverty in Ontario shows no sign of succumbing.

Welfare payments, in Ontario, are funnelled through two separate systems: Family Benefits, which is a provincial operation designed to help people with permanent, long-term needs, and General Welfare Assistance, which is — in theory — an emergency fund for people in temporary trouble, and is run by the municipalities.

(This separation is primarily designed for administrative convenience, and does not rise out of any deep thought about the nature of poverty. People in general do not bounce on to welfare rolls in times of sudden, unforeseen crisis and then bounce off again. Most of those who are reduced to applying for public assistance at any time are in serious long-term financial or social difficulty.)

The rates for each category are set by provincial authorities, and work out roughly equal, although municipal administrators are allowed considerable leeway in setting their own levels for General Welfare Assistance.

There are a number of categories of eligibility for Family Benefits. Generally, they're given to the aged, the blind and disabled, mothers with children and no husbands, foster mothers, or other people in clear need of long-term financial assistance. They're not very generous; in fact, they're not even close to any reasonable living standard.

Ontario's Family Benefits program, as noted, is restricted to people who are unlikely ever to be able to support themselves, but the principle of "work incentive" — that is, the attempt to encourage people on welfare to earn some of their daily bread, if possible — is still applied, in a rather half-hearted way.

Obviously, the more a recipient is allowed to keep from his own earnings, the more likely he is to go after a job in a serious way. Exemptions, however, must under the present system be kept low enough to avoid making the total pay-off from work *and* welfare combined much more attractive than the amount of money that can be earned from work alone. In other words, earnings incentives, and the incentive to get off welfare, are inextricably mixed up with the going rate for unskilled labour: where the prevailing wage is kept at or around the poverty line, and at or below the welfare-benefit level, incentives must be kept tiny or nonexistent; if they are raised, minimum-wage workers will give up the fight and apply for welfare. Once people without valuable skills are on welfare, there can be very little earning-exemption incentive provided for them to bestir themselves. It is an uneasy compromise all around.

These constraints show up very clearly in the levels of earnings exemptions provided in Ontario, which are set out in table V.4.ii.

The rates don't look very high, even on a yearly basis. When broken down into a smaller time scale, they are reduced almost to the vanishing point. A deserted mother with a child below the age of nine receives a basic Family-Benefits allowance of $2234 ($43 per week), and can earn an extra $432 ($8.30 per week) and keep all of it, which brings her income up to $2666 ($51.30 per week).[9] Anything she earns above that, she gets to keep a quarter of; her Family-Benefits cheque is reduced by seventy-five cents for every extra dollar she brings in. In other words, she may work for a bit more than four hours per week at the federal minimum wage of $1.65 per hour, and keep all four hours' earnings. Any extra hours of labour are rewarded at the princely rate of about forty-one cents each. (There is a statutory requirement, furthermore, that mothers with children not work more than 120 hours per month. It is uncertain why any of them would want to work more than a quarter of that.)

Ontario has solved the dilemma of the earnings-exemption/minimum-wage tangle by keeping its exemption levels low. Other provinces have reduced them almost to invisibility. Manitoba has a ceiling on outside income of $20 per month, as does New Brunswick. There is a difference: if a Manitoban earns $21, the province takes $1 from his cheque; if a resident of New Brunswick earns $21, the province takes the extra $1 and the original $20 along with it, and leaves him right where he started.

---

9. Recipients are not allowed to earn their yearly quota in one burst; earnings for each month must be below the monthly allowance.

TABLE V.4.ii
Annual earnings exemption, application to social-assistance levels

FAMILY UNIT	Social-assistance budget	Income exemption	Earnings beyond which ineligible
1 person			
(living alone)	$1,380	$288	$2,126
(disabled)	1,560	288	2,366
2 persons			
(1 child 0-9)	2,234	432	3,409
(1 child 16)	2,544	432	3822
3 persons			
(2 adults, 1 child 0-9)	2,772	576	4,270
(1 adult, 2 children 16)	3,026	576	4,606
4 persons			
(2 adults, 2 children 0-9)	3,156	720	4,926
(1 adult, 3 children 16)	3,576	720	5,486
5 persons			
(2 adults, 3 children 0-9)	3,540	864	5,582
(1 adult, 4 children 16)	4,128	864	6,366

a. 75% of all earnings above this amount deducted until gross earnings reach the cut-off level indicated. Source: Ontario Department of Social and Family Services brief to the Special Senate Committee on Poverty (Feb 1970).

So earnings exemptions, in Ontario as in other provinces, are token efforts only, and do not make much difference to the standard of living available to recipients of Family Benefits. This bleak picture improves, just a little, with the addition of Family and Youth Allowances, the exemption of benefits from income tax and free medical insurance. Furthermore, as the Ontario brief to the Senate committee on poverty points out, people on welfare do not have work expenses. And so people on Family Benefits are considerably better off than those working at the federal or provincial minimum wage. But, in the long run, the difference is almost academic; both are still well below any reasonable standard of living.

General Welfare Assistance is run by the Ontario municipalities and regions, and is aimed at people in need who are not eligible for Family Benefits, or are waiting for their Family Benefits eligibility to come through. The costs are covered by the municipalities, which later pick up eighty per cent of their expenditures from the provincial government. (The "first-dollar" approach again, and easier for the more affluent cities to cope with than rural areas on starvation budgets.)

The municipalities are required to pay a certain minimum benefit level, and are then given the option of providing certain other payments — supplements to Family-Benefits or Old-Age-Security recipients, and money for drugs, medical services, prosthetic appliances, and so on. The province picks up the usual eighty per cent of the bill for supplementary payments to Family-Benefits and Old-Age-Security recipients, but only fifty per cent of the bill for the "extras" — a fairly explicit disincentive to provide eyeglasses and false teeth for people on short-term welfare.

If these extras are provided, of course, they're likely to be cut short without notice when the money is needed for traffic lights or ceremonial dinners. Mrs. Audrey Burger, Welfare Committee chairman of the Toronto Association of Women Electors, told the Senate Committee on Poverty:

> I happen to know, observing the Metro Housing and Welfare Committee, that there was an allocation made for blankets in, I think, October of last year [1969]. Suddenly there were no more blankets, and even though the Commissioner of Welfare would very much like to have given people blankets, he just had no more money left for blankets.[10]

Recipients of General Welfare Assistance are usually much more likely than Family-Benefits recipients to be able to hold a job, at least part time; in times of economic recession, for example, the GWA rolls are likely to include numbers of unskilled people who have been knocked out of the labour market, and have no resources to tide them over until they find another job. When these "unemployed

10. Evidence of the Association of Women Electors of Metropolitan Toronto to the Special Senate Committee on Poverty (27 Jan. 1970) 26:34.

employable" persons try to supplement their welfare benefits with a little honest work, they run head-on into the paradoxical GWA work-incentive policy, which is stated delicately by the Ontario brief to the Senate committee on poverty:

> Restrictions on employment and the supplementing of earnings apply to the first group only, that is, to unemployed employable persons. In order to be eligible for assistance under the Act an employable person cannot be engaged in remunerative employment at the time he makes application for assistance. However, there is no administrative definition of "remunerative employment;" as this pertains to conditions of eligibility it may be determined locally. Similarly, the definition of "regular full-time employment" is a matter for the local welfare administration to determine. Patterns vary according to the discretion exercised by local administrators.
>
> . . . The other groups listed are not subject to work restrictions. (Many of these are, of course, unlikely to be able to find employment.)[11]

What that means, after the underbrush has been cut away, is that work incentives must be provided for those unlikely to be able to use them, and offered only *at the discretion of the municipality* to those who are likely to need them. And, since earnings exemptions chop money out of welfare budgets, municipalities are usually reluctant to let welfare recipients on GWA earn a nickel. R. S. Godfrey, commissioner of the Social Welfare Department of the Ottawa-Carlton region, told the Senate committee on poverty:

> At the present time the legislation requires us to deduct 100 per cent of any part-time earnings of a family. Applicants have to declare earnings, and if they do not and we find out, the result is a reduction of their allowances. It destroys any incentive that is likely to be there or that might be developed, because they will say what is the point of getting a job if the

11. Brief of the Ontario Department of Social and Family Services to the Special Senate Committee on Poverty (25 May 1970) 43:56-7.

moment I do so you are going to take away what little I might earn?[12]

In other words, welfare systems, and GWA in particular, discourage any impulse a recipient might have to go out and make a living. The tendency of welfare recipients to become dependent on welfare systems is not due to any moral collapse or social addiction, but is the direct result of the way welfare systems are set up.

Employers of people who have been on welfare think differently; many exhibit considerable suspicion of people who are trying to break the welfare cycle. One Toronto woman, who spent three years working in a dog-food processing plant, described her relations with her boss:

> He started treating me like dirt and saying poor people were lazy, no-good bums while all the time I was working just to keep even financially and not getting ahead at all. Finally, I asked him for a transfer to another job under another chemist. He refused and I quit. He called me back the following Monday and told me I was fired.[13]

This state of affairs puts direct pressure on the family unit itself. First, General Welfare Assistance — short-term welfare — may be extended to complete families headed by an unemployed male, but Family Benefits — long-term, and more secure, welfare — may be granted only if that unemployed male is separated from his wife and children. Many workers, acting out of a sensible and human concern for the security of their families, do just that.

Second, a man who does stay by his family is put under extreme emotional strain, not only as a result of the loss of his employment,

---

12. Proceedings (27 Jan. 1970) 15:10. This situation has evidently been changed, as far as Ottawa-Carlton is concerned; and some attempt is now being made to supplement certain kinds of people with jobs that yield extremely low wages.

13. *Toronto Daily Star* (7 Aug. 1971), p. 11. The Toronto *Globe and Mail* of the same date found it necessary to run a first-page story about damage done to property rented by a welfare family in Winnipeg. The *Star,* to give it credit, buried the same story on an inside page.

but also as a result of the loss of identity a life on welfare inevitably brings about. This particularly nasty result of welfare systems is not restricted to Ontario, but is an integral part of welfare systems everywhere. The American writer, Irving Kristol, recently observed:

> The family is, in our society, a vital economic institution. Welfare robs it of its economic function. Above all, welfare robs the head of the household of *his* economic function, and tends to make of him a "superfluous man."[14]

It is a persuasive indication of the inadequacy of the Ontario benefits — which are among the highest in the country — that welfare officials are unable or unwilling to explain to welfare recipients just how they are to manage on the money allotted to them. The amounts available are simply referred to as "pre-added budgets,"[15] which are not open to analysis, but are quite simply all the provincial government is prepared to pay.

These rates are rigid. No cost-of-living escalator is built into the schedule; instead, welfare rates are raised whenever the politicians in control feel like it. This happens, in Ontario, roughly once every three years — and at the end of the cycle, just before an increase, the benefit levels have been eroded almost beyond the starvation point. Commissioner Godfrey of Ottawa told the Senate committee on poverty what life was like for welfare recipients just before the last increase:

> Our home economist took a family, a so-called typical family of four children plus a husband and wife, and determined what, in her professional opinion, was needed to feed that family for a month. In 1966, it would have cost $132 to buy the items that are listed . . . these are basic necessities. In 1969, it takes $157, approximately a 19 per cent loss in purchasing power. . . . With a given amount of money you could buy 22 quarts of milk in 1966, but only 18 quarts of milk today (1969), and similarly

14. Irving Kristol, "Welfare: The Best of Intentions, the Worst of Results," *Atlantic* (Aug. 1971), p. 47.
15. "Pre-added budgets" dole out lump sums for food, clothing, personal supplies and so on.

down the line . . . there has been no off-setting increase in the rates.[16]

The raising of welfare benefits, even when they have become catastrophically inadequate, is generally about the last priority on any politician's list. J. H. Craigs, a member of the executive committee of the Ontario Welfare Council, described to the Senate committee the results of an attempt to pry a few concessions from the Ontario cabinet:

> *Mr. Craigs:* I was part of the delegation before the Robarts Cabinet only last Thursday, and, perhaps to misquote the late Winston Churchill, it was a sort of mystery wrapped in an enigma. . . . As far as organized labour is concerned, we have no evidence to convince us that the present portfolio has any real status within the cabinet. In other words, it has no political crunch. For that reason it is relegated to a lower order of priorities as the cabinet sees them.
> *Senator Cook:* You mean, the labour portfolio or the welfare one?
> *Mr. Craigs:* Both. Emphatically, both portfolios.[17]

The result, for the poor, of the Robarts assessment of political crunch was that welfare benefit levels that were barely adequate in 1966 continued in effect until 1969.

In 1966, for each member of a family of six, about one dollar per week was available for the purchase of clothing and all other personal requirements. In 1969, prices for absolute necessities had risen, and even clothing was likely to go; that dollar was now required to pay for food and rent. In 1966, the rates considered adequate for rental of housing space were unrealistic; in 1969, they had become unbelievable. The following report, which presents the results of this erosion in a particularly pointed way, is from a social worker's casebook submitted to the Senate committee by Ottawa's Commissioner Godfrey:

16. Proceedings (27 Jan. 1970) 15:25.
17. Proceedings (5 Mar. 1970) 25:22. The delegation was attempting to find out just why the Ontario government was making no use of major parts of the Canada Assistance Plan.

Description of living accommodation. Woman deserted — five children. Living conditions—rented property. Three-room row house. Exterior well painted, interior in very poor condition.

Basement. Holes in walls dividing unit from others which allowed rats entrance from other units. Holes in floor and front and back walls which allowed rats entry to unit from outside. No door on basement and holes around pipes and in corners which allowed rats access to living quarters.

Holes in upstairs walls (corners) allowed rats access to bedroom. Defective electrical switch in hall with semi-exposed and exposed wires. Glass in front door out for over a month without replacement. Windows and doors uninsulated. Repairs of some holes substandard. Wall broken around kitchen light switch.

Comment on tenant: This woman kept her house well in spite of its poor condition. Her floors were always as neat as could be expected with five children in the house. She complained often to landlords agent but had trouble contacting him and received only empty promises when contact was established.

On December 5, 1969, woman reported to the social worker that rats had been driven in by snow. She reported food spoiled and rats acting very boldly in living quarters. At 100 per cent municipal aid holes were patched and an exterminator was engaged.

Rent allowance: $95.00. Heat allowance: $27.20. Total: $122.20.

Difference between actual rent and rental allowance: $80.00.

This woman is therefore obliged to take $80.00 from the pre-added budget figure of $164.00 (food, clothing, etc.) to meet this excess rent figure every month.[18]

Food, clothing and personal care for one mother and five children: fifty cents each, per day.

Life on welfare, then, is not easy; and it becomes harder as time

18. Proceedings (27 Jan. 1970) 15:56.

goes on. But the suspicion remains among welfare administrators and the general public that large numbers of people will, if given the chance, flood the welfare rolls whether the rates are adequate or not.

Politicians and bureaucrats prevent this phantom onslaught by keeping welfare rates as low as possible, and by publicly stigmatizing welfare recipients. This last and most vicious procedure is, again, characteristic of welfare systems everywhere. The British social critic Richard Titmuss notes:

> Many need-eligibility programmes are basically designed to keep people out; not to let them in. Moreover, they are often so administered as to induce among consumers a sense of shame, guilt or failure in using a public service.[19]

Welfare systems, then, are quite simply and deliberately set up to discourage the poor from making use of them. The techniques are crude and brutal. Alphonse Nadeau, moderator of the Assemblée Générale de l'Ile de Hull, describes procedures in that city:

> First of all, when you try to reach the welfare by telephone, it does not work; if you wish to speak to a Mr. So-and-So, who would be in charge, you cannot reach him; the calls are screened by a receptionist who transfers your call to another gentleman, who asks you to which subject you are referring, and so on; you are unable to reach the persons in charge. Then you are received by the accounting people; you enter a large room . . . there are no chairs, and you must remain standing, and when it is your turn, you go to the counter, where there are three or four persons in charge, with reports — the public statement that can be heard by everybody in the room; they can hear what you say. Then, you wait for months, you do not receive an answer, it drags on, and you just come back . . . what happens is that the people end up by being discouraged, and when they have to return to the welfare three or four times, they return home and say: there is nothing we can

19. Richard M. Titmuss, *Commitment to Welfare* (London: George Allen and Unwin, 1968), p. 68.

do, and I will endure my misery and crawl in my hole. It is like that.[20]

The Social Planning and Research Council of Hamilton reported to the Senate committee:

On occasion an applicant waits all morning to be seen at the Public Welfare Department of Hamilton, only to learn that he should have gone to the Social Services Department of Wentworth County. . . . The Hamilton Public Welfare Department takes automobile plates from recipients, making these licence plates available to them again on the basis of specified needs which are approved by the Department.[21]

When reporters turn from examinations of welfare frauds to investigations of the real workings of welfare systems, they find routine examples of callousness:

Loretta says she was occasionally forced to beg and forage for pop bottles to supplement the welfare allowance of about $26.00 weekly provided for her and her son.

For several months in the final stages of her pregnancy, she says, the Metro welfare department made her walk once a week from her home in the Danforth-Woodbine area to the welfare office at Queen and Coxwell — a round-trip journey of about 40 blocks — to pick up her cheque.

"That's the sort of thing they're always doing to you," Loretta says. "There seems to be little or no consideration for your personal feelings and they won't go one inch out of their way to make things a little easier. I asked them for enough for carfare but they said, 'No, you can go on walking.' "[22]

This kind of system is as demoralizing to administer as it is disastrous to deal with. The proceedings of the Senate committee on poverty contain anguished appeals for reform from the very

20. Proceedings (29 Jan. 1970) 16:24.
21. Proceedings (12 Mar. 1970) 28:93-4.
22. *Toronto Daily Star* (7 Aug. 1971), p. 11.

people who run the welfare systems. Ottawa's Commissioner Godfrey, in his evidence before the committee, said:

> The investigatory processes which are required by law, and that must be carried out, are in themselves humiliating. The persistent inquiry into a person's circumstances, the inquiry over and over again into: How much do you earn? What have you done? When did you last work? Why have you not worked? Why have you not done this? — all tend to humiliate people. This checking-up process does nothing, in our opinion, to enhance the inherent dignity of the individual. There is at all times a delicate situation and a matter of acute embarrassment and discomfort for people and yet these are the areas in which we have to probe. . . .[23]

So, finally, the villains of the piece are not to be found on either side of the wire mesh in the welfare offices; some welfare clerks, working at or around the minimum wage, take home less money each week than the people to whom they give the cheques. The villains, if there is villainy beyond the qualities of stupidity and ungenerosity, are to be found in the legislatures that create and control the welfare systems, and in the public that ignores them.

Welfare systems treat people like animals. They encourage dependency. They do not provide enough money to ensure a decent living for the people trapped within them. They reinforce, they do not break, the cycle of poverty. They are corrupt and ugly embodiments of prejudice and brutality, and they cannot be reformed; they must be replaced.

23. Proceedings (27 Jan. 1970) 16:24.

VI

A New Tax and Transfer System

VI.1 OBJECTIVES

If poverty and inequality are to be eliminated, and if poverty and inequality are produced by Canada's economic system, it makes sense to start any action against poverty and inequality inside that system. In chapter IV we set out a general program of earnings and employment policies to make the economic system — the world of jobs, wages, salaries and profits — perform better for all Canadians, not just the few at the top, and so to reduce the inequalities that are the root of poverty.

But earnings and employment policies alone won't eliminate poverty and inequality. For, as chapter V indicated, there are many people in Canada who are not in the world of jobs, wages, salaries and profits, and who wouldn't be affected much by employment and earnings policies. These are the old, the handicapped, female heads of families — in short, most of the people now caught in the welfare system, or living on inadequate pensions.

In fact, employment and earnings policies won't completely eliminate poverty and inequality even for everyone who can work. For some of those policies — full employment, for example — cannot always be fulfilled, particularly in times of great change or upheaval in the economy. Some workers will have to pay for the imbalances; less than full employment means that somebody is unemployed. Those workers will have to be compensated for their unemployment, and an earnings and employment policy alone won't do that. There is, furthermore, no guarantee that employment and earnings policies will work at top efficiency all the time; needs change, and Canadian governments, as they have amply demonstrated in recent years, can make mistakes.

There is one further limitation. As we have pointed out, even a fair wage can be quite inadequate to provide a decent standard of living for a large family. Wages are given to workers, not to families, and a wage that may be perfectly satisfactory for a single man may be totally unsatisfactory for a man with a wife and three children.

In other words, an affluent society must guarantee all of its citizens a minimum living standard. And that standard must not be below the Relative Poverty Line; that is, nobody — widow, orphan, blind man, unemployed worker or anyone else — should be living at less than half the average living standard of the nation as a whole.

That relative income standard is certainly not going to make anybody rich. It is, as we have indicated in chapter I, enough to keep people out of poverty; but it still leaves enough economic incentive to give anybody who can work reason to do so. But the transfer system will at least protect people from absolute financial catastrophe through sudden loss of employment or illness.

Any society that claims to respect the principle of equality must provide that kind of insurance; and, conversely, any society that does provide that kind of insurance will become more egalitarian. Economic inequality produces political inequality; and the idea of democracy demands at least some basic guarantee of rough equality, in power and in security, to each citizen. Nobody should be left out of the system of economic protection, and nobody should be allowed to escape paying its costs if they are able to; and if wives and children are to be considered people, eligible for protection, obviously some assessment of need, based on family size, will have to be built into the guarantee.

There are some essential lessons to be drawn from the present state of Canada's welfare systems, for if the more loathsome aspects of those systems are to be avoided, the assessment of need for protection will have to be done in a way that is not degrading to the person in need. Protection in case of need is a right, and should be treated that way; everyone should understand that right, and be helped to take full advantage of it.

This is not to say that financial protection should operate as a money machine, without supervision or flexibility. Its controllers must somehow be given the ability to respond to unique circumstances without being allowed to exercise bureaucratic arbitrariness. This is possible, surely; for the workings of present-day welfare systems indicate that bureaucrats can be quite arbitrary without responding to unique situations in any way.

One area in which the current welfare system breaks down completely is in its connection with family life. In many cases, families disintegrate, not because of their poverty, but because welfare systems prevent them from climbing out of poverty as a complete unit. Transfer systems should not necessarily encourage people to stay together if they don't want to, but they certainly should not discourage people from staying together when they do want to.

There are two obvious financial traps a transfer system must avoid. First, it should not penalize people so that they have no reason to work; and, second, it should not cost so much to run that it cuts down on the work and savings incentives of the affluent.

What Canada needs, then, is an income-support program that guarantees everyone a certain minimum decent standard of living; a social-insurance program that protects people against sharp drops in income; and a tax system to pay for the first two by drawing money from the affluent and so evening out economic inequalities from the other end of the scale.

A program of social insurance, as opposed to income support, generally makes sure that an individual has the responsibility of looking after himself if he can. It is, in fact, a kind of standardized saving against emergencies and it still maintains some relation between the work a man does and the money he gets for it. So, in most cases, social insurance should be the basis for any transfer program; and income-support measures, which are much closer to "something for nothing," should be kept for those cases in which social insurance won't work.

VI.2 THE GUARANTEED ANNUAL INCOME

The case for a guaranteed annual income is unassailable. Many people will always be unable to survive on the terms of the labour market; and these people have a right to dignity, decency and a standard of living that will allow them to enjoy the liberties of a democracy.

The idea of a guaranteed annual income is hardly radical. It has been suggested, in fact, as the basis of a system in which government would actually do less for the individual than it does now. Robert Theobald, an American authority on the guaranteed annual income, points out that even the conservative economist Milton Friedman approves of the scheme:

> Professor Friedman hopes that once such an allowance is available, society would not only cease to demand the introduction of further measures of government intervention, but would acquiesce in the dismantling of the vast majority of the measures already in existence that were passed to help those less able than themselves.[1]

This is not to say that a guaranteed annual income is a good thing because both liberals and conservatives approve of it. For a guaranteed annual income of the kind Friedman would like to see, one that provides an income floor of only $1600 for a family of four, would have nothing to do with changes in the pattern of inequality in North America, and would do more to perpetuate poverty than to eliminate it. The introduction of a guaranteed annual income of the wrong kind (or *any* guaranteed annual income, as a measure taken in isolation from other policies) would amount to a cop-out, an excuse for government to declare the problem of inequality irrelevant.

There will, of course, be tremendous political pressure on the Canadian federal government to adopt a guaranteed annual income of precisely that kind. The Canadian economist Trevor Lloyd has noted:

> In general terms, if the guaranteed income is applied at any level that ensures a decent standard of living it involves a large

1. Robert Theobald, *The Guaranteed Income: Next Step in Socio-Economic Evolution?* (New York: Doubleday, 1966), p. 18.

redistribution of income in an egalitarian direction, and it also involves freeing the able-bodied poor from the compulsion to accept any job available as a necessary condition of getting assistance from the government. The second point is even more radical than the first; taken together, they are too much for governments to face. On the other hand, a guaranteed income at a level somewhat below a decent standard of living has neither of these effects, and so is more acceptable to a state capitalist government. It need not cost very much, and as it keeps the recipients very close to the subsistence level it still leaves them with a very considerable incentive to work to get up to a reasonable standard of living. This is why, when Nixon's government in the United States and Heath's government in Britain suggest guaranteed income schemes, in both cases the suggested level of support is low enough to mean that nobody would live on it if they had any choice in the matter.[2]

In other words, a guaranteed annual income at a low level is a glorified welfare program. And a dangerous one — for its introduction would allow the Canadian government to make political hay out of a minor adjustment in bookkeeping.

The guaranteed annual income, to be useful, must have as its basis the concept of poverty as relative to affluence. In other words, the income level must be set at or above the relative line, and it must rise as that line rises, in relation to the overall well-being of the country.

The poverty line set out in chapter I needs adjustment before it can be used as the basis of a guaranteed annual income, however; for the poverty-income line amounts to one-half of the average income *before taxes*. (The before-tax poverty line was needed to estimate the extent of poverty; and the data were provided on a before-tax basis.) The income guarantee, however, should be one-half of the average income *after* taxes, adjusted for family size, since that represents spending power. Appendix III sets out the average living standard, after taxes, and the corresponding poverty-income

2. Trevor Lloyd, "State Capitalism and Socialism: The Problem of Government Handouts," in *Essays on the Left,* Laurier Lapierre et al eds. (Toronto: McClelland and Stewart, 1971), pp. 171-172.

line, or the basic income floor for families of various sizes at which a guaranteed annual income would be paid.

One common objection to schemes of this kind is that they discourage people from working. What the objectors mean by this is that the provision of a guaranteed annual income will have a bad effect on the national psyche, for people will no longer be *compelled* to work. This argument implies that the maintenance of poverty is essential to the well-being of the nation; for some people must be forced to work at ugly and degrading jobs, and they can be compelled to do so only if absolute deprivation is the sole alternative. (It also implies that the present welfare systems encourage people to work — which they do not.)

Compulsion of that kind is out of place in a democratic society. And, for that matter, so are the jobs that (it is argued) require compulsion; technology will increasingly replace human with mechanical drudgery. Furthermore, the compulsion may be inefficient. Robert Theobald points out that

> . . . the historical and anthropological record makes it clear that economic motivation is not the only way to get people to work — indeed there is considerable evidence that it is not necessarily the most effective way.[3]

Erich Fromm agrees that compulsion can be replaced — and in most cases compulsion already *has* been replaced:

> Material incentive is by no means the only incentive for work and effort. First of all there are other incentives; pride, social recognition, pleasure in work itself, etc.
> . . . Secondly, it is a fact that man, by nature, is not lazy, but on the contrary suffers from the results of inactivity. People might prefer not to work for one or two months, but the vast majority would beg for work, even if they were not paid for it.[4]

The results of a number of experiments with guaranteed-income schemes in the United States have suggested that guaranteed-income

3. Theobald, *Guaranteed Income,* p. 23.
4. Erich Fromm. "The Psychological Aspects of the Guaranteed Income," in Theobald, *Guaranteed Income,* pp. 186-187.

programs do not discourage people from working,[5] but may actually encourage many, perhaps by providing them with enough emotional security to hold a job.

Certainly, one of the objectives of all democratic societies should be the elimination of any policy that compels people to work or to starve, and the guaranteed income will free people from jobs that they cannot abide. But, at the same time, people should be allowed, and encouraged, to work at things they want to work at — not only because they will save the public money by doing so, but also because the idea of work is closely bound up with the idea of self-respect.

This will be possible only if there is a fairly high demand for labour. But it will also be possible only if a certain proportion of earnings can be retained by people who are receiving the guaranteed annual income. The costs of an income scheme skyrocket with each extra amount people can retain of the money they earn; but recipients should be allowed to keep at least forty per cent of their earnings. If that kind of exemption is not allowed, there will be no reason for low-income people to work.[6]

The mechanics of the guaranteed income are quite simple. Each family unit has a certain minimum income guarantee, according to its size. This is calculated through living-standard equivalence points, as shown in appendix II. The members of that family may then work, and keep two-fifths of their earnings; the other three-fifths will be deducted from their guaranteed income. Finally, if the members of the family earn enough, they pass the *break-even point*, at which they are earning enough not to need any money from the government.

For example: a family of four, in 1971, would be entitled to a guarantee of $4100; that's how much that family gets from the government if no money at all is earned. If the head of that family earns

5. These results are for urban centres only; the effects might be different in rural areas, where jobs of any attractiveness are scarce. For US results, see Harold W. Watts, "Adjusted and Extended Preliminary Results for the Urban Graduated Work Incentive Experiment" (University of Wisconsin: Institute for Research on Poverty, 1969), discussion paper 69-70.
6. There will, furthermore, be no reason for people to save for their old age, if the income from their savings will be taxed away from them completely. Some people have suggested that the old be given a higher subsidy, but no retention of other income; the same argument applies.

$1000 in the year, he gets to "keep" $400 of it; that is, $600 is deducted from his guaranteed income by the government, which reduces his government income to ($4100 minus $600) $3500. His *final* income, from the government and his earnings combined, comes to ($3500 plus $1000, or $4100 plus $400) about $4500.

If that family head earns $3000, his government income is reduced by $180, and he keeps $1200 on the deal; so his government income is $4100 minus $1800) $2300; and his final income ($4100 plus $1200) is $5300.

If that family head earns $6900 or so, however, he has reached the break-even point at which sixty per cent of his income ($4100) equals the amount of guaranteed income he is eligible for.

There are, then, three figures to be kept in mind; the *basic guarantee,* which is the poverty-line living standard for any family size; the *marginal transfer rate,* which is the amount the government takes from earnings of families; and the *break-even point,* at which the amount of subsidy given by the government equals the amount taken by the government from earnings. Appendix II sets up the relationship in graphic form.

Two real problems — as opposed to the phony "destruction of the work-ethic" problem — arise here.

First, the tax structure of Canada will have to be modified to allow for the guaranteed annual income, or the whole idea of marginal transfer rates, break-even point, and so on, will be lost. For if people are taxed below the break-even point, the government will in effect be taxing their incomes twice — once to recover the guaranteed-income subsidy, and a second time for straight tax purposes. This means that instead of keeping forty cents out of every dollar earned, people working and receiving part of the guaranteed annual income will be keeping much less — possibly as little as fifteen cents or so. The solution, of course, is to raise tax exemptions to the break-even point — that is, not to charge anybody any money for taxes until they're beyond the point of needing any subsidy from the government.

Second — and this is not a mathematical problem, but a political one — is the question of subsidies for the young. Certainly there would be a violent storm of protest if children became eligible for the guaranteed income when they were sixteen, and a lot of them dropped out of school; but unquestionably, that is what a lot of them would do.

To some extent, the problem looks bigger than it is. Most young people, for better or worse, still accept the consumer society, and want to get ahead in it; the "youth culture" — that is, the one everybody worries about — is still the province of a minority. Furthermore, there is some reason to think that some of the young people who don't want to work are only beating technology to the gun, and are finding something useful to do with themselves before the machines take over.

We will quite frankly have to duck this one. Or, as the politicians would say, an experimental approach is required; but even if members of the counter-culture begin to rip off guaranteed annual incomes in large numbers, the solution is not necessarily to remove them from the rolls, but to attempt to make satisfactory work and training available to them. They are, after all, citizens; and if enough of them find work pointless, then the nature of work itself will have to be changed.

Even for people over twenty-five, the assessment of need will not be determined simply on the basis of income. For living standards — and poverty is relative to those standards — are not determined only by money income.

In the next section, it will be suggested that taxation ought properly to take into account a number of things that are not taxable at present, in the sense that they amount to a "command over resources." The resources of the poor are already checked thoroughly before much government help is extended to them, but it is important to remember that rent-free housing should be counted as income. And, if possible, fringe benefits from employment, and produce from family farms, should be counted as well.

The most important of the missing components, however, from the point of view of fair measurement, is wealth. There has been some resistance to taking wealth into account in the calculation of living standards, and not only from the wealthy — for, as is explained in the next section, such calculations are difficult, and finally arbitrary. But some basis for measurement — and for taxation — is essential, and a fair one might be to consider five per cent of net assets part of a family's annual standard of living. This five per cent measurement would be used not only for tax purposes, but also in the determination of eligibility for the guaranteed annual income.

If eligibility for government help is to be influenced by non-money income and wealth, then any estimation of the average living standard should be as well. Appendix III is based *only* on money income, and even that is under-reported by about five per cent, as noted in chapter I — which means that the poverty line in chapter I is below the mark even in terms of money income, and greatly below the mark set by a living standard that includes wealth, property, and so on. As these measurements are added into the calculation of the average living standard, that standard — and the poverty line, and the guaranteed annual income — will rise.

It is important to use the family as a basis for these measurements. Living in a household is considerably cheaper than living on your own; and there is no reason to pay a separate guaranteed annual income to a mother living in the house of her rich son. Furthermore, a little work will have to be done on the taxation of gifts between members of family units, so that the son of rich parents does not receive both support from his father and a guaranteed income while he toots around college in a sports car — a situation that might explode the whole program as far as the general public is concerned.

(At this point, it might be noted that the poor are unlikely to be encouraged to raise larger families by a guaranteed annual income; family and youth allowances haven't increased the birth rate, as a Brookings Institution study makes clear.[7] And so there is no reason to restrict a measurement of the poverty line — or the benefit level of a guaranteed income — to a certain number of children, as the Economic Council of Canada poverty line does; children exist, and cost money, whether one approves of them or not.)

The usual government response to any proposal for a guaranteed annual income is that we can't afford it, or, if we can afford it, that it would be inflationary. Demonstrably, we can afford it, or we could if we were less afraid of stepping on some corporate toes; and the inflation involved can be prevented.

As long as the program is paid for from taxes, and not through

7. See Christopher Green, *Negative Income Taxes and the Poverty Problem* (Washington: Brookings Institution, 1967), pp. 47-48, 130-133.

budget deficits, the scheme will not be inflationary; most consequences of the redistribution involved could be softened by phasing the program in over three years.

One special result of the sudden redistribution of a lot of money from the rich to the poor might be a sharp increase in the price of housing, which would be inflationary in itself, and would also blunt the point of the entire program; so some form of rent control, at least on older housing, might be necessary.[8]

Many businessmen worry about the effects of a guaranteed annual income on regional economies that pay low wages; workers might suddenly demand higher wages, and destroy jobs where they are needed most. Certainly higher wages will have to be paid, and there's nothing wrong with that. But there will also be a lot more money, and a lot more consumer demand, floating around in the depressed regions, which will stimulate the industries of the area, which produce for the local market. Workers with more security will be in a better position to look around for high-paying jobs, and go after them; so employers will have to start competing to keep workers in the area at all. The general rise in wages in depressed regions should be balanced by increased demand and, therefore, increased volume and profit, without large price increases. All things considered, the effect of a guaranteed annual income can only be beneficial for depressed regions; so there should be no variation in guaranteed-income payments for residents of those areas.

The guaranteed annual income, then, can act as an economic lever to improve conditions in depressed and underdeveloped areas. But, primarily, it is the bottom level of a series of social-security programs for Canada — programs that include the Canada Pension Plan, for example, and Unemployment Insurance. Only when these programs prove inadequate for an individual will the guaranteed annual income come into use.

There may be initial hitches in co-ordinating the guaranteed income with existing programs, or even with the improved programs; workers in jobs that pay less than poverty-line wages will have a real incentive to try to get on to the unemployment-insurance and guaranteed-annual-income combination. (This is not necessarily disastrous, for it will tend to push wages up to a level higher

8. See IV.6.

than the poverty line, and so will act less as an employee incentive than an employer incentive.)

It is fairly clear, then, who should get the guaranteed annual income, how much it should pay for each person, and how it could pay off for the country's economy; but there remains one important technical question. How is it to be delivered?

This bothers people, and it's not hard to see why. There are two main proposals, and they both sound awkward — the negative income tax, and the demogrant.

The negative income tax asks people to declare themselves in need; the Department of Finance checks what they have been earning over the previous period, and then pays them the appropriate amount.

This involves trouble, probably more trouble than it's worth. For one thing, people would have to be in need for some time before it could be estimated how much they were likely to require — a mechanism for emergency help would have to be set up, and that would very likely be as messy as the present welfare system. Or, under a tax-credit version of this approach, applicants could forecast their income for the year and receive payments on that basis, which would be cumbersome and would also invite retrieval problems or swindle. In any case, the applicant would still have to file for his benefits in a rather complicated manner, and the system would retain at least a shadow of the welfare system's stigma.

The second alternative sounds unlikely, but would in fact work better. Under a demogrant approach, everybody would be given an income subsidy, and then people who didn't need it would have it taxed back from them, either through a special tax or through a revision of the whole tax system. The retrieval would be done through payroll check-offs, in exactly the same way taxes are collected now, so there would be no build-up of loose money that might be spent before it is retrieved.

This would not involve application, would be basically fair and a lot less trouble to administer. And it would finally give people access to the money they need, without picking them out of the population and marking them as poor.

The costs of a guaranteed annual income, as noted above, vary tremendously with the marginal transfer rate, or the amount the government takes from the money recipients earn. At a marginal transfer rate of sixty per cent — in which the recipient keeps forty per cent of his earnings — the total cost of the program itself, installed, checked and running, would be about 2.3 per cent of yearly GNP. That sounds astronomical.

These costs are high, simply because a guaranteed annual income, at any reasonable level, is extremely expensive when unemployment is high, when there is no adequate social insurance, and when the economy is victimizing a lot of people. If other structural measures were introduced, the guaranteed annual income would not be needed by as many people, and costs would fall drastically.

The demogrant approach — paying out money to everyone and then taxing it back from people with high incomes — would not necessarily cost more than the negative income tax if payments were retrieved on a weekly or monthly basis, and would probably, in fact, cost less.

VI.3 A SOCIAL-INSURANCE PACKAGE

The guaranteed annual income should draw a line below which nobody, single or member of a family, will be allowed to fall. But the guaranteed income is only the bottom layer of a number of other programs that prevent workers from falling to the poverty line in the first place. Some of these programs are structural policies, which ensure demand for labour and so prevent large-scale unemployment, and training programs, which help workers to cope with jobs of increasing complexity. Others are programs of social insurance, which help workers to maintain their standards of living when they do become unemployed or are disabled or retire.

Up to a point, social-insurance schemes — to which workers contribute premiums, and receive benefits when they need them — work better than noncontributory programs like the guaranteed income. They are a lot less expensive for the public, for one thing; and they emphasize the relationship between the worker and his job, rather than the worker and his government. In a healthy economy, these social-insurance programs would allow a worker and his employer to make sure that his standard of living will not be destroyed, either in the short or the long term, by unemployment, sickness or old age, and that he will not be forced down to dependence on the guaranteed annual income alone.

There are two basic parts to the social-insurance package: Unemployment Insurance and the Canada Pension Plan. The insurance programs should work on a rough actuarial basis; that is, people should pay into the scheme, on the average, approximately as much as they are going to get out of it, plus a bit more to pay for the scheme's overhead. Insurance companies that pay out more in benefits to people than they take in in premiums from people go broke. Insurance companies that take in more than they pay out make a profit. (About ninety-nine out of one hundred insurance companies get the knack of this with very little trouble.)

And the benefits from both programs combined with the guaranteed annual income should be roughly in line with the living standards of the people who pay into them. The Canada Pension Plan should help ensure that a worker does not go broke, or suffer hardship, when he retires or is disabled; Unemployment Insurance should do the same for a worker who is laid off.

There is no reason why social-insurance schemes cannot meet both conditions, if the worker who stands to gain more through benefits — that is, a worker who has a relatively high standard of living — pays higher premiums than a worker with a lower standard of living, who will need less money to avoid disaster if he loses his job, or gets sick, or needs help for any other reason.[1] (Standard of living, of course, is not merely a function of earnings, but of guaranteed income payments *and* earnings.)

Furthermore, if these social-insurance programs are going to act as supplements to the guaranteed annual income, and help to keep the costs of that basic public program down, they should be set up to interlock with it.

This can be done, as far as Unemployment Insurance is con-

1. This is not as hard-hearted as it sounds. Social-insurance programs, by themselves, are insurance against the consequences of lost income, and work to maintain income, whatever that income may be. Recipients with low incomes have their benefits supplemented with large GAI payments as indicated; contributors with high incomes — who tend to pay high premiums — are less likely to lose their jobs, less likely to draw insurance, and so subsidize low-income recipients, who draw benefits more often.

cerned, if the benefits a worker may draw from the scheme run at fifty per cent of his previous earnings.[2]

That ratio, combined with the guaranteed-income payments, will make sure that the living standard of his family does not drop too sharply; but it will also make sure that he does not receive almost as much in benefits and guaranteed income combined as he did from his earnings and guaranteed income combined, and so has no reason to work until his benefits run out.

For example: a man who earns $115 a week (about $6000 a year), and is head of a family of four, would be entitled in 1971 to a guaranteed-income subsidy of about $10 per week — raising his earnings and guaranteed income combined to $125 per week.

When he lost his job, his Unemployment-Insurance benefits would come to $58 a week (half of $115); and, since for the purposes of the guaranteed annual income his benefits are counted as earnings, his guaranteed-annual-income payments would rise to $45 a week, for a total of $103 a week. So when he became unemployed, his income would drop from $125 a week to $103 a week, a loss stiff enough to give him incentive to find another job, but not so stiff as to destroy his family's standard of living completely.

If the worker were unemployed for so long that he ran out of benefits, his guaranteed-annual-income payment, by then his only source of income, would rise again, but not as high as his benefits and guaranteed-income payments combined; he would be allowed approximately $80 per week to provide the minimum standard of living for a family of four. But at least the drop would have been relatively gradual, and easier to adjust to.

The same general principle can be applied to the Canada Pension Plan, except that for purposes of the CPP the level of benefit is not calculated in the same way; the "earnings," rather, are taken as an average of the worker's standard of living over the last fifteen or twenty years, and adjusted for family size. (It is important to make sure that CPP benefit levels reflect the previous living standard —

2. At the moment, fifty per cent must be a maximum, because with a guaranteed income that makes up sixty per cent of the gap with respect to the break-even level, the benefits are close to the worker's previous earnings level as it is. Eventually, unemployment insurance should pick up a larger share of the burden. But first, the marginal transfer rate will have to drop from sixty per cent. A fifty per cent marginal transfer rate could probably be worked in combination with a 70/100 ratio of benefits to previous earnings.

which is affected by family size, and not merely by savings. And entitlement to CPP benefits should be detachable — that is, divorcées should not be left in the lurch.) This will smooth out any real decline in income towards the end of a worker's earning life, and will also allow for the fact that children leave families as they grow older, and that retired people generally live in units of one or two. Since no work incentive is required, the benefits for CPP may be higher in relation to previous living standard than in unemployment insurance.

The Canada Pension Plan, furthermore, can be expanded to incorporate the job the present Workmen's Compensation programs are now supposed to be doing, but aren't. A worker who is disabled should immediately be put on to Canada-Pension-Plan disability benefits, and he should be given the right to sue his employer for negligence, or, in fact, to sue anybody for negligence, regardless of his membership in the Workmen's Compensation plan. If the suit were successful, the plan could retrieve the benefits it had paid out before the settlement; if it were not, the disabled worker could continue on his plan benefits.

In addition, the plan administrators could be given the power to sue a negligent person or company on behalf of the disabled worker. In any case, some intervention is required into the present scheme of things, to redress the lopsided balance of resources between the worker and the Workmen's Compensation Boards. If the compensation programs are designed to be employers' insurance funds, then they should be that and nothing more.

This is not to say that the actuarial principle should be abandoned for social-insurance schemes; it should not be, for in times of reasonable labour demand, social-insurance programs should take most of the burden of looking after the needs of members of the work force, and leave to the guaranteed-annual-income scheme the main job of providing for those who are helpless, and bringing poor wages up to scratch. The changes could be phased in over time, to maintain the actuarial principle, with one exception: pensions under the Canada Pension Plan are so inadequate that they should be raised *now*, actuarial principle or not. This is particularly important if Old-Age Security and the Guaranteed Income Supplement are to be replaced by a guaranteed annual income.

This can be done by dipping into the present mammoth reserve of contributions being held in the form of low-yield provincial and municipal securities; provinces and municipalities should be supported in ways that do not affect the living standards of the elderly.

VI.4 AN EQUITABLE TAX SYSTEM

In Canada, the tax system and the welfare or social-security system have been kept apart.

The government has treated affluence as something quite different than poverty. In terms of taxation, affluence has been defined as the ability to pay a certain amount of tax; in terms of income maintenance, or welfare, there has always been a consideration of both the applicant's need for help, and anything he has that would allow him to get along without that help. For example, people in taxable ranges of income, affluent or not, may use several methods to reduce taxes — such as splitting them between two earners — that are not available to people applying for welfare. Assets are calculated for purposes of determining need for welfare, but are not considered to contribute to ability to pay taxes. One kind of bookkeeping, then, for affluence, and another for poverty.[1]

It is difficult, finally, to make a case for that separation. For wealth and poverty are closely related. Poverty is the lack of affluence; affluence, freedom from poverty.

So the tax system, which deals with affluence, and the income-maintenance program, which deals with poverty, should be seen as a package, the one an extension of the other. Both have to do with the determination of an individual's standard of living, which is, as noted in I.3, the core of any real consideration of economic equality and inequality.

1. One of the most revealing insights into the incompetence and biases of the federal government is that two major reforms, each dealing with one side of the same coin (income equality and taxes), have been effected, *totally* without co-ordination between the two. In addition to the different definitions of the family, and of income, noted above, the tax system taxes the poor, and taxes them hard. Moreover, in the white paper on taxation, it was promised that the problem of tax exemptions for children would be discussed in the white paper on income security; when that paper was released, there was no satisfactory discussion of the subject. This was either unforgivable absent-mindedness, or subterfuge, or simple callousness.

This involves looking at affluence in the same way as poverty. If assets, like a house, are considered in determining poverty (or in figuring out the welfare system's balance between means and need), then assets should be considered in determining affluence.

The key concept here is one of "command over resources." That is what the ability to pay taxes is, and it includes not only money income, but also assets that can be converted into money — things like mansions, Ferraris and purebred racehorses, as well as $20,000 homes and five-year-old Chevrolets.

The Royal Commission on Taxation considered that something like command over resources should be used as a basis for determining how much tax people should pay. The commission used the phrase "economic power," and defined it as

> . . . the power of a tax unit to command goods and services for personal use, whether the power is exercised or not.[2]

Or, in other words, economic power that is being sat on in the form of savings or great works of art or little places in the country is just as powerful as income. A man's economic power can be determined by the market value of a man's net assets at any particular point in time:

> The money he holds and the money he could obtain by exchanging his other assets for money, determines his personal command over goods and services.[3]

Of course, for most people, income makes up a great part of economic power. Income, of course, is not only the weekly pay cheque, but also, as the commission pointed out,[4] gifts and bequests, payments in kind, a gain in the value of property and the possession — that is, the personal use and enjoyment — of property that could have been rented to other people for income. This is all command over resources, and as such should be taxable, as far as it can be managed without clogging administrative machinery with detail.

2. Royal Commission on Taxation, *Report* 3 (Ottawa, 1966): 5.
3. Ibid, 3:22.
4. Ibid, 3:40.

It is, of course, difficult to find a way to get at this kind of wealth, figure out its value and tax it, without providing destructive loopholes. The royal commission threw up its hands in despair:

> If the tax base of each taxable unit were measured by the market value of each unit's assets . . . on a given date each year, the units that derived all of their income from personal effort could easily arrange their affairs so that they received and spent large sums between these dates and yet had no marketable assets on these dates. Such a tax-planning prodigal who received employment income could arrange to have little if any economic power on the crucial date if such a measure were used, despite the fact that he had exercised economic power whenever he consumed goods and services during the year. The financial and physical assets of the saver would, however, be taxed year after year.[5]

As the royal commission saw it, a playboy with a high income could arrange to fly to the Riviera at the end of the fiscal year, spend his substance in a week of delirium, and be conveniently (and happily) penniless when the Department of Finance inspectors arrived to assess his economic power for tax purposes. The responsible man, however, who soberly placed half his salary in a bank each week, would have to pay tax on it.

As far as the commission was concerned, the loopholes were unpluggable; and there was also the problem of estimating the values of skills (or "human capital," as the theoreticians would have it) as a part of assets. So the commission essentially jettisoned the idea of taxing economic power, and decided instead to tax *changes* in economic power.[6]

But the commission gave up too soon. The kind of tax evasion outlined above can be nailed by keeping track of income — as is done now — and including it in the estimate of the amount to be taxed. And wealth can be taxed simply by estimating its value and taxing part of it — say, the annuity value; that is, estimating the command of resources a man's wealth would give him for the rest of his life if he never increased it at all.[7] (There is a certain problem

5. Ibid, 3:22-23.
6. Ibid, 3:23-24, 27.
7. See Burton Weisbrod and W. Lee Hansen, "An Income Net-Worth Approach to Measuring Economic Welfare" (University of Wisconsin: Institute for Research on Poverty, 1968) 70—2543.

here with savings, which might wind up being taxed first as income, and then again as wealth. If necessary, savings can be made tax exempt, at least for those without significant wealth.) And there is no compelling reason to tax skills and knowledge as assets at all; a concentration of skills or knowledge is not undesirable, as a large concentration of wealth usually is.

Everyone should be assessed (and taxed) on an equal basis — on the basis of their command over resources, or their share of the country's total wealth and rewards. And that kind of taxation will tend to cut down on large concentrations of wealth.

Large chunks of economic power, or command over resources, concentrated in a single pair of hands can be dangerous. For one thing, they can be converted into political power:

> A main danger of great wealth concentration lies in the political sphere. Although the day is gone when the men who controlled the Southern Pacific railroad could also control the state of California, there remain some legislatures that can be, and occasionally are, bought for a price. Of greater importance is the differential advantage of those candidates for public office who obtain the support of wealthy people. Political campaigns above the local level have become highly expensive, largely eliminating potential candidates who cannot command, in some way or other, substantial financial backing. Wealthy groups are considerably overrepresented in legislative bodies because of the financial support they are prepared to give to candidates sympathetic to their views.[8]

And, according to R. H. Tawney, the power is increasingly concentrated in the hands of those who are already powerful:

> In an industrial society, the tendency of economic power is not to be dispersed among numerous small centres of energy, but to be massed in blocks. It is gathered at ganglia and nerve-centres, whose impulse gives motion to the organism, and whose aberrations or inactivity smite it with paralysis. The

8. Earl A. Rolph and George F. Break, *Public Finance* (New York: Ronald Press, 1961), p. 206.

number of those who take the decisions upon which the con-
duct of economic affairs and, therefore, the lives of their fellow-
men, depends is diminished; the number of those affected by
each decision is increased. . . . Lord Metchett smiles, and there
is sunshine in ten thousand homes. Mr. Morgan frowns and the
population of two continents is plunged in gloom.[9]

The concentration of great wealth in the hands of few people is
not only undemocratic, it is actively anti-democratic, and the tax
system should act so as to break up large concentrations of money
and power and pass them out to people who don't have much money
or power of their own.

The most obvious kind of tax that does this is the tax on inheritance and gifts. As James Meade has pointed out,[10] there are four
quite distinct alternative ways of setting up such taxes. First, one can
tax the estate itself, according to its size, and hit a large estate with
large taxes, no matter who it's going to. This does nothing at all to
encourage the man who owns the estate to pass it out to a large
number of people; the tax is the same, no matter who benefits by his
gift or will.

Or second, one could tax each individual gift or estate as it passed
into the hands of its recipient; a man who inherited a million dollars,
then, might pay a very stiff rate of taxation, but if the same million
dollars were carved up among a hundred people, each of them would
receive only $10,000, and their rates of taxation might be more
lenient. This will encourage rich people to carve up their estates and
gifts into smaller packages — but there is nothing in the idea to
encourage them to pass the money on to people who need it, and
even the smaller and more numerous estates and gifts of the rich
would probably go to people who were quite well off already.

Third, it would be possible to tax each gift or estate according to
its size, and according to how much the person getting it has already;
a rich man receiving $10,000 would pay a higher rate on it than a
poor man. This is more in line with the principle of ability to pay.

Fourth, it might be possible to keep a register of all gifts and
bequests received by any one person throughout his lifetime, and
tax those gifts progressively as the total rose.

9. Tawney, *Equality*, p. 161.
10. Meade, *Efficiency, Equality and Ownership*, pp. 55-58.

For Canada, the third alternative seems better than the fourth one, and certainly much better than the first two; for that kind of tax directly tackles concentrations of wealth and power, and sees to it that a substantial portion of all gifts and bequests gets passed either from the rich to the non-rich, or to the government.

Clearly, death taxation, set up in a sensible way, can be useful. But by themselves, estate and gift taxes will not be enough to break down large blocs of wealth and power. For one thing, there are too many ways to get around them. Furthermore, as American public-finance authorities Earl Rolph and George Break have pointed out:

> If the objective is the erosion of plutocracy, death taxation of the estate tax type is not especially efficient. Granted the value judgment that great wealth in the hands of a person is objectionable *per se,* there is no reason to wait until a person dies to begin undermining his wealth. An annual graduated net worth tax with a large exemption would be more effective than any death tax.[11]

Of course, there is no particular reason to give up on a death and gift tax simply because a net-worth or net-wealth tax is more efficient. Both of them are useful — in fact, both of them are essential.

There is nothing particularly startling about the idea of a yearly tax on net wealth. Some fourteen countries already have one, including West Germany, Switzerland and the Netherlands, which are not ordinarily considered to be bastions of radicalism. The exemption level for wealth — that is, the point above which wealth becomes taxable — varies from a low of $2500 in West Germany to a high of $16,000 in Sweden. Usually, the tax is a straight rate of one or two per cent; some countries, however, use a progressive tax on wealth that can go as high as 2½ per cent, as in India.[12]

The current wealth taxes are not tremendously important in terms of raising money; no country gets more than three per cent of its revenues from wealth tax. But the fact that these measures do exist is proof enough that wealth taxation is both possible and practical.

---

11. Rolph and Break, *Public Finance,* pp. 270-271.
12. James Cutt, "A Net Wealth Tax for Canada?" *Canadian Tax Journal* 17 (July-Aug. 1969): 299-302.

Rates of one and two per cent are not worth much in terms of breaking down concentrations of wealth and power; logically, the rates of taxation on the tremendously rich — those with holdings of $100 million or more — should go a lot higher than that. Rolph and Break have proposed a net-worth tax that amounts to about twenty per cent annually for wealth in that bracket,[13] because net-worth taxes are really the fairest and least disruptive kinds of taxation possible:

> Of the progressive tax devices known, a net worth tax is probably as neutral a tax device as can be devised. It is not likely to have significant effects upon the work-leisure choice [which means people don't stop working], upon the choice among the types of assets to own, or upon the choice between holding assets and consuming.[14]

When Rolph and Break argue that a net-worth tax will have no effects on the choice between holding assets and consuming — that is, between spending and saving — they part company with James Meade, who argues that:

> This tax like all progressive direct taxes is bound to reduce the level of private savings; it reduces the ability to accumulate capital by the richest citizens who are the most able to save.[15]

Meade is quite happy about that, however, for he feels that any reduction in the saving power of the most wealthy can be compensated for through an increase in the saving power of the less well-off, which can be stimulated by government.[16] Furthermore, the wealthy would find it very difficult to shift the effects of wealth taxation on to somebody else.[17] There is, as noted above, a problem in the area of savings, which may be taxed twice, once as income and a second time as assets. This can be gotten around by making savings, up to a point, exempt from income tax, but taxing them as wealth or assets; beyond a certain figure, however, savings should be taxable, whether

13. Rolph and Break, *Public Finance*, pp. 206-208.
14. Ibid, p. 201.
15. Meade, *Efficiency, Equality and Ownership*, p. 53.
16. Ibid, pp. 53-54.
17. Rolph and Break, *Public Finance*, pp. 203-204.

that amounts to double taxation or not, in order to break up massive concentrations of wealth.

This kind of taxation of wealth could be directly harmful only to those people — almost always elderly — who have a fair bit of property in the form of a house and land, but relatively little income to pay the taxes with. The answer for them would be to sell the house in return for a lifetime annuity and the right to live in the house; the return on the annuity would be taxed as income, not as wealth, and nobody would have to move. A government agency would be set up to take care of this, for people who wanted it, to avoid the exploitation of old people by private companies. The harshness of this kind of taxation can be relieved by an exemption based on family size.

As was indicated in the previous section, some sensible estimation of wealth will have to be made in order to operate the guaranteed annual income; otherwise, to take one example, some hot-shot with immense wealth but no income (say, in a year of business losses) could declare himself eligible for income assistance. So five per cent of all assets should be included as income in the estimation of both assessment of need and ability to pay taxes. There should be no exemption for wealth — in the context of a guaranteed income, exemptions become obsolete in any case — and that percentage should be progressive, rising to ten per cent at $1 million, fifteen per cent at $10 million, and up to twenty per cent at $100 million. Wealth tax, then, would become a part of the income tax, or, rather, the personal-living-standard tax, which would apply to wealth *and* income.

The previous section also indicated that the tax base, for the purposes of calculating eligibility for the guaranteed annual income, should include as much as possible — the equivalent of rent from owner-occupied houses, for example, which could be figured as a percentage of the value of the houses, which has already been estimated for the purposes of the wealth tax.

The guaranteed annual income will have to be integrated with the tax system in other ways. The break-even point, for example, will have to serve as the beginning of the tax bite, or people below the break-even point will be paying very stiff rates on their earnings. And the tax system will have to become a lot more progressive in the top ranges; for there is nothing to justify the screwy judgments that led the Royal Commission on Taxation through a daisy-chain of "discretionary" and "non-discretionary" types of expenses, and ended in a commission recommendation that progressive taxation stop at fifty per cent — for the rich, after all, really do *need* all that money. (When one is used to a Rolls-Royce, presumably riding in an Oldsmobile could cause severe psychic damage.)

Tax deductions, as opposed to tax exemptions, are another story. There should be only two kinds; for things like employment expenses, which are necessary and cannot be considered "command over resources," and should therefore be straight deductions; and for socially desirable expenses, like contributions to charity, which, if genuine, should be allowed small tax credits.

There could be a surcharge on income from investments to keep down the tax on other incomes. Such a tax would not seriously affect any incentive to work, and would tend to shift money from the rich to the poor; or at least it would discourage people from working less than a tax on employment income. And it would be primarily focussed on people with wealth. On that basis, capital gains should be taxed *more highly* than employment income, not half as much.

A few notes on regressive taxes, of which Canada could employ a lot fewer. Excise and sales taxes should be eliminated, except when they are used as part of an economic policy — that is, to make industries compensate government for expenditures forced on government by those industries: for the highways required by the automobile industry, for example, or for pollution programs. Under-handed subsidies to industry through tax concessions should be eliminated wholesale; any form of subsidy to industry should be visible. The recommendation by the Royal Commission on Taxation that corporation income tax be integrated with personal taxes paid by individuals should be put into law. (In other words, corporations should go tax-free; but individuals should be taxed on what they *get* from corporations.) And municipalities will have to be wheedled out of the property tax, which is, in any case, used largely — and improperly — for education. The property tax will have a parallel — and fairer — incarnation as a part of the tax on income and wealth. The shift from regressive to progressive taxation will, of course, require a new revenue-sharing formula between governments.

It is quite possible that if these changes were instituted, the wealthy would threaten not to be quite so wealthy any more, which would be fine. One area in which the wealthy might react to these changes would be to reduce their savings, an area that they dominate at the moment; and so future concentrations of wealth would be discouraged right at the start.

Instead of being bulldozéd by the threat of a sudden reduction in savings, government can do a lot more in the area of savings than it is doing now. For savings are important in the maintenance of a reasonable rate of economic growth. Savings should be stimulated, through tax incentives, among those who do not save much now: the poor. (This opens a number of intriguing areas of social investment — the Canada Development Corporation, in fact, could be made a corporate spearhead for the poor, allowing them to invest relatively small amounts of money, and still paying off in good returns. That would force other financial institutions that wished to remain competitive to open up their services to the poor.)

Policies should be introduced to make it easier for low-income people to buy their own houses, which can be seen as a form of saving, and which would improve the distribution of wealth. And public saving — that is, public spending on investment — can be used to make up for any reduction in private savings; the profit from such investment would benefit all Canadians, not just an affluent few.

These recommendations are made to head the government in the direction of real control over the economy — a control that can be used in the interests of all Canadians.

VI.5 SUMMARY

Employment and earnings policies are important; but they are not enough on their own. Canada needs a guaranteed annual income that would ensure that nobody, in any category, fell below the poverty line, and would allow low-income workers to retain some of their earnings.

This would be backed up by a compensation system of social insurance that would protect workers against a collapse of their living standards in time of unemployment and sickness, and all Canadians in retirement or disability.

Canada's tax system needs to be turned around. Affluence and poverty should be considered two aspects of the same measure of "command over resources," and the same standards should apply to those who will use the guaranteed annual income and those who will finance it. Wealth should be taxed. The personal income tax should be fitted to the guaranteed annual income, and it should be made a lot more progressive over the middle- and upper-income range. Canada should get out of the regressive-taxation business as much as possible; and savings policy should aim at a better distribution of wealth and its benefits.

VII

Public Services and the Poor

II.1 THE STARVATION OF THE PUBLIC SECTOR

Canadians prefer to spend their own money, rather than have governments spend it for them.

The proposed new tax legislation will remove some of the burden of payment for government services from the poorest of the poor, and will shift a little of that burden on to the affluent, but the proportion of national revenue available to the government will not rise by much. Canadians funnel a relatively small proportion of the proceeds of their national output into the public sector; other nations, particularly those of Western Europe, that have public political philosophies not markedly different from Canada's, assign up to half of the money available in the nation to public services.

There is a general prejudice in Canada in the area of public services, a prejudice fostered largely by the corporations. It centres around a convenient conviction that any service that is in the least profitable should be left to private interests, and public services should include only those areas that will not yield a buck.

When government begins to move into areas in which private interests are profitably entrenched — as in the recent controversy over auto insurance in Manitoba — all hell breaks loose, even though these areas may *obviously* be better arranged and organized in the public sector. The auto-insurance industry in Manitoba raised a large slush fund to fight the public bill. Saskatchewan doctors reacted the same way to the introduction of public medical insurance.

But full organization of public services in the public sector has yet to be attempted. In terms of national priorities, then, public services that benefit the poor are relatively low on the list. And the problem goes deeper. For even a superficial investigation of the condition of the poor in Canada indicates that they are not getting an even break in the two essential sectors of public service: education and health.

The health of the poor is fragile; the education available for their children is insufficient. And the social-service agencies that exist to overcome these disparities are disorganized, mismanaged and obsolete.

VII.2 EDUCATION

The links between education and affluence, and lack of education and poverty, are almost absolute.

The numbers are conclusive. At least two-thirds of the heads of low-income families have no more than elementary-school education.[1] Workers with little or no education lose their jobs faster and oftener than anyone else.[2] And over the last decade, the number of jobs available to high-school graduates has risen by about forty per cent, as it has *declined* by ten per cent for nongraduates.[3]

The connections are just as clear at the other end: a university degree will increase the lifetime earnings of its recipient by seventy-five per cent.[4] In other words, education is worth cold, hard cash. The route to security in a decent job at decent wages runs directly through the educational system.

That route has traditionally been closed to the children of the poor. As the Economic Council of Canada has pointed out, a poor man's child has the dice loaded against him:

The education levels of family heads were very likely influenced

1. Brief of the ECC to the Special Senate Committee on Poverty (22 Apr. 1969) 1:44. See also ECC, *Fifth Annual Review* (Ottawa, 1968), table 6-3, p. 111. Estimates of low income are by the ECC definition, based on the census of 1961, when the ECC poverty line was more generous than the Relative Poverty Line.
2. DBS, *Special Labour Force Study #1* (Ottawa, 1965), table 9, p. 14.
3. Brief of the Canadian Home and School and Parent-Teacher Federation to the Special Senate Committee on Poverty (19 Feb. 1970) 22:24.
4. DBS, *Profile of Poverty in Canada* (Ottawa, 1965), table E-1.

by the income and related circumstances of *their* parents; and their circumstances in turn are likely to influence the educational levels attained by their children.[5]

Education, then, has failed as a weapon against the transmission of poverty from one generation to another, despite a recent surge of public spending on schools. As Charles Taylor points out, the boom in educational investment has done little more than scratch the surface:

> Provincial education budgets have sky-rocketed in recent years. But this has done little more than dent the scandalous backwardness in this field evident in certain regions of Canada in absolute terms, and in Canada as a whole relative to the United States. Yet everyone recognizes that one of the keys to economic survival in the last third of the twentieth century is education; and everyone recognizes that it is an essential weapon against poverty among less-favoured sections of the population. If public spending has risen relative to the Gross National Product, this is because there was a big backlog of need to make up; and it is clear that this is not yet made up — far from it.[6]

There is real reason to suspect that increased spending did not arise primarily out of a desire to help the poor catch up to the rich; if the educational planners had anything like that in mind, their new programs did not reflect it. As one recent study points out, the children of the affluent got just as much, or more, than the children of the poor from the improved educational system:

> It is quite possible (although the evidence is by no means irrefutable) that the trend towards later school leaving between 1951 and 1961 raised the general level of educational attainment without effectively disturbing class differentials in educational opportunity, at least not at the extremes of the class spectrum.[7]

5. ECC, *Fifth Annual Review*, p. 116.
6. Taylor, *Pattern of Politics*, p. 40.
7. Robert M. Pike, *Accessibility to Higher Education in Canada* (Ottawa: Assoc. of Universities and Colleges of Canada, 1970), table 15, p. 60.

The children of the poor, then, are tending to stay in school one or two years longer than their parents; but so are the children of the rich. The gap between the two groups is not closing. As weapons against poverty, Canada's schools are a bust.

The reasons for the failure, as always, can be reduced to money: who spends how much, and on whom.

Canada's educational systems are constitutionally under provincial control, and the regional disparities that are evident in Canada's welfare systems and industrial structures show up very clearly in the schools. Education systems cost money, and, as table VII.2.i shows, only the affluent provinces can afford adequate ones.

As the Economic Council points out, expenditures on education "are generally correlated with average income levels in the various provinces."[8] In other words, you get what you pay for; if your child goes to school in Newfoundland, which can't pay for much, he's out of luck.

The varying levels of spending on education by the provinces have

TABLE VII.2.i
Operating expenditures per full-time student, by province

PROVINCE	Elementary and secondary [a] $	Universities [b] $
Newfoundland	180	1,460
PEI	250	
Nova Scotia	260	2,350
New Brunswick	250	1,900
Quebec	410	2,060
Ontario	420	3,130
Manitoba	350	2,340
Saskatchewan	410	2,290
Alberta	450	2,800
BC	440	2,420
Canada	390	2,490

a. Expenditure data for the calendar year 1966 are related to 1965—66 enrolment.
b. Based on data for the 1966—67 academic year.

Source: ECC *Sixth Annual Review*. (Ottawa, 1969), p137. Based on DBS data.

8. ECC, *Sixth Annual Review*, p. 137.

led to real differences in the quality of schooling available from one province to another. Any estimation of "quality" in an educational sense is difficult to come by. But, all other things being equal, a teacher with a university degree tends at least to be more informed than a teacher without one; and in 1966-67, the percentage of elementary-school teachers with university degrees ranged from twenty-five per cent in British Columbia to three per cent in Prince Edward Island.[9] In any case, the education systems in the poor provinces are a lot less successful in hanging on to the students beyond the term required by law, as table VII.2.ii shows.

TABLE VII.2.ii
Retention rates, by province

PROVINCE	1960-61	1967-68	Percentage change
Newfoundland	38	49	29
PEI	36	66	84
Nova Scotia	47	65	37
New Brunswick	44	60	35
Quebec	33	70	113
Ontario	56	73	32
Manitoba	61	80	32
Saskatchewan	56	70	26
Alberta	64	79	23
BC	68	82	22
Canada	50	71	42

Note: The retention rate refers to enrolment in grade 11 as a percentage of grade 2 enrolment nine years earlier. The data underlying the estimates have been adjusted to remove the effects of student migration.
Source: ECC, *Sixth Annual Review*, (Ottawa, 1969), p 128.

Schools in depressed provinces, then, tend to be of lower quality, and are on the average less successful than schools in the affluent provinces.

The federal government has resolutely refused to do anything much about this; there are no interprovincial equalization payments for education at the elementary- and secondary-school levels, with the exception of a trickle of funds for capital costs through Depart-

9. Ibid, p. 134.

ment of Regional Economic Expansion programs. Federal involvement in the financing of education is restricted to the universities — places the children of the poor usually don't get to. (A child whose parents earn $3000 per year has about one-quarter the chance to get to university of a child whose parents earn $12,000 per year.[10]) Provincial spending is also loaded in favour of university education; and that, statistically, amounts to a considerable public subsidy to the children of parents above the poverty line.

The disparities in the quality of education between one province and another are broad; the differences in the quality of education *within* each province, as the Economic Council points out,[11] may in fact be broader. Schools in the poor sections of Canada's large cities tend to be underequipped, understaffed and outmoded. The brief of the Canadian Teachers' Federation to the Special Senate Committee on Poverty noted:

> Many of the schools in Canada are community schools in the worst sense of that concept. The children of the poor may have few if any books at home — so why not omit libraries from their schools? They regularly play in the streets at home — so why make the school's playground significantly bigger or better? Surroundings at home may be drab and dreary and run-down — a depressing run-down school should fit in perfectly. Better to concentrate resources in the affluent areas, where the parents might otherwise complain.
>
> It will no doubt be pointed out that the disparities in facilities are accidental rather than intentional. While Canadian school systems were going through a period of rapid expansion in the nineteen-fifties and early sixties, funds were not available for replacing or renovating older schools. Moreover, it is a result of certain trends in urban development that the poor have fallen heir to the older, less adequate schools. And, finally, variable zoning requirements contribute to the perpetuation of small school grounds in the inner city by raising property values to commercial rates.

10. Home and School Federation, brief, 22:24.
11. ECC, *Sixth Annual Review*, p. 138.

It will no doubt be argued that replacement of inadequate facilities has begun. On the other hand, the process is hardly proceeding with undue haste.[12]

In some cities, substandard schools in poor areas may continue to be neglected because they are not successful — some educational administrators may suspect that expensive equipment will be wasted on the children of the poor. Certainly, many administrators don't expect that the poor will have much need for secondary education. John Sewell, an alderman from a low-income area of Toronto, told the Special Senate Committee on Poverty:

> In our ward there are 17 elementary schools. There is not one five-year high school. That is what education is about for the poor.[13]

Children in rural areas may even be worse off than children in the inner city. Table VII.2.iii, drawn up by the Canadian Council on Rural Development for the Senate committee on poverty, demonstrates that teachers in the country are markedly less qualified, in terms of university degrees, than teachers in the city.

Poor children then, are not receiving a fair share of public investment in education. And even the share they do get tends to do them little good. Education in Canada is designed by and for members of the middle class; it is aimed quite specifically at the "average" — that is, middle-class, middle-personality, middle-intelligence — child or adolescent. Textbooks promote a dream of suburban consumption. Discipline is geared towards the polite and submissive. In a brief to the Senate committee on poverty, staff members of the Duke of York public school in Toronto pointed out that this kind of set-up is of little use to the children of the poor:

> These children come to school sorely equipped to benefit from what could be called a standard educational program. They tend not to trust adults. They fear new experiences. They are not motivated towards academic learning. They settle differ-

12. Brief of the Canadian Teachers' Federation to the Senate Committee on Poverty (2 June 1970) 46:47.
13. Proceedings (11 Mar. 1970) 27:19.

TABLE VII.2.iii

Percentage of rural and urban elementary and secondary-school teachers with university degree for nine provinces,[1] 1967-68

PROVINCE	% of urban teachers with degree (s)	% of rural teachers with degree (s)	% of all teachers with degree (s)
Newfoundland	24.3	11.1	18.2
PEI	25.9	14.5	19.1
Nova Scotia	40.7	25.4	34.5
New Brunswick	30.3	14.3	23.6
Ontario	35.9	15.8	35.1
Manitoba	38.5	19.3	33.4
Saskatchewan	38.9	20.2	30.3
Alberta	49.0	30.2	44.2
BC	52.3	37.2	48.5
Canada	39.0	22.9	35.9

1. Comparative information not available for the province of Quebec.
Source: Brief of the Canadian Council of Rural Development to the Special Senate Committee on Poverty (5 Feb 1970) 18:51. Figures from DBS, Education Division.

ences by physical rather than verbal means. They are explosive in behaviour. They are not adequately rested or fed.[14]

In other words, children born in poverty do not grow up suburban. And a suburban school system, or a system built on suburban premises about education, is not equipped to deal with them — or they with it. This poses difficulties for the teachers; and Canadian teachers, by and large, have competed in avoiding them. The brief of the Canadian Teachers' Federation to the Senate committee on poverty makes the point:

> There has been a distinct reluctance on the part of teachers generally to seek or stay in schools in isolated areas or in schools where the children do not respond quickly to the usual teaching methods. This problem was compounded in the past through somewhat dishonest recruitment procedures which did

14. Brief of the staff members of the Duke of York Public School in Toronto to the Special Senate Committee on Poverty (Jan. 1970) 26:177-178.

not provide teachers with an honest picture of the situation they were likely to encounter.[15]

The teachers that do wind up working in slum areas become jailers for the children of men and women they despise:

> Teachers in schools for the poor do not usually live in the same area as their students. Thus they tend to look upon the adult community that surrounds the school from the point of view of outsiders, seeing the parents as shiftless, apathetic, lacking interest and responsibility, and, in general, inferior.[16]

Callousness towards the poor in general quickly becomes quite specific callousness towards poor students. Stories like this one, taken from the Catholic Women's League brief to the Senate committee on poverty, are fairly common:

> Young people from grade seven up must use large (about 10″ by 14″) triplicate forms to purchase their books and other needed supplies for school. It is not uncommon for their social status to be clearly announced over the PA systems. "All welfare students are reminded to come to the office for their vouchers at 3:30." The average young student will not get up and be humiliated in front of his friends and teachers, but if he does, he is not yet finished. He must have this large voucher filled in and then signed by the teacher or principal, then go to the department manager. This creates extra paper work and time, and often the harried teachers and clerks take out their anger by insulting the young student.[17]

15. Canadian Teachers' Federation, brief, 46:53.
16. Ibid, 46:54.
17. Brief of the Catholic Women's League of Canada to the Special Senate Committee on Poverty (3 Mar. 1970) 24:73. Another perspective on these attitudes may be found in Robert Rosenthal and Lenore F. Jackson, "Teacher Expectations for the Disadvantaged," *Scientific American* 218, no. 4 (April 1968): 19-23. The authors found that when teachers were told that certain children in their classes had been estimated to be of high potential, the performance of these children improved markedly; when children were not designated improved, the teachers tended to be critical of them and considered them "difficult." Rosenthal and Jackson concluded (p. 22), somewhat placidly, "It would seem that there are hazards in unpredicted intellectual growth." It may at least be hazarded that intellectual growth on the part of most slum children will be unpredicted and therefore discouraged.

For Indian children, or black children, or other visibly non-standard children, the economic inequality is intensified with a little extra stupidity. George Munroe, executive director of the Indian and Métis Friendship Centre in Winnipeg, told the Senate committee on poverty:

> They have always transported the Indian people from God knows where to somewhere 500 or 600 miles from their own home communities and this hasn't worked for the simple reason that the type of education these people get is completely unsuited to their special needs.[18]

Harold Cardinal — who was born in 1945 — describes his own education in his book *The Unjust Society:*

> In grade eight I found myself taking over the class because my teacher, a misfit, has-been or never-was sent out by his superiors from Quebec to teach savages in a wilderness school because he had failed utterly in civilization, couldn't speak English well enough to make himself understood. Naturally, he knew no Cree. When we protested . . . we were silenced as "ungrateful little savages who don't appreciate what is being done for you."[19]

Black children, in the Maritimes, get in school a taste of the blank lack of understanding they will experience in the outside world. Joseph Drummond, executive advisor of the New Brunswick Association for the Advancement of Coloured People, told the Special Senate Committee on Poverty:

> The school is all geared to the white majority. We have been neglected, sadly neglected, in the schools. It has been a calculated neglect. We have never learned anything about ourselves. When I came through the school system, the only thing you saw concerning black people was *Little Black Sambo*. After we

18. Brief of the Indian and Métis Friendship Association to the Special Senate Committee on Poverty (18 Nov. 1970) 7:12.
19. Cardinal, *Unjust Society*, 54.

reacted and they took that out, it left three lines in the history book: Black people are slaves. They could sing and dance. They were happy.[20]

The various improvements in the educational system that came about with the increased demand of the 1950s and 60s has not, then, done much good for the children of the poor. Schools in poor areas are inadequate; schools in depressed provinces are starved for funds; almost no attention is paid to the special needs of the poor, white, red, yellow, brown or black; and the result has been the continuation of those barriers that stand between the poor child and a decent education.

The human wastage involved here is incalculable. But certain figures do give some idea of the proportion of the failure visited on the poor who went to school before education became fashionable. Twenty per cent of the population of the northern Prairies have less than a grade-four education. And, in Canada as a whole, according to the 1961 census, there are over a million people over the age of fifteen who have had either no education at all or less than four years of it.[21]

The vast majority of these people are locked into the desperate indignity of the illiterate. Almost all of them are restricted to low-paying, low-security jobs. And very little is being done to ensure that their children will do better.

II.3 HEALTH

People who live in bad housing, who eat bad food and cannot afford decent clothing, get sick.

So the health of the poor is worse than the health of the affluent; and that deficiency can be traced directly to an economic system that will not allow them enough money to stay well.

The problem has been studied so often, and so thoroughly, that the poor have become sick of hearing about their own sickness.

20. Brief of the New Brunswick Association for the Advancement of Coloured People before the Special Senate Committee on Poverty (4 Aug. 1970) 61:39.
21. Brief of the Canadian Association for Adult Education to the Special Senate Committee on Poverty (3 Mar. 1970) 24:52.

Investigators have found consistently that the health of the poor in Canada is weak. Even — or especially — that of the babies:

> Children of the poor suffer more from ill health and run much greater risks of dying from illness and disease than do children from higher income groups. Across Canada there is a correlation between income levels and the likelihood of dying in infancy. Between 1959 and 1961, Ontario, with a per-capita income of $1,807, had an infant mortality rate of 23.5 and Newfoundland, with an income of $874, had a rate of 37.5.[1]

Some of those infants who survive suffer from diseases associated with the worst slum conditions of the nineteenth century. The incidence of rickets in children from three months to two years of age actually *increased* from 1962 to 1967; over five years, about fifty children with the disease were admitted annually to the Montreal General Hospital alone.[2]

Rickets is a direct result of an insufficient diet, as are anemia, low resistance to infectious diseases, and as mental illness and — perhaps most important — mental retardation[3] may be as well. (The poor performance of many low-income children in the school systems may be determined by their diets before they even get to school.) And this kind of deficiency, along with the others associated with poverty, plague the poor throughout their lives. Pregnant women are as likely to be damaged as their unborn children:

> The risk of malnutrition is greater for specific population groups, due to increased needs at certain stages of life; pregnant and nursing women are among the most vulnerable. A Canadian study has shown that malnutrition was prevalent among a sample of pregnant women in low-income groups in Montreal.[4]

But the problems of bad health have their most drastic effects on

1. Robin F. Badgley and Samuel Wolfe, *Doctors' Strike* (Toronto: Macmillan, 1967), p. 147.
2. Canada Department of National Health and Welfare, brief, 23:192.
3. Ibid, 23:62.
4. Royal Commission on the Status of Women, *Report,* p. 316. The study referred to may be found in Montreal Diet Dispensary, "A Preliminary Report of a Nutrition Study on Public Maternity Patients," mimeographed (Montreal, 1970).

the poor when they involve family wage earners, and so cause loss of essential income; a survey of Canadian sickness has shown that low-income male workers lose much more time in terms of "disability days," than comparable working men with higher incomes.[5]

The patterns of ill health among specific groups of the poor are even more striking. Canada's native peoples, for example, are much more vulnerable to disease and early death than other Canadians.

The effects of a marginal existence, which is the common experience of most Indians and Eskimos, are apparent in related health statistics.

The infant mortality rate in 1968 was 21 per 1,000 live births for all Canadians, 49 per 1,000 for Indians, and 89 per 1,000 for Eskimos. Among Indians as a whole, infant mortality has declined during the past decade from three times the national rate to just over twice the rate.

. . . in 1968, 56 per cent of all Eskimo deaths, and 35 per cent of all Indian deaths, involved children under five years old. High death rates reported for Indian and Eskimo babies occurred in spite of the fact that 90.6 per cent of all births in the Northern Region took place in medical institutions under professional supervision. The chief causes of early mortality were respiratory infections such as pneumonia and bronchitis, followed by gastro-enteritis and associated disorders.[6]

The health of the poor in general, and of Canada's native people in particular, is greatly below the level enjoyed by Canada's affluent. And this gap has persisted, in spite of the fact that Canada's public spending on health has risen markedly over the last decade. In 1959-60, government expenditures on health amounted to about 2.3 per cent of Canada's gross national product; by 1968-69, that expenditure had almost doubled, to 4.0 per cent. (Expenditures on other social-welfare programs remained relatively constant, at 6.2 and 6.6 per cent respectively.[7])

5. The Canadian Sickness Survey, cited in the brief of the Canadian Medical Association to the Special Senate Committee on Poverty (28 May 1970) 45:41. The loss of income is almost never compensated for through insurance, and is therefore absolute. See the brief of the Canadian Welfare Council, 12:470.
6. Canada Department of National Health and Welfare, brief, pp. 50-51.
7. Ibid., table 3, p. 20.

There are a number of reasons for this situation.

First, the poor are less likely than the affluent to recognize symptoms like loss of weight, lumps in the breast or abdomen, or blood in stools or urine as signals serious enough to consult a doctor.[8] So the poor are less likely to seek out medical help for problems that are not totally incapacitating, even though those problems may develop into crippling ones later on.

Second, a great many doctors and other medical personnel tend to be rather less sympathetic towards the indigent patient than the wealthy one. This lack of empathy may have a lot to do with the fact that very few poor people become doctors. Bernard Blishen, former research director of the Hall commission on health services, has written:

> In Canada, both general practitioners and specialists tend to come from families in which the father has a managerial or professional occupation. This tendency is particularly evident in the case of specialists. When comparing the occupational distribution of the fathers of present-day physicians with that of the total labour force, it is evident that the managerial and professional occupations are over represented. All other occupations are under represented.[9]

Blishen's analysis is in fact a severe understatement; for the statistics upon which he bases his opinion show that, of a sample of doctors who entered medical school in 1962, 54.4 per cent of the general practitioners and 65.8 per cent of the specialists were children of managerial or professional men, and only 2.3 and 1.5 per cent were the children of labourers.[10]

People who become doctors, then, are urban and middle class, and like to stick to cities and comforts — which contributes directly to medical shortages in rural areas, an anomaly the British Columbia government has been attempting to remedy by law.

The medical schools themselves, through rigorous admission

---

8. Bernard R. Blishen, *Doctors and Doctrines* (Toronto: University of Toronto Press, 1969), table 1, p. 19. Some symptoms may be recognized as dangerous, but go untreated because there is no money to pay for medical consultation.
9. Ibid, p. 34.
10. Ibid, table 4, p. 33.

procedures, ensure that the children of the affluent get a head start — even though the doctors being produced may not be much good for any humane practice of medicine. Dr. Daniel Cappon, of the Canadian Medical Association, told the Senate committee on poverty:

> We have determined that one of the great drawbacks to doctors becoming family practitioners — and we did not put this on the record — is the question of medical student selection. When you have got to make 80 or 85 per cent to get into Ontario medical schools, for instance, you have to be an introverted book-worm who is not much good in general practice, and they want you to have degrees and laboratory and medical facilities, but nothing to do with human beings.[11]

This kind of procedure produces a medical caste that has little comprehension of the social needs of its clients. Donald Tansley, the original chairman of the Saskatchewan Medical Care Commission, who bucked that province's doctors through a bitter medical strike over public health insurance, later commented:

> I have never encountered a group which has so little understanding of the normal social process operating in our society. . . . One can only speculate as to why the profession should have such a gap in its knowledge. It can be attributed in part to the time required for the study of technical subjects in medical schools [and] the fact that doctors work long hours which leaves little time for keeping abreast of developments in other fields. . . . Society as a whole is partly responsible for placing the members of the profession in an exalted position and letting them believe for so many years that their word in any field should be the final word.[12]

Certain events during the medical strike in Saskatchewan revealed that the doctors' associations were only the spearhead of an offensive by the professional and managerial classes to deny *any* public protection against the effects of disease:

11. Canadian Medical Assoc., brief, 45:38.
12. Badgley and Wolfe, *Doctors' Strike,* p. 100.

The trend of support and opposition varied by the social class or position of correspondents whose letters were published in newspapers. For example, of signed letters printed in one large daily paper, 71 per cent of the writers who were professionals or managers, or who held comparable positions, were against the legislation; in contrast, 75 per cent of those whose work ranged from unskilled to skilled supported the medical plan.[13]

And the social convictions of some doctors still lead to episodes of routine brutality. Claire St. Aubin, of the Pointe Claire Community Clinic in Quebec, told the Senate committee on poverty:

> There are many doctors in Verdun, which is a town right beside Pointe Claire, and many of those doctors refuse the card from people on welfare. I know this to be a fact, because I know a woman who died of that. She was so shy she did not ask for anyone else to come. They had to get her to the hospital at the last minute, and she died two days later.[14]

The success of the government in Saskatchewan in setting up a medical-insurance program, and subsequent successes in other provinces, should have helped to narrow the gap between the poor and the health services they need. In fact, there are still serious shortcomings in these programs. The brief of the federal Department of Health and Welfare to the Senate committee on poverty pointed out:

> Levies in Ontario, Alberta and British Columbia are high enough to constitute a significant percentage of disposable income for families just above the cut-off lines entitling them to premium subsidies. Voluntary enrolment, as in British Columbia and for individuals not in employee groups in Ontario, can result in failure of some families to enrol because the demands made upon them for food, shelter, transportation, and clothing may be even more immediate. Compulsory enrol-

13. Ibid, p. 74.
14. Brief of the Pointe Claire Community Clinic to the Special Senate Committee on Poverty (28 May 1970) 45:26.

ment in Alberta can result in a diversion of available funds from spending requirements that marginal-income families may believe to be even more pressing, such as food.[15]

Furthermore, specific services for the poor, or services that the poor are more likely to need than anyone else, are still extremely scarce. Even traditional programs of this kind are running into trouble:

> In 1966, 8.6 per cent of the total number of professional nurses employed in Canada were working in public health (general public health, schools, occupational health, visiting nursing). In 1968, this figure was only 8.3 per cent and of these only 6 per cent were in general public health and visiting nurse positions. If the visiting nurse services are examined separately, it is seen that the percentage has also decreased from 1.5 per cent to 1 per cent in 1965.[16]

And the poor in isolated areas are still short of services of any kind. The brief of the Canadian Nurses' Association to the Senate committee on poverty gave an example:

> When a nurse sympathizes with a mother who says she will have to start milking the cows at 4:00 a.m. in order to catch the bus at 7:30 a.m. to keep a 9 o'clock appointment at an out-patient clinic miles away in the city, where the nurse knows she will probably be left to wait until 11:00 a.m. before she is seen, the nurse is well aware of the inaccessibility of health services.[17]

The pressures of poverty have drastic effects on the mental health of the poor. A number of studies have found that the incidence of mental illness increases as social status declines;[18] and this may be

15. Canada Department of National Health and Welfare, brief, 23:117.
16. Brief of the Canadian Nurses' Association to the Senate Committee on Poverty (4 June 1970) 47:43.
17. Ibid, 47:40.
18. See John A. Clausen, "Mental Disorders," in *Contemporary Social Problems,* Robert K. Merton and Robert A. Nisbet eds. (New York: Harcourt, Brace & World, 1961).

related to the fact that low-income workers are usually considered much more ill than affluent patients with the same symptoms.[19] One survey notes that:

> There is a definite tendency to induce disturbed persons in Classes I or II (upper classes) in a more gentle and "insightful" way than is the practice in class IV (working) and especially class V (unskilled), when direct, authoritative, compulsory and at times coercive brutal methods are used.[20]

Generally, facilities for treatment of mental illness are much better for the affluent than for the poor, who find it difficult to obtain treatment for anything short of complete breakdown. When that breakdown occurs, the poor are more likely to be given shock treatment than therapy.[21]

The gap between the health services available to the poor and the services available to the affluent is not being closed. Medical personnel tend to be somewhat uninterested in their problems. Government medical-insurance programs are still defective, and cause hardship for many poor families. And specific programs to overcome the difficulties — outreach programs, either rural or urban, increased public-health facilities, and so on — are still rudimentary.

If you are poor — and especially if you are Eskimo or Indian — you are likely to get sick sooner than the rich. Your children are more likely to die than the children of the affluent. And very little is being done about it.

VII.4 THE SOCIAL SERVICES

The poor do not have, and have never had, equal access to publicly provided services like the educational and health systems.

---

19. See August B. Hollingshead and Frederick C. Redlick, *Social Class and Mental Illness: A Community Study* (New York: John Wiley and Sons, 1958).
20. Ibid, p. 192.
21. Ibid, pp. 267, 289. For Canadian data, see "Social and Mental Health Survey" (Montreal: Urban Social Redevelopment Project, 1966), in Mann, *Poverty and Social Policy.*

Some of the barriers, like premiums for health care, are quite simply financial. Other barriers are consequences of lack of money that have gathered a momentum of their own: alcoholism, for example, is associated with poverty because alcohol, for many poor people, represents their sole, temporary escape from a life of drudgery — even though the incidence of alcoholism seems to be similar for all classes.

Social-service agencies — organizations both publicly and privately supported — exist to try to help people with problems they can't handle. In every city in Canada there are a number of these agencies, which employ large numbers of people in an attempt to solve, or at least to help out with, those problems of the poor that do not immediately yield to a transfusion of cash.

These agencies are numerous, and cover a range of purposes: there are agencies to visit the elderly, provide psychiatric assistance, protect abused children, treat alcoholism, sort used clothing, fix teeth and do a variety of other useful things.

The performance of these agencies is largely a mystery. Information about them is scarce, and getting information from them is difficult. What they are supposed to be doing, however, is fairly clear: their job is to bridge the gap between the poor and the services the poor need — and to provide specific answers to specific problems of the poor.

A great many such agencies are compromised into ineffectiveness from the very beginning. They are the organizations that are connected to the welfare system; whose services are forced on those poor people who are, for one reason or another, on relief. The Manitoba brief to the Senate committee on poverty pointed out just how senseless that was:

> At the present time, we submit an applicant for public assistance to a long, degrading application and interview process before granting financial assistance. The purpose of this procedure, in addition to establishing need, is to determine what social services such as personal or family counselling, health services, employment assistance, vocational retraining or other rehabilitative services are required by the applicant. The acceptance of these services is then established as a pre- or co-requisite to the receipt of financial assistance.

> This approach fails to recognize two important facts. First, not all persons who require financial assistance also require social services. This point follows directly from a recognition of the societal causes of poverty. Second, social services are of minimal benefit if entered into under compulsion. Voluntarily accepted social services are much more likely to assist the individual person.[1]

In other words, people who apply for welfare are treated to a helping of compulsory advice about the state of their psyches, the inadequacy of their personalties and the shape their families are in. The advice may or may not be sensible, but it is almost always, and quite rightly, resented.

The welfare applicant treats this process as further proof — if any more were needed — that welfare workers consider his lack of money to be a kind of flaw of character. Of course, welfare workers do tend to think of him in precisely that way; social services are provided, not from some disinterested compassion for the suffering of poor families, but from a bookkeeper's desire to get them off the welfare rolls.

And, of course, if and when the family manages to become self-supporting, the problem is considered to be solved, and the services of the welfare-department social worker are customarily withdrawn. This results in a kind of intermittent treatment that does little good, and results in increased depression, for families who are consistently beaten by the labour market.

The process is just as damaging to the people who give the advice as to the people who have to listen to it. Most social workers bail out of welfare-department work fairly quickly. The ones who remain retreat into one of two defensive attitudes, blaming either the system that makes their work ineffective, which is correct but solves nothing by itself, or blaming the poor who fail to respond to their work, which is not only wrong but makes the whole problem worse.

The problem of hostility on the part of social workers is not restricted to the welfare system, but it is strongest there. The poor are faced with an unspoken assumption that they are inadequate

1. Proceedings (4 Nov. 1970) 9:32.

because they are not able to maintain themselves at a middle-class level, and it is assumed that the job of a social-service agency is to turn substandard material into middle-class citizens. There is no questioning of middle-class values. These are assumed, always, to be supreme.

Not all social-service agencies are directly involved with welfare departments, and it might be expected that the ones that aren't are performing more effectively. It is difficult to tell. For almost all agencies are working in a kind of information vacuum. They have no real idea of their performance in relation to social-work agencies in other fields, or in relation to nonprofessional institutions (schools, for example) or even in relation to other organizations that are tackling the same problems they are.

This conclusion is drawn from the Winnipeg social-service audit, which is, to date, the most complete inventory of social services that has ever been undertaken in Canada. The Winnipeg audit set out to discover just how the various social-service agencies in that city were working, what they were doing, what they thought they were supposed to be doing and whether the whole network was accomplishing much good. The audit quickly came to the conclusion that the city's agencies were in a serious mess:

> There is not, in Metropolitan Winnipeg at the present time, comprehensive social-welfare planning; neither is there provincial-wide comprehensive planning. Planning has been undertaken up to the present time by all the agencies within their own sphere of operation. . . . The basic limitation at present is that what planning is taking place is unilateral; it lacks comprehensiveness. There are no commonly-agreed-upon goals, and the information and analysis upon which sound decision-making depends are not presently available. There is not sufficient co-operation in social planning with planning in other fields, such as education and employment.[2]

The primary trouble, then, was not a lack of money, or even necessarily a lack of trained personnel; the difficulty was that nobody

2. Social Services Audit Inc., *Report* (Winnipeg, 1969), p. 24.

had any overall sense of where social-service agencies in Winnipeg were going, or even, in fact, what was going on at the time. This, predictably, was not working out well for the customers:

> With a total of 278 health, welfare and recreation agencies in Metropolitan Winnipeg, it is to be expected that people in need of help are baffled as to where to go. Agencies . . . confirmed the fact that clients are often frustrated and demoralized, by going from door to door, office to office, trying to find their way through the labyrinth. . . .
>
> The effect of this lack of follow-up and continuity means that clients get lost in the gaps between agencies, miss services where connections break down, and never do get their problems resolved. As an example, a counselling agency may refer an individual to a public welfare office for financial assistance, and not check back to see that the needed help was given.[3]

The potential for chaos in this situation is obvious, and fully realized. The audit reported that the agencies often became as confused as their clients:

> One family, or even one individual, may, and often does, receive help from three, four or even six agencies at any one time. Apart from the confusion and fragmentation that can result from this for the family, it means costly duplication of records and administrative structures. Time and money are wasted in the intricacies of referral, repetition of records, and reports.[4]

This buggy-whip approach to administration and organization within the social-service agencies is not restricted to Winnipeg. The Premier's Task Force on Extended Care and Alcoholism Treatment Facilities in Prince Edward Island reported, in its brief to the Senate committee on poverty:

> The historical traditions in the development of our helping services have resulted in these services becoming fragmented

3. Ibid, pp. 25, 27.
4. Ibid, p. 27.

into isolated professional and administrative empires which communicate badly with each other and collaborate hardly at all in their efforts.[5]

These "historical traditions," apparently, are that agencies typically spring up to deal with specific problems whenever these problems are perceived, on an ad hoc basis, and are never integrated into any kind of organized whole. This procedure, as the audit reported, means that certain problems, new or old, tend to get left out: Winnipeg was seriously behind in the provision of day-care centres, diagnostic services for emotionally disturbed children, services for the mentally retarded and services for transients. Once the difficulties in these areas reached crisis proportions, agencies would no doubt be set up to deal with them — but the agencies would likely be organized in exactly the same independent and unco-ordinated way the others had been.

This sort of procedure, of course, means that social-work agencies are restricted to coping with problems that already exist in a major way. As the audit pointed out, Winnipeg had little or no machinery available to prevent developing problems from becoming crises in the first place, or for eliminating problems in their entirety:

> Remedial action is designed and taken for precisely that purpose, and usually fails to diminish or eliminate the source of the problem. It also fails to prevent a repetition of the problem. The bulk of the time spent by health and welfare agencies is on the urgencies of remedial services.[6]

This lack of preventive service is likely to hurt the poor much more than the population at large. As Richard Titmuss points out,

> . . . in relative terms there are more unmet and unexpressed needs among the poor, the badly educated, the old, those living alone and other handicapped groups. Their needs are not expressed and are not met because of ignorance, inertia, fear, difficulties of making contact with the services, failures of co-

5. Proceedings (6 Nov. 1969) 4:58.
6. Social Services Audit, *Report*, p. 30.

ordination and co-operation between services, and for other reasons. These are the people — and there are substantial numbers of them in all populations — who are difficult to reach. Yet they are often the people with the greatest needs.

By contrast, middle-income groups make more and better use of all services; they are more articulate, and more demanding. They have learnt better in all countries how to find their way around a complicated welfare world.[7]

In other words, social-service agencies, like the welfare systems, are involved in staving off the immediate effects of poverty — not in the prevention of poverty, or in an attack on the roots of poverty, or in any attempt to eliminate poverty.

It follows, then, that a social worker's life must be one of quiet, or noisy, desperation. The problems never decrease; the worker is lucky if they stay constant. The supply of social workers, meanwhile, is falling constantly behind the demand. One young Toronto social worker has reported that her caseload in a good week runs to between thirty-five and forty interviews, a schedule that demands between seventy and eighty hours of work; a reasonable caseload rarely runs higher than fifteen interviews.

The agencies, in trying to bridge the gap between inadequate supply of trained professionals and increasing demand for professional services, have resorted to the use of nonprofessionals, even in areas in which professional training is crucial. One Ontario study discovered that, in 1964, seventy-three per cent of the social-work positions in the Ontario Children's Aid Society were filled by people with no social-work training.[8]

At least some of this unpleasant and unwieldy jumble will be eliminated when local welfare systems — as they must be — are phased out; and until that elimination takes place, there will be no real point to the work of a large sector of Canada's social-service agencies.

7. Titmuss, *Commitment to Welfare*, p. 66.
8. Study of the Canadian Association of Social Workers (June 1964); cited in Titmuss, *Commitment to Welfare*, p. 80.
   In 1971, the Ontario Municipal Association received a report that recommended that the provincial government take over the field of children's protection. The society's Toronto director claimed that this would move children into the "political" arena. See Toronto *Globe and Mail* (24 Aug. 1971), p. 6.

But the introduction of a guaranteed annual income, or any other income-security scheme, will not eliminate, or even affect, many of the problems: the chaos in planning the work and objectives of social-service agencies, the emphasis on remedial rather than preventive services, and the increasing shortage of trained social workers.

A great deal of this can be traced to the fact that social-service agencies are typically run by businessmen, on a voluntary basis; and so are the various social-planning councils that attempt to advise and co-ordinate their work.

Businessmen generally resist any attempt, particularly on the part of government, to co-ordinate their work, and relationships between agencies run by businessmen tend to be competitive. When the interests of professionals and of clients clash with the beliefs of the businessmen who run agencies, the convictions of the businessmen usually win out. In one recent Toronto skirmish, the local social-planning council was threatened with withdrawal of support from Toronto fund raisers if "radicals" were voted into office. The radicals in question were mostly poor people; the fund raisers mostly were not.

The problems in social-service work, then, are various: lack of planning, co-ordination and co-operation; lack of research into new problems and lack of preventive work of any kind. The social-service network is not doing its job.

II.5 REORGANIZATION OF THE PUBLIC SERVICES

Obviously, no set of specific recommendations can pry new funds from a government or a nation that refuses them. And so no specific recommendations are made in this area.

But new funds for education, benefits, housing and other areas that concern the poor are desperately needed; and that money will have to come from somewhere.

What is required is no less than a national commitment to eliminate poverty and to head this country in the direction of economic equality. That demands that most of Canada at last acknowledge its obligation to provide justice for the poor.

Specific recommendations follow in the areas of education, health and the social services. These call for political changes that will make changes in the budgets of the public services trivial.

Education: Recommendations

The British North America Act, which Canadian governments preserve in lieu of a sensible constitution, gives responsibility for education to the provinces.

The federal government has nibbled away over time at the edges of this assignment of jurisdiction. It now finances a considerable part of Canada's university expenditures, and has introduced training programs for unemployed workers. But solid authority for the supervision and financing of the formal education systems remains in the provincial sector; and, as any child who has moved from one province to another has already found out, this has led to extreme disparities in the variety and adequacy of educational services available across the country.

There can be no excuse for the kinds of differences that exist between the schools of Newfoundland and the schools of British Columbia. These disparities in quality are wasting the talents of a generation of children in depressed areas.

Provincial governments should be offered massive equalization payments for education; or, alternatively, be allowed to opt out of the education field entirely and leave the area to be financed by the federal government.

The federal government should attempt to raise the levels of schooling available across the country, and to that end should:

— declare any region that is producing high school graduates at a per-pupil rate of more than twenty per cent under the national average an academically deficient area, and therefore eligible for federal assistance at the option of the region;

— offer premiums in salary to teachers with high qualifications who will work and live in these areas;

— allocate at least a majority of the capital budget for educational hardware (nonsalary expense) to the renovation of substandard schools, and to the construction of new schools in deficient areas;

— offer paid sabbaticals to any teacher working in deficient areas to study new techniques and procedures at professional institutes;

— finance and manage centres for research into new techniques of teaching children with backgrounds of poverty;

— offer manpower retraining programs for teachers' aides and paraprofessional workers, with guaranteed employment in the system after successful completion of the course.

Health: Recommendations

The medical profession, as a whole, has shown itself to be consistently unsympathetic towards the poor as a class, and towards their individual and collective needs for protection against illness. And public health insurance has not been living up to the standards demanded of any public system — that it be complete, and that it be easy to use.

Certain steps may be taken to overcome the general failings of the profession, but the health of the poor will not improve significantly until their incomes are made adequate and they are guaranteed decent housing, clothing and food. If these things are done, the following recommendations will make sense:

— Medical insurance should be extended to the whole of the population, and should include uniform coverage for all medical expenses, including drugs, dental work, psychiatric and optical services.

— Payment should be made from public revenues, with no deterrent fees.

— Hospital and medical services should be raised to a uniform standard across the country, and within each province. This can probably be done through equalization grants; alternatively, provinces should be allowed to opt out of the medical field.

— Capital expenditures for hospitals and clinics in each province should be subject to federal control and financing to the end of providing uniform service.

— Medical manpower should be drastically expanded and increased financial help should be given to low-income students.

— A premium payment should be made to those doctors and

medical personnel who will work in family service, and another to those who take up practice in medically deficient areas. These payments should be federal, and medically deficient areas should be designated in the same way as educationally deficient areas, by surveys of the population.

— Public-health doctors and medical personnel should be given materials, equipment and office space in neighbourhood service centres that will also include other social-service outlets.

Reorganization of Social Services: Recommendations

If poverty produces a network of inter-related problems, obviously no social-service agency can operate in a vacuum. Yet that is what most of them have been doing. Certain measures are in order:

— Control over social services must be delivered to public authority. No public funds should be given to agencies that will not submit to public direction and co-ordination.

— The public authority should consist, on the municipal level, of social-planning councils, which should contain a clear majority of clients and professional workers.

— On the provincial level, public authority should be given to co-ordinating bodies, drawn from social-planning councils, to make use of social-service programs on a provincial basis.

— These centres should be adequately staffed with "client advocates," who will represent the poor in their dealings with bureaucracies.

— Services should be delivered, if at all possible, through neighbourhood centres, which will contain medical and government personnel as well as trained social workers.

— A sufficient number of "outreach" personnel should be attached to neighbourhood centres, with responsibility to discover, report on and plan for emerging social needs in the community.

—Mobile centres should be set up to cover the needs of rural populations.

VIII

Costs and Sources of Financing

But can we afford it?

The fast answer to that one, of course, is that we cannot afford *not* to afford it; for poverty and inequality are not only antidemocratic, oppressive and directly harmful to all Canadians, but also intolerably expensive and wasteful.

Poverty and inequality mean that people who could be working aren't, and that people with the equipment and desire to work at demanding jobs are working at crummy ones. The simple, cold economic total of this wastage, according to the Economic Council, may amount to some six per cent of the potential gross national product that is going unproduced.[1]

And that estimate is a gentle one: it does not include the expense of picking up after poverty — medical care, police forces, penitentiaries, welfare systems and the rest.[2]

Economic considerations are not final, or even primary. The best argument against poverty remains the moral one: poverty is intolerable in a humane society.

There remain, however, people (like the prime minister of Canada) who claim that this society cannot afford to be humane, and that morality, in this context, has nothing to do with the running of a country. The argument is indefensible, both logically and morally. For, given the estimate of the Economic Council, the costs of elimin-

1. ECC, "Measuring the Costs of Poverty: Some Considerations and Estimates," *Sixth Annual Review* (Ottawa, 1969).
2. Ibid, p. 110.

ating poverty would have to be staggering to match the costs of sustaining it.

But in many crucial areas of public action against poverty, questions of cost and expense are irrelevant. For a large number of anti-poverty programs of the type that have been outlined are regulatory, designed not to spend money on the poor, but to eliminate their exploitation by the rich. This involves no outlay of cash — merely a resolve to make humane laws and to enforce them. These laws will more than pay for their own enforcement, for they are designed to increase the productivity of low-wage workers, and so increase the efficiency of the economy.

A number of other proposals do have a financial base, but are self-supporting; both social-insurance programs and industrial-training boards, for example, will sustain themselves, the one from contributions from workers, and the other through levies on industries that benefit from training.

Some programs that require initial investment by the government — skill development for the disadvantaged, for example — will pay off quite noticeably in increased production. So they can be designed, in part, to be responsive to benefit-cost analysis, although the definition of "benefit" should be extended well beyond the nickel-and-dime increase in gross national product that is now the basis of government calculation. Increased redistribution of income, for example, is patently a good thing, and should be counted as a benefit; programs that affect distribution, then, should be mounted whether they contribute to the national output or not.

The one area that does require subsidy — the transfer system and, in particular, the guaranteed income — will be expensive, but not in economic costs. The costs will be financial. In other words, the guaranteed income will not affect the gross national product, will not pull money irretrievably out of the economy and will not force the government to print a single new dollar bill. It will require distribution of existing money from the rich to the poor, which is, in the final analysis, merely a matter of bookkeeping.

It is possible that the guaranteed annual income could affect national output in only one way — through the creation of work and savings disincentives. But the type of work that would be given up in favour of a guaranteed income would likely be so low paying and so unpleasant as to be indefensible in any case; and incentives to protect reasonable jobs can be built into the transfer system. (It is risky to predict government actions, but we are quite certain that the government of Canada will *never* institute a system to support the poor without building healthy work incentives into it.) Savings disincentives can be dealt with through institutional change, as outlined in chapter VI.

The bookkeeping required to finance the transfer system should be fairly simple. For one thing, an equitable tax system, along the lines of the one proposed in VI.4, would generate a great deal of revenue. The inclusion of five per cent of wealth and assets in the personal income-tax base, for example, should boost incomes, on the average, by about one-fifth for the purposes of tax and the guaranteed annual income — and the bulk of this money will come from a relatively small and well-heeled group at the top of the income scale. A sensible — that is, sceptical — approach to the provision of tax concessions and subsidies to business will eliminate a lot of pointless spending.

Furthermore, a great deal of government expenditure is now concentrated in areas that benefit minorities that do not pay for them. The production of cars, for example, requires government to build highways; polluting industrial plants require government expenditure on clean-up programs and treatment centres; companies with lousy working conditions produce demand for medical services, and so on. All these are now being provided by government, without fee; they should be charged for, and priced the more steeply because they tend to run counter to the public interest in cleanliness, health and safety.

In VI.4 we recommended the abolition of indirect taxes — sales, export, and so on — which are assessed at a flat rate on goods and services. But these can be replaced quite simply with selective taxes on products or processes that require public outlay; a pollution and highway tax, for example, could quite reasonably be placed on the sale of new cars. The consumer, then, would be paying for both the private and the public costs of his consumption; and those who did not consume in these areas would no longer be forced to pay for those who did.

One source of revenue remains. The Senate of Canada costs about

$5 million a year to run.[3] This is $5 million a year too much. The money should be distributed each year to five poor people, so that they, too, could be introduced to the pleasant sensation of being millionaires; the office space should be rented out to those who would make good use of it; and the bagmen should be returned to the arms of the interests they have served so well. This will be directly in the public interest. It will have the added benefit of preventing any future reports on poverty by the Senate of Canada, leaving the subsidy of fantasy to others.

3. Canada Department of Finance, Budget Papers for 1971-72, in *Hansard* (18 June 1971): 189.

Appendices

APPENDIX 1
Relationship between industrial structure and wage rates in manufacturing, 1964 [a]

WAGES	CONCENTRATION		
	Low	Medium	High
High	printing, machinery	industrial chemicals, pulp and paper, soaps, motor-vehicle parts, structural steel	petroleum and coal production, iron and steel mills, motor vehicles, smelting and refining, aircraft, ship building, electrical industrial equipment, electrical wire and cable
Medium	wire fabricating, saw and planing mills, clay and glass products, architectural metals, hardware, tools and cutlery	beverages, boiler and plate work, meat products, metal stamping, major electrical appliances, tobacco, rubber, misc metal production, paints, heating equipment, grain mills, paper boxes and bags, plywood and veneer, misc paper products	non-ferrous metal rolling, iron foundries, communications equipment, cement products, radio and television
Low	dairy products, pharmaceutical, misc electrical products, bakery products, misc manufacturing, furniture, woollen mills, misc textiles, leather, men's clothing, women and children's clothing, knitting mills	canners, fish processing	synthetic textiles, cotton mills

a. The different degrees of concentration were defined in terms of the percentage of total sales that were made by the eight largest firms; low if fifty per cent or less, medium if over fifty but under eighty, high if more than eighty per cent. The 1964 hourly wage rates were defined as low if less than $1.80, medium if between $1.80 and $2.24, high if between $2.25 or over.
Sources: G. Rosenbluth, "Foreign Control and Concentration in Canadian Industry," *Canadian Journal of Economics* 3 (Feb. 1970): 20-21, table 1. DBS, *Review of Man-Hours and Hourly Earnings, 1957-67*, cat. no. 72-202 (1969), table 5.

APPENDIX II

The mechanics of the guaranteed income and its integration with social insurance

An income equal to the after-tax poverty line is guaranteed as a minimum. For every additional dollar of independent income, the income subsidy is reduced by sixty cents. This means that at an income level equal to 166.7 per cent of the minimum income guarantee, the subsidy disappears and positive taxation begins. This is shown in chart 1.

If the guaranteed income is improved and the reduction of the subsidy is only fifty cents for every dollar of independent income, the level at which the subsidy disappears and positive taxation begins (the "break-even" level) is two hundred per cent of the minimum income guarantee. (The intersection is at two hundred per cent on both graphs.) It is therefore more expensive and is consequently recommended for implementation in the future.

The introduction of social insurance complicates the picture somewhat. Chart 2 represents a situation in which unemployment benefits are fifty per cent of the previous earnings level, with a ceiling on these benefits equal to the break-even level for the guaranteed income, and in which the guaranteed income is based on a sixty per cent subsidy-retention rate. A person whose earnings are equal to the after-tax poverty line will, while working, get a guaranteed-income payment of sixty per cent of the difference between his earnings and the break-even level at 166.7 per cent of the poverty line. This leaves him at 140 per cent of the poverty line.

If this person then becomes unemployed, he will receive fifty per cent of his previous earnings in unemployment-insurance benefits plus guaranteed-income payments covering sixty per cent of the difference between those benefits and the break-even level at 166.7 per cent of the poverty line, which difference is seventy per cent of the poverty line. His final income while unemployed, then, is 120 per cent of the poverty line. The drop from 140 per cent of the poverty line while working to 120 per cent of the poverty line while unemployed would mean, in 1971, a drop from $48 to $41 per week for a single person, from $111 to $95 per week for a family of four, and from $206 to $177 for a family of ten.

If the worker's level of earnings were equal to the break-even level at 166.7 per cent of the after-tax poverty line, he would not be receiving any guaranteed-income payments. If he became unemployed, his unemployment-insurance benefits would cover 83.3 per cent of the poverty line and the guaranteed income payments would cover another fifty per cent, bringing him up to 133.3 per cent of the poverty line. The drop from 166.7 per cent to 133.3 per cent of the poverty line would mean, in 1971, a drop from $57 to $45 per week for a single person, from $132 to $106 for a family of four, and from $246 to $197 for a family of ten.

For workers whose earnings exceed 333 per cent of the after-tax poverty line, unemployment-insurance benefits will be at the maximum level of 166.7 per cent and no guaranteed-income payments will be paid during unemployment. This ceiling would in 1971 amount to $57 per week for a single person, $132 for a family of four and $246 for a family of ten.

If the subsidy-retention rate of the guaranteed income is reduced—from sixty per cent to fifty per cent, for example—and the unemployment-insurance benefits in terms of percentage of earnings increased—from fifty per cent to seventy per cent, for example—then the break-even level of the guaranteed income would rise and more would be paid out in unemployment-insurance benefits. For the changes given as examples, the break-even level would be two hundred per cent of the poverty line, which would become the ceiling for unemployment-insurance benefits for earnings of more than 286 per cent of the poverty line. In other words, the maximum unemployment-insurance benefits would be reached at a somewhat lower earnings level, even though the maximum is considerably higher.

The relation between the guaranteed annual income and pension benefits is similar to its relation to unemployment insurance. However, since a work incentive is not important, the pension benefit can be a higher proportion of the preceding living standard than the fifty per cent rate under unemployment insurance. If, for example, a seventy-five per cent pension-benefit rate is combined with a guaranteed income that has a sixty per cent subsidy-retention rate, the persons who have had poverty-line incomes in the past would maintain an income after retirement of 124 per cent of the poverty line. This would amount to $183 per month for a single person and $305 for a couple. If income in the past were at the break-even level for the size of the person's family, then he would get 125 per cent of the poverty line in pension benefits, plus twenty-five per cent of the poverty line in guaranteed-income payments; he thus is kept at 150 per cent of the poverty line, which, in 1971, amounted to $221 per month for a single person and $369 for a couple. Of course, even without pension benefits, no one could fall below the poverty line, which for 1971 is $148 a month for a single person and $246 for a couple.

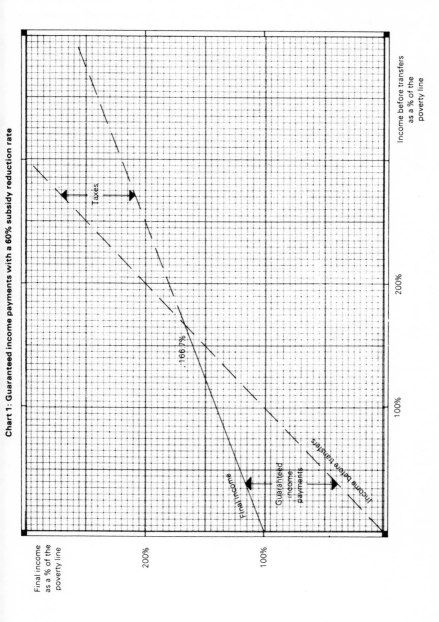

Chart 1: Guaranteed income payments with a 60% subsidy reduction rate

Chart 2: Unemployment insurance benefits and guaranteed income payments

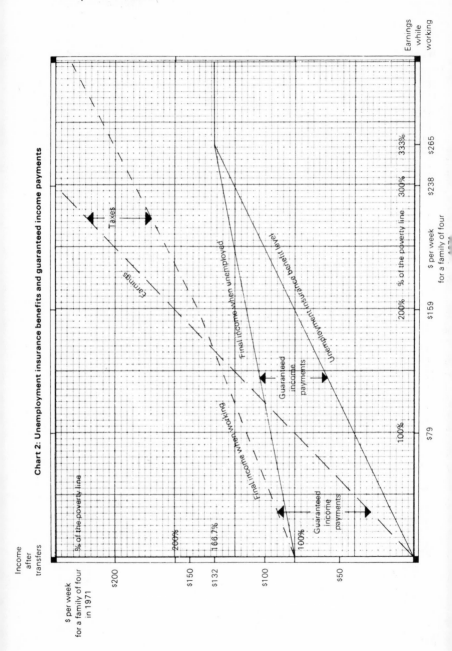

APPENDIX III

The cost of a guaranteed annual income

The data used were a finer break-out of the data from the *Survey of Consumer Finances, 1967,* used to produce *Income Distributions by Size in Canada, 1967* (cat. no. 13-534, December 1970), on an economic family basis, showing family income from thirteen different sources, by twenty-one income groups and nine family sizes and types. Each family-income/size/type cell was taken as an average, with a number count for each item. It was possible to identify Old-Age Security and Family-Allowance payments for each cell, and these were removed. The average GAI payment per cell was then worked out for various assumptions as to the subsidy-retrieval rate and benefit level. These were summed over income groups and family-size types to yield gross program cost. The benefit level used was one hundred per cent of the Relative Poverty Line, and estimates were prepared for costs at fifty per cent and seventy per cent subsidy-retrieval rates. The benefit levels for each family size in 1967 were:

Family size	Benefit levels	RPL after taxes
1	$1600	$1392
2	2700	2320
3	3300	2784
4	3800	3248
5	4400	3712
6 and over	5000	4382

The group "6 and over" was taken to represent 6.23 people. The survey data was for families of sizes one to five and over, and the groups "5" and "6 and over" were split out by using a size distribution of all families in 1961, taken from DBS, *Population Statistics 1961,* special census bulletin 5X-10, statement 2, p. 7. The percentage composition of all families size five and over was constrained to equal one hundred per cent, and the proportion thus obtained was applied to create a new five and six-and-over category out of the existing five-and-over category.

To adjust the cost figures to a disposable-income basis, the ratio of personal disposable income to personal income in 1967 (.85) was used to deflate the Relative Poverty Line and, consequently, the benefit level. The costs are:

1. At a subsidy-recovery rate of fifty per cent:

Program cost = 3.800 billion dollars
Lost tax revenue = .683 billion dollars
Conversion adjustment[a] = .342 billion dollars
Savings[b] = —2.315 billion dollars
Net cost: 2.510 billion dollars

2. At a subsidy-recovery rate of seventy per cent:

Program cost = 2.550 billion dollars
Lost tax revenue = .163 billion dollars
Conversion adjustment = .114 billion dollars
Savings = —2.315 billion dollars
Net cost: .512 billion dollars

a. This is needed to adjust program costs for the additional costs accruing when the income of those with incomes under the break-even point is converted to a personal disposable-income basis. For example, with a subsidy-recovery rate of fifty per cent, a loss of income of .683 billion dollars for this group would increase program costs by .342 billion dollars.

b. 1.815 billion dollars was spent on the Old-Age Security and Family-Allowance programs in the calendar year 1967. About .500 billion was spent on CAP. We propose that these programs be dropped.

Unemployment was four per cent in 1967, and higher unemployment rates will increase GAI costs, although there was not time to calculate by how much.

The tax calculations were done for federal taxes only, on the basis of the rates applicable for detailed tax calculations in 1967. Standard exemptions were used, except for children, where a uniform $350 exemption was used; this reflects the age distribution of children living at home.

Taking net costs at a sixty per cent subsidy-recovery rate, to be about halfway between the costs at fifty per cent and seventy per cent, we estimate the net costs at sixty per cent to be about $1.5 billion. The assumption of a linear relationship between subsidy retrieval and costs is unwarranted, but unavoidable. We didn't have the time to drop it and recalculate. This should not commit much violence on the figure.